...*l Journal of Psychology* (IJP) is the journal of the *International ...ogical Science* (IUPsyS) and is published under the auspices of the ...ks to support the IUPsyS in fostering the development of ...ychological science. It aims to strengthen the dialog within psychology around the world and to facilitate communication among different areas of psychology and among psychologists from different cultural backgrounds. IJP is the outlet for empirical basic and applied studies and for reviews that either (a) incorporate perspectives from different areas or domains within psychology or across different disciplines, (b) test the culture-dependent validity of psychological theories, or (c) integrate literature from different regions in the world. IJP does not publish technical articles, validations of questionnaires and tests, or clinical case studies.

Regular issues include two types of articles: empirical articles and review articles. Empirical articles report data from single or multiple studies in one of the major fields of scientific psychology. Review articles provide overviews of the international literature on a particular topic; authors are especially encouraged to include in their review relevant publications from regions of the world not typically cited and/or not published in English. Special topical issues or sections are also published two or three times a year. All articles include a detailed abstract in English, French and Spanish.

The International Platform for Psychologists
Associate Editors: M. Bullock (USA) and P.L.-J. Ritchie (Canada)
Many of IJP's issues include a second section, the International Platform for Psychologists, which provides an opportunity to exchange news and opinions on psychology as an academic and applied profession. This section also contains information about the IUPsyS, about major international meetings, and about the activities of the National Psychological Societies. Finally it offers an opportunity to express opinions and to discuss internationally significant psychological issues. There is also a United Nations section with the International Platform for Psychologists.

Publication. The *International Journal of Psychology* is published by Psychology Press, 27 Church Road, Hove, East Sussex, BN3 2FA, UK, on behalf of the International Union of Psychological Science.
Psychology Press is an imprint of the Taylor & Francis Group, an informa business.

The International Journal of Psychology is now available online: *Psychology Online* on www.psypress.com/ijp for more information (online ISSN: 1464-066X).

Subscription rates to Volume 41, 2006 (6 issues) are as follows:
Individuals: UK: £95.00; Individuals: Rest of world: $159.00
Institutions: UK: £413.00; Institutions: Rest of world: $681.00
Plus free *Psychology: IUPsyS Global Resource* CD-ROM to all subscribers

International Journal of Psychology (USPS permit number 016263) is published bi-monthly in February, April, June, August, October, and December. The 2006 US Institutional subscription price is $681.00. Periodicals postage paid at Jamaica, NY by US Mailing Agent Air Business Ltd, C/O Priority Airfreight NY Ltd, 147-29 182nd Street, Jamaica, NY 11413, USA. **US Postmaster:** Please send address changes to Air Business Ltd, C/O Priority Airfreight NY Ltd, 147-29 182nd Street, Jamaica, NY 11413, USA.

Subscription orders should be addressed to:
Psychology Press, c/o T&F Customer Services, Informa UK Ltd, Sheepen Place, Colchester, Essex CO3 3LP, UK; Fax: +44 (0) 1256 479438; Tel: +44 (0) 20 7017 5544; E-mail: tf.enquiries@tfinforma.com. Please give six weeks' notice of changes of address and include both old and new addresses.

Disclaimer: Psychology Press makes every effort to ensure the accuracy of all the information (the "Content") contained in its publications. However, Psychology Press and its agents and licensors make no representations or warranties whatsoever as to the accuracy, completeness or suitability for any purpose of the Content and disclaim all such representations and warranties whether express or implied to the maximum extent permitted by law. Any views expressed in the publication are the views of the authors and are not the views of Psychology Press.

The *International Journal of Psychology* is covered by the following abstracting, indexing, and citation services: Assia; Biosis; Bell & Howell Learning (formerly University Microfilms); Current Contents – Social/Behavioural Sciences (ISI); Ergonomics Abstracts; Linguistic and Language Behavior Abstracts; NISC/Family Studies Database; Psychological Abstracts/PsychINFO; Research Alerts (ISI); Social SciSearch (ISI); Social Science Citation Index (ISI); Social Services Abstracts (formerly SOPODA); Sociological Abstracts; and UnCover.

Typeset by Charlesworth, Wakefield, UK

Manuscripts are invited for submission. All submissions should be made online, in a standard document format type such as Word or Rich Text Format, at the *International Journal of Psychology*'s **Manuscript Central site (http://mc.manuscriptcentral.com/pijp)**. New users should first create an account. Once a user is logged onto the site submissions should be made via the Author Centre. If any assistance is needed with this, please feel free to e-mail on ijp@uni-halle.de

If for any reasons, surface mail submission is preferred please send one copy of the manuscript AND a disk version to: **Prof. Dr. Claudia Dalbert**, Martin Luther University, Institute of Education, D-06099 Halle, Germany.

All manuscripts should be submitted in American Psychological Association (APA) format following the latest edition of Publication Manual of the APA (currently 5th edition). All manuscripts must include a 300-word abstract in English. Submission of empirical papers must be accompanied by the author's confirmation that they have access to the original data on which the manuscript reports.

Manuscripts should be presented double spaced. Please leave wide margins. Instructions on preparing tables, figures, references, metrics, and abstracts all appear in the *APA Publication Manual* (5th edition). Any manuscript which does not conform to these guidelines may be returned for necessary revision before reviewing. The Editor retains the right to reject manuscripts that do not meet established scientific or ethical standards.

In case of rejection, manuscripts cannot be returned.

Reviews are conducted in a single-blind fashion, thus the reviewers remain anonymous. Every effort is made to have the initial review process completed less than three months after submission, but there are occasional delays due to circumstances beyond our control. Most accepted manuscripts require some revision; suggestions to facilitate the preparation of the revision will be communicated to the author(s) in the editorial decision letter. Accepted papers written in incorrect English may be returned to the author for language correction; in that case, the authors are advised to contact a native speaker.

Manuscripts should not be submitted for concurrent consideration in other journals. Duplicate publication— that is, the publication of a manuscript that has already been published wholly (in the same or another language) or in substantial part in another journal—is also prohibited. It is the responsibility of the author to ensure that the paper contains nothing that is libellous or infringes copyright.

Any change of contact details after submission must be sent promptly to the Editor's or an Associate Editor's office. If available, e-mail addresses and fax numbers should be included in the covering letter.

Proofs: Page proofs will be emailed to the corresponding author as a PDF attachment to check for typesetting accuracy. Other than the correction of errors, no changes to the original typescript will be permitted at this stage. A list of queries raised by the copy editor will also be emailed. Proofs should be returned promptly with the query sheet.

Early electronic offprints (e-prints): Specified corresponding authors will receive their article by email as a complete PDF. This allows the author to print up to 50 copies, free of charge, and disseminate them to colleagues. In many cases, this facility will be available up to two weeks prior to print publication of the article. One copy of the journal issue in which their paper appears will be sent by post to all specified corresponding authors free after print publication. Paper offprints can still be purchased by authors. For a price list and details please email web.queries@tandf.co.uk

International Platform Section
Manuscripts for publication in the *International Platform* should be sent to either of the Associate Editors: **Pierre L.-J. Ritchie**, School of Psychology, University of Ottawa, 145 Jean-Jacques Lussier St., PO Box 450, Stn A, Ottawa, K1N 6N5, Canada, or **Merry Bullock**, Science Directorate, APA 750 First Street NE, Washington DC 20002, USA

Copyright: It is a condition of publication that authors vest or license copyright in their articles, including abstracts, in the International Union of Psychological Science. This enables us to ensure full copyright protection and to disseminate the article, and the journal, to the widest possible readership in print and electronic formats as appropriate. Authors may, of course, use the material elsewhere after publication providing that prior permission is obtained from Taylor & Francis. Authors are themselves responsible for obtaining permission to reproduce copyright material from other sources. To view the 'Copyright Transfer Frequently Asked Questions' please visit www.tandf.co.uk/journals/copyright.asp.

Permissions and fee are waived for the photocopying of isolated articles for non-profit classroom and library reserve use by instructors and educational institutions. This consent does not extend to other kinds of copying, such as copying for general distribution for advertising or for promotional purposes, for creating new collective works, or for resale.

Back Issues: Taylor & Francis retains a three-year back issue stock of journals. Older volumes are held by our official stockists: Periodicals Service Company, 11 Main Street, Germantown, NY 12526, USA to whom all orders and enquiries should be addressed. Tel: +1 518 537 4700; Fax: +1 518 537 5899; Email: psc@periodicals.com; URL: http://www.periodicals.com/tandf.html

INTERNATIONAL JOURNAL OF PSYCHOLOGY, 2006, 41 (6), 433–435

Prologue: Behaviour analysis around the world

Rubén Ardila

National University of Colombia, Bogotá, Colombia

Behaviour analysis has traditionally been one of the main areas and main approaches to psychology. It is based on laboratory research and in conceptualizations from distinguished figures of the discipline, such as Skinner, Pavlov, Mach, and even Watson and Thorndike. It has generated a science (the experimental analysis of behaviour), a philosophy (behaviourism), and numerous practical applications (applied behaviour analysis). For several decades it was even considered to be the dominant paradigm in psychology.

In the last few years, cognitivism has emerged as a paradigm that is supposed to be an "alternative" to behaviour analysis. Some regard cognitive psychology and not behavioural psychology as the dominant paradigm in present psychology. Nevertheless, behaviour analysis continues to hold a place of great importance in psychology as well as in other disciplines, such as education, anthropology, pharmacology, neurosciences, political science, and even philosophy.

Behaviour analysis emerged in its definitive form with the publication of Skinner's book, *The Behavior of Organisms* (1938). This area was initially developed as a laboratory science with animal subjects (rats, pigeons, and others), and with human participants. It gave origin to a philosophy, to a methodological conceptualization (an inductive methodology, based on Mach's philosophy of science), and to an immense series of applications in such diverse fields as the clinic (behaviour therapy), education (behaviour analysis applied to education), the world of the organizations (organizational behavioural management), rehabilitation of delinquents, sports, special education, health psychology, autism, and many others.

This Special Issue of the *International Journal of Psychology* is devoted to behaviour analysis at the global level. It shows that behaviour analysis is an international enterprise, not solely limited to the United States or the English-speaking nations. It is also revealed that behaviour analysis is very active and in process of extensive growth around the world. The post-Skinnerian developments are very relevant in basic areas (for example verbal behaviour), and in applied areas.

This Special Issue contains papers from Belgium, China, Colombia, France, Greece, Iceland, Mexico, Poland, Spain, Switzerland, and the United States. It is a sample of the work carried out in behaviour analysis, basic and applied, at the international level.

A few of the articles are theoretical and conceptual, and refer to the basic foundations of behaviour, both human and nonhuman. Some others are historically oriented. Most refer to practical applications in the area of big social issues like education, organizational behaviour, clinical psychology, autism, health, and others.

In the first article, Emilio Ribes Iñesta (from Mexico) presents his theoretical and experimental program on human and animal behaviour. This taxonomy of behaviour was proposed initially in 1985 following the interbehavioural field model developed by J. R. Kantor. In the present paper he summarizes the main concepts and assumptions of this taxonomy and describes some of the relevant methodological preparations and experimental data. The model includes basic animal behavioural processes, complex human behaviour, human learning, social behaviour, and extensions to natural and social settings: health, *education*, scientific behaviour, mother–child dyadic interactions, and interactive styles.

In a very original discussion of the concept of "person" and its place in psychology and the analysis of behaviour, Marino Pérez-Álvarez and José Manuel García-Montes (Spain) indicate that the concept of person is fundamental in any

Correspondence should be addressed to Rubén Ardila, PO Box 88754, Bogotá, Colombia (E-mail: psycholo@aolpremium.com).

http://www.psypress.com/ijp

DOI: 10.1080/00207590500495180

psychology worthy of that name, but is not among the technical terms of behaviourism. Indeed, behaviourism was reticent about the concept of person, not surprisingly, given its traditional substantialist and intrapsychic sense. However, behaviourism, particularly Skinnerian radical behaviourism, has the ideas from which a perfectly acceptable concept of the person can be developed. The difficulties refer to the "inner world" and to individual freedom. Solutions are presented.

The experimental synthesis of behaviour was proposed by Ardila as a paradigm for the unification of psychology. The central core of the theory is behaviour analysis, and its aim is to explain the findings of contemporary psychology in behavioural concepts. The experimental synthesis of behaviour is not "eclectic." Following a post-Kuhnian description, the author states that psychological schools were analogous to paradigms, and that a state of normal science (in Kuhn's terms) could be reached. The main characteristics of the experimental synthesis of behaviour, as a program for the unification of psychology, are as follows. (1) A behavioural level of explanation; psychology has its own level, which includes the behaviour of organisms and their varied relations to the environment; behaviour is not reducible, in a strict sense, to biology or to social science. (2) The method is experimentation, but in the initial stages importance is given to observational and correlational procedures. (3) Emphasis is on learning: Human behaviour is primarily learned, with a biological (genetic) basis. (4) The wide range of phenomena to be explained include all the traditional fields of scientific psychological research. (5) Emphasis is also on the environment, both social and physical. (6) Importance is given to the basic technology derived from behavioural research.

French culture has not been traditionally receptive to analytic approaches in psychology, including the experimental analysis of behaviour. Skinner, behaviourism, and behaviour therapy did not find enough acceptance in France and other French-speaking countries, with the possible exception of French Canada (Quebec). In their article, Marc Richelle (from Belgium), Esteve Freixa i Baqué (currently in France), and Jean-Luc Lambert and Valentino Pomini (from Switzerland), show that the influence and development of behaviour analysis in French-speaking territories of Europe has been different from the developments in France and in the French-speaking parts of Belgium and Switzerland. French psychology has shown persistent reluctance towards behaviour analysis, except for a few

individuals in a few institutional circles. On the other hand, Belgium has been the main centre from which behaviour analysis has propagated to the French-speaking area as a whole. Territorial specificities, both in experimental analysis and in applied behaviour analysis, are described and placed in context.

Moderato and Presti (Italy) describe the development of behaviourism in their country, beginning with Virgilio Lazzeroni, who in 1942 published a paper in which he claimed that behaviour was the subject matter of psychology. The behaviouristic tradition is relatively young in Italy, due to the influence of the cultural environment centred on idealistic philosophy. The tree of Italian behaviourism has two roots, which can be labelled Pavlovian-reflexiological-psychiatric, and Skinnerian-operant-psychological. The founding of the Italian Association for Behaviour Analysis and Modification (AIAMC in Italian), in 1977, was particularly influential. National and international scientific meetings have been organized, and also 4-year postgraduate courses in behaviour analysis and therapy. Almost all of the main books of the behavioural literature have been translated into Italian, and a number of original books by native authors have been published. There is research and practical work on theoretical, clinical, educational, and organizational topics.

In their article on observational *learning*, Greer, Dudek-Singer, and Gautreaux point out that recent evidence suggests distinctions between the effects of observation on: (1) the emission of previously acquired repertoires, (2) the acquisition of new repertories, (3) the acquisition of conditioned reinforcement, and (4) the acquisition of observational learning as a new repertory. The authors describe investigations reporting procedures leading to: acquisition of observational learning, acquisition of operants and higher-order operants by observation, and the acquisition of conditioned reinforcment as a function of observation. They indicate that in their efforts to build a more robust science of teaching, it is necessary to make distinctions between types of behaviour change from indirect contact with contingencies. Those distinctions are likely to be important to inquiries in other areas of psychology, neuroscience, environmental influences on genetically predisposed behaviour, and others.

Collective violence is one of the most urgent problems of our time. It includes war, terrorism, violent political conflicts, genocide, repression, organized criminal activity, disappearances, torture, other abuses of human rights, etc. Mattaini and Strickland explore the roots of collective violence from the perspective of the natural science of behaviour. The analysis indicates that policy-makers often rely on responses and preventive strategies that are weak or contraproductive. Potentially more powerful strategies, based on the science of behaviour, remain largely unrecognized. The authors present programs that expand strategic options, and point out that pursuing this work will require courageous scholarship conducted in solidarity with those at risk.

Suchowierska (Poland) works on teaching language and reading to typically and not-typically developing children. She indicates that a primary goal of behavioural intervention is to establish generative responding. Recombinative generalization is defined as the demonstration of novel arrangements of previously established linguistic units. She reviews recombinative generalization, discusses the conditions necessary for successful recombinations (e.g., teaching conditional discriminations and abstraction), and makes suggestions for practice relating to recombinative generalization.

A sample of the applied work carried out in China is seen in the paper by Guo Yanqing, from Beijing University. He presents a training program with two parts. (1) Professional training is received by graduate students at the Institute of Mental Health of Beijing University, based on the principles of behaviour assessment and modification, radical behaviourism (Skinner), and applied research methods. (2) Parent training focused on parents with autistic children, using the behaviour analysis and modification methods. There is a great need in China for this kind of work, but there are few professionals with the appropriate scientific knowledge and skills to work with autistic children. These professionals will help to further develop the area of behaviour analysis in China.

Sigurðardóttir and Sighvatsson (from Iceland) worked with people with chronic aphasia, using operant conditioning and errorless learning procedures. Treatment lasted 7 months, and the effects were evaluated with a multiple-baseline design across behaviours. Prompts were used in training, but faded out as performance improved. The performance of all participants improved significantly in all tasks; they all reached 100% correct performance without prompts. Generalization took place across stimuli and settings. The authors indicate that the treatment variables (performance feedback, social reinforcers, instructions, recycling, etc.), must be evaluated in relation to individual variables (age, level of education, size and location of a cerebral lesion, etiology of lesion, etc.). The importance of operant conditioning procedures for treating people with chronic aphasia was clearly demonstrated.

The next article, by Angeliki Gena (from Greece) considers the inclusion of autistic children in regular schools. Autism is an important area of work in applied behaviour analysis. The issues associated with inclusion of children with autism have been discussed, and we are still far from having a global appreciation of the needs that arise in these situations. The present study demonstrates that social reinforcement in combination with prompting procedures, provided by a "shadow teacher," were effective in increasing social initiations and appropriate responding to peers' initiations of children with autism during interaction with their classmates in preschool. The treatment benefits were obtained in a natural setting; initiations and replies were not cliché statements but involved generalized language use appropriate to the social context. The author points out that the issues of inclusion concern not only children with disabilities, but also the entire school community.

Staddon indicates that operant learning is considered as interplay between response emission (variation) and reinforcement (selection). When applying his ideas to teaching, Skinner emphasized selection almost exclusively, but the real puzzle is not selection but the sources of variation that cause an action or an idea to appear for the first time.

From the perspective of the behavioural systems analysis approach, Malott and Salas Martinez describe a higher education change initiative. In a teacher training university in Veracruz (Mexico), three types of complexity were analysed: environment, hierarchy, and component. Four improvement strategies were identified and implemented: an adult literacy program, options for terminal requirement of educational programs, diversification of programs, and redesign of student-centred administrative processes. The article and its implications show that behaviour analysis can be useful for complex organizational change.

This Special Issue of the *International Journal of Psychology* has covered a broad spectrum, from theoretical and conceptual problems, to experimental and applied work. We hope that the reader gets a balanced and up-to-date image of behaviour analysis at the world level. The Skinnerian and post-Skinnerian contributions have much to offer to contemporary psychology.

INTERNATIONAL JOURNAL OF PSYCHOLOGY, 2006, 41 (6), 436–448

Psychology Press
Taylor & Francis Group

A theoretical and experimental program on human and animal behaviour

Emilio Ribes Iñesta

University of Guadalajara, Zapopan, Mexico

*I*n 1985 the author proposed a theoretical taxonomy of behaviour functions that followed the interbehavioural field model developed by J. R. Kantor. The formulation of the taxonomy is an attempt to overcome logical, conceptual, and empirical limitations in prevailing behavioural approaches, especially operant theory. A molar analysis of behaviour is provided. In this paper, the author summarizes the main concepts and assumptions of this taxonomy, and describes some of the relevant methodological preparations and experimental data. The proposed interbehavioural field taxonomy (IF) consists of a classification of stimulus-response functions that describe the structural relations of a given behaviour segment. A behaviour segment consists of an organism interacting with stimulus objects and other organisms in a given setting. The behaviour segment contrasting with traditional conditioning framework includes categories with different logical functions. These categories are: (1) the interactive history, (2) the situational factors, (3) the medium of contact, (4) the field boundaries, and (5) the distinctions between object/organism, stimulus/response, and the stimulus-response function. Five general research programs are presented by the author: (1) basic research on animal behaviour, (2) complex human behaviour, (3) behavioural development processes, (4) extension to natural and social settings, (5) conceptual and theoretical analysis. Several experimental and theoretical developments are presented.

*E*n 1985, l'auteur a proposé une taxonomie des fonctions du comportement qui a suivi le modèle d'études inter-comportemental par J. R. Kantor. La formulation de la taxonomie est une tentative pour surpasser les limites logiques, conceptuelles et empiriques dans l'établissement des approches comportementales, particulière-ment de la théorie opérante. Une analyse molaire du comportement est offerte. Dans cet article, l'auteur résume les concepts principaux et les postulats de cette taxonomie et il décrit quelques préparations méthodologiques appropriées. La taxonomie du champ d'études inter-comportemental proposée est composée d'une classification des fonctions stimulus-réponse qui décrivent les relations structurales d'un segment de comportement donné. Un segment de comportement consiste en un organisme qui interagit avec des objets-stimuli dans un contexte donné. Le segment de comportement qui contraste avec un cadre de conditionnement traditionnel inclut des catégories avec des fonctions logiques différentes. Ces catégories sont: (1) l'histoire interactive, (2) les facteurs situationnels, (3) le moyen de contact, (4) les frontières du champ d'études et (5) les distinctions entre objet/organisme, stimulus/réponse et la fonction stimulus/réponse. Cinq programmes de recherche généraux sont présentés par l'auteur: (1) la recherche de base sur le comportement animal, (2) le comportement humain complexe, (3) les processus du développement comportemental, (4) l'extension à d'autres contextes naturels et sociaux, et (5) une analyse conceptuelle et théorique. Plusieurs développements expérimentaux et théoriques sont présentés.

*E*n 1985 el autor propuso una taxonomía teórica de las funciones de la conducta que seguía el modelo de campo interconductual desarrollado por J. R. Kantor. La formulación de la taxonomía es un intento de superar las limitaciones lógicas, conceptuales, y empíricas de los enfoques conductuales dominantes, especialmente la teoría operante. Se presenta un análisis molar. En este artículo se resumen los principales conceptos y presupuestos de esa taxonomía, y se describen algunas de las preparaciones metodológicamente relevantes y algunos datos experimentales. La taxonomía interconductual de campo (IC) propuesta, consiste en una clasificación de las funciones de estímulo-respuesta que describe las relaciones estructurales de un segmento dado de comportamiento. Un segmento de comportamiento consiste en un organismo que interactúa con objetos de estímulo y con otros organismos en un ambiente dado. El segmento de conducta contrasta con el marco de referencia tradicional del condicionamiento, e incluye categorías con diferentes funciones lógicas. Estas funciones

---

Correspondence should be addressed to Emilio Ribes Iñesta, University of Guadalajara, Center for Studies and Research on Behavior. PO Box 5-374, 45040 Zapopan, Mexico (E-mail: ribes@cencar.udg.mx).

http://www.psypress.com/ijp

DOI: 10.1080/00207590500491130

son: (1) La historia interactiva, (2) los factores situacionales, (3) el medio de contacto, (4) los límites de campo, y (5) la distinción entre objeto/organismo, estímulo/respuesta, y la función estímulo-respuesta. Se presentan cinco programas generales de investigación: (1) investigación básica sobre conducta animal, (2) conducta humana compleja, (3) procesos de desarrollo comportamental, (4) extensiones a contextos naturales y sociales, (5) análisis conceptuales y teóricos. Se presentan algunos desarrollos experimentales y teóricos.

INTRODUCTION

Twenty years ago, with Francisco López, I proposed a theoretical taxonomy of behaviour (Ribes & López, 1985) that followed the interbehavioural field model developed by J. R. Kantor (1924–1926). The formulation of this taxonomy was an attempt to overcome logical, conceptual, and empirical limitations in prevailing behaviour-theoretical approaches (especially operant theory), and was conceived so as to provide a molar analysis of behaviour. The limitations of operant theory have been discussed elsewhere (Ribes, 1982, 1985, 1986, 1994, 1996, 1997, 1999, 2000, 2001, 2003a, 2003b, 2004b, 2005, in press). The taxonomy was developed as an effort to systematize as many observational and experimental phenomena as possible, and as a conceptual instrument that would open new empirical horizons to be studied.

A FUNCTIONAL TAXONOMY OF BEHAVIOUR

The proposed interbehavioural field taxonomy (IFT) consists of a classification of stimulus-response functions that describes the structural relations of a given behaviour segment. A behaviour segment consists of one organism interacting with stimulus objects and other organisms in a given setting. The behaviour segment, contrasting with traditional conditioning framework, includes categories with different logical functions. These categories are: (1) the interactive history; (2) the situational factors (including biological states); (3) the medium of contact; (4) the field boundaries; and (5) the distinction between object/organism, stimulus/response, and the stimulus-response function.

Categories (1) and (2) deal with *setting events* (Kantor, 1959) and play the logical role of dispositional terms or statements (Ryle, 1949). Dispositional terms or statements refer to collections of simultaneous or successive events, and do not qualify as causal statements. Dispositional statements are predictive and actuarial in nature, and concepts of this kind describe facilitating or interfering effects. Thus, dispositional concepts and statements deal with the *probability* of occurrences but not with causal relations between

occurrences. Category (3) includes *enabling* concepts, which refer to the *possibility* of an occurrence or relation given certain conditions. The medium of contact may be examined at different levels: physico-chemical (e.g., light, air, water, etc.), ecological (e.g., adaptive niches and species-specific patterns), and conventional (e.g., institutions). Finally, categories (4) and (5) are concerned with the functional structure of proximal or distal contacts of organisms with stimulus objects and other organisms. Stimulus-response functions (SRF) and the field boundaries describe the spatial and temporal organization of the individual organism interacting with particular objects or organisms. These categories, to the extent that they refer to relations between occurrences, are the components of causal or law-like statements in the form of conditional propositions. Summing up, the environment is composed of stimulus objects, media of contact, situational factors and boundaries, while the organism is related to reactional systems, situational factors (biological states and conditions), and a history of interactive functions.

The IFT outlines a classification of SRFs conceived as contingency fields. The various functional stimulus and response elements are seen as the organization of reciprocal, interdependent factors, in such a way that the functional properties of each element depends upon the entire system of conditional relations between stimulus and response factors. In accordance with four criteria, five different types of SRFs may be identified: contextual, supplementary, selector, extrasituational substitution, and transituational substitution. The four criteria consist of the form, mediation, detachment, and adjustment of any given interaction (Ribes, 2004b). Each SRF involves a particular arrangement of these four criteria. As an example, the contextual function consists of a contingency system mediated by a biologically significant stimulus element, in which responding is detached from its biological relation to the stimulus, and the adjustment is attained by differential responding to isomorphic relations between stimulus events. Similar analyses can be made for the other four SRFs along each criterion. Thus, the form of the interaction may be isomorphic, operative, permutative, transitive, or reflexive, while the criteria of adjustment may obtain through differential, effective, precise, congruent, or coherent responding. Mediation may take place through conventional or nonconventional stimulus or response elements, progressively including larger and more complex relations. The functional detachment of responding may consist of establishing new functions within the interacting situation, or of extending the boundaries of responding either to contingency relations not present in the situation, or to conventional contingencies based on language as a symbolic system. The IFT sets a qualitative boundary between human and nonhuman behaviour in terms of the differences in medium of contact (conventional media in humans: language and institutions), and the possibility provided by conventional reactional systems (language in a broad sense) to mediate contingencies between and across situations (substitutional contingencies).

The IFT is conceived both in terms of processes and of evolution. Functions are conceived as progressively inclusive contingency fields, in which the simpler functions are contained as components of the more complex functions. The IFT rests on three assumptions: (1) that processes deal with the structure of contingencies resulting from different kinds of mediation; (2) that complex processes always include simpler processes, although their functional parameters may vary within each function; and (3) that psychological evolution is an asymmetrical process in time represented by the emergence of progressively more complex functions, including previous ones. The IFT serves various purposes: (1) it identifies and classifies observational and experimental phenomena as instances of different forms of organization of behaviour; (2) it points to the variables and parameters that are relevant to each SRF; (3) it looks for the necessary and sufficient conditions responsible for the transition between SRFs; (4) it allows for the comparison of parametric functions in different SRFs, preventing the confusion between procedures and processes; (5) it provides a *psychological representation* of variables related to the media of contact, field boundaries, and setting factors, usually neglected or misrepresented in traditional conditioning theory as private events or as pseudomolar variables such as the "verbal community," "phylogenic contingencies," etc.; and (6) it promotes the design and development of observational and experimental preparations for the study and analysis of theoretically meaningful phenomena.

A REVIEW OF EXPERIMENTAL PREPARATIONS AND FINDINGS

Figure 1 describes the various experimental and observational programs stemming from the IFT, as well as some extensions to the analysis of natural social settings. I will deal only with some of the programs and extensions.

The central core of the theoretical proposal deals with five general research programs: (1) basic processes in animal behaviour, (2) complex human behaviour, (3) behavioural development processes, (4) extensions to natural and social settings, and (5) conceptual and theoretical analyses. Each of these programs is subdivided into different projects or topics, such as mother–child interactions, interactive styles, human learning, social behaviour, knowledge and beliefs, temporal parameters of stimulation, segmentation of responding, and the analysis of scientific behaviour, education, and health. In this paper, I will review and summarize some of the advances achieved along three projects: (1) response segmentation, (2) human learning and problem solving, and (3) social behaviour. I will describe the goals, experimental preparations, and findings of these projects.

Segmentation of the response function

Although Skinner (1938) acknowledged the continuous nature of behaviour in time and space, the methodological preparation of operant conditioning ignored this claim. On the one hand, the procedure partitioned the occurrence of behaviour in terms of responses and nonresponses. On the other hand, the spatial dimension of behaviour was neglected by either setting up a fixed location for the behaviour to occur and be measured (a fixed operandum), or by equating the temporal allocation of responding with the spatial properties of behaviour (Baum & Rachlin, 1969). This attitude is still present today, in spite of the observations of Schoenfeld and Farmer (1970) and Schoenfeld (1976) about the functional relevance, in the operant situation, of behaviour that is not being measured directly.

The IFT has been concerned with the identification, analysis, and conceptualization of the spatial dimensions of behaviour, in order to provide a molar account of animal behaviour interactions. An initial approach to the spatial dimensions of behaviour must deal with the quantitative analysis of the physical properties of responding, in order to provide a picture that goes beyond the temporal organization and morphology of

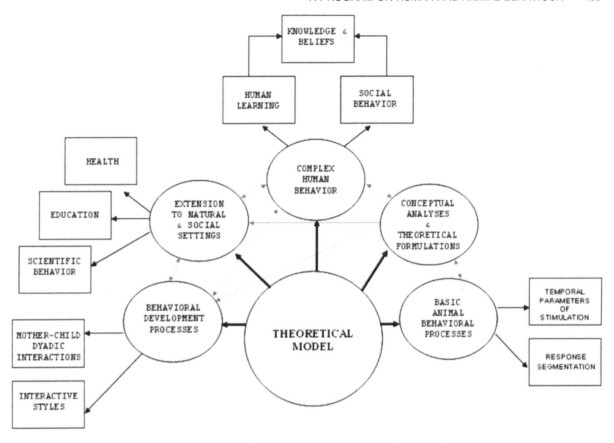

Figure 1. Description of the research program and its relation with the theoretical taxonomy.

behaviour (Silva & Timberlake, 1998; Staddon & Simmelhag, 1971). Physical properties of behaviour involve dynamic and spatial dimensions. On the one hand, intensity (effort) and duration stand out as dynamic properties, while bidimensional (geography or topography) and tridimensional location (orography) stand out as spatial properties. Physical dimensions of responding may not be entirely independent of each other. Thus, for instance, changes in the orography of behaviour may covary with changes in effort and duration, and changes in geography and orography are always changes in the duration spent in a given location. Geography, orography, and duration of behaviour may be recorded and measured, either through unaided observation or through sensing devices. Effort may also be directly measured in relation to specific manipulative responses, such as bar-pressing (Notterman & Mintz, 1965), but must be inferred through indirect measures such as speed or persistence when the analysis focuses on displacement or free movement conditions.

Two experiments were run in order to evaluate changes in the relative duration of rats' locations; a modified operant chamber (Med Env-008CI), and under different values of a response-independent schedule of water delivery (Ribes &

Torres, 2000). In both experiments, fixed-time schedules delivered water in two dispensers that were located at opposite ends of the chamber. In one experiment, the two schedules provided complementary frequencies of water delivery while the overall number of deliveries stayed constant. In the other experiment, one of the schedules delivered water twice as frequently as the other; this proportion was kept constant while the overall density of water deliveries changed systematically. The experimental chamber was divided into six locations (two water dispensers, two adjacent areas, and two lateral areas) and four different positions of the rat were recorded (lying down, standing on all four legs, standing on hind legs, and standing still). The location and position of the rats were videotaped continuously and transcribed by two observers. In both experiments, a single position (height) of the rat was pre-eminent. Also, the percentage of time allocated to each dispenser was roughly proportional to the percentage of water deliveries associated with the dispensers.

Three additional experiments were run (Ribes, Torres, Montes, & Correa, 2006c) to extend the evaluation of the effects of temporal contingencies on the spatial distribution of rats' behaviour.

These experiments used random time and location-contingent schedules of water delivery, and behaviour was automatically recorded by means of a set of photocells. When random-time schedules were used to provide complementary frequencies of water delivery in two opposed dispensers, rats spent more time in the areas adjacent to the dispensers than in the dispensers themselves, and the percentage of time allocated to each area was not proportional to the percentage of water deliveries associated with the corresponding dispenser. In the other two experiments, water delivery was contingent on the location of the rat in the area adjacent to the functional dispenser (proximal condition) or to the area adjacent to the opposite dispenser (distal condition). Water was delivered according to a fixed-interval or a random-interval schedule. In these experiments, no relation was found between the percentage of water delivered by each dispenser and time allocation to the dispenser or its adjacent areas. Irrespective of the location required by the schedule, the rats spent more time in the area adjacent to the dispenser where water was delivered, suggesting that spatial contiguity, not contingency, determined the allocation of behaviour. These experiments show that the spatial distribution of behaviour results from an interaction of the regularity and contingency of water deliveries, and that no single function, principle, or "law" is sufficient to describe these interactions.

We designed a new prototype in order to evaluate not only the spatial distribution of behaviour but also the effects of contingencies dependent of spatial properties. This experimental preparation (Coulburn Habitest Lablinc L91-165), which will replace the standard operant chamber, consists of a space of 92 × 92 cm with 20-cm high walls. Behaviour is recorded by a digital camera that parses response position and location continuously into 0–25 s events. A replication of the previous experiments was carried out, exploring the effects of fixed-time and random-time (independent) schedules on the spatial distribution of behaviour in a larger setting. In a first study with complementary fixed-time schedules (Ribes, Torres, García-Leal, & Isiordia, 2006b), results were different from those of Ribes and Torres (2000). Behaviour was allocated not to the water dispensers but to the adjacent areas, and the percentage of behaviour allocation was not proportional to the percentage of water deliveries in each dispenser. In the initial experimental phase of a second study with complementary random-time schedules (Ribes, Avalos, Torres, Mayoral, & García Leal, 2006a), most behaviour was allocated to one water dispenser, in which all water was delivered. However, in later phases of this study, behaviour was not distributed proportionally to the percentage of water delivered in each dispenser. Behaviour was also allocated to adjacent and lateral areas, suggesting that the rats moved along different routes within the session.

The molar analysis of behaviour under simple concurrent schedules of water delivery does not replicate the findings usually observed when discrete, punctate responses (bar-pressing or key-pecking) are used. Nevertheless, it is not sufficient to compare continuous measures of response allocation under modified experimental environments. It is necessary to look for new units of analysis of behaviour in time and space, which provide increased ecological validity to our observations. We are currently developing descriptions of rats' behaviour that go beyond simple percentages of time allocation in various areas. Digitalized data are being transformed into molar measures such as trajectory, route, distance sweep, speed, acceleration-deceleration, permanence (including entries in, and exits from, areas), and variability (type and number of changes of location and position). These new measures may provide a molar, field-based analysis of how behaviour becomes organized in time and space according to complex spatial and temporal arrangements of events in the environment.

Human learning

The operant study of complex human behaviour has been largely influenced by Skinner's analysis of verbal behaviour (1957). Recent formulations based on the concepts of rule-governed behaviour and equivalence relations have expanded such analysis (Hayes, Barnes-Holmes, & Roche, 2001; Sidman, 1994), although the conceptual and logical relations of such formulations with original operant theory are quite questionable (Burgos, 2003; Ribes, 2000; Tonneau, 2001). Elsewhere I have discussed the inadequacy of the operant analysis of language and complex symbolic processes in terms of verbal behaviour and complex stimulus control relations (Ribes, 1992, 1999). Language is not only a conventional reactional system, with functional properties different from those of strictly biology-bound reactional systems, but it also plays the role of a medium of contact, through social and cultural institutions (Kantor, 1982; Ribes, 1993). Although language involves the activities taking place in speech, writing, and gesturing, it is something more than these activities. Language constitutes a conventional system that mediates and makes possible all human practices. The characteristics of each linguistic system (and its correlated cultural practices) determine three dimensions of human behaviour (Ribes, Cortés, & Romero, 1992): (1) the functional properties of the medium and environment, (2) the instrumental properties of behaviour as a conventional reactional system, and (3) the potential contingencies within, across and above the situations mediated by the properties of (1) and (2). The analysis of human behaviour must focus on the various interactions that may develop between the three dimensions of language. From this perspective, all human behaviour is linguistic (assuming that "verbal" and "linguistic" are not synonyms).

The main goal of this project is to systematically explore the development of cognition. Cognition is understood as the transition from interactions regulated by factors present in a situation to interactions regulated by implicit events dependent on linguistic factors. This transitional process is evaluated in terms of the acquisition, maintenance, and transfer of complex discriminations, both in problem-solving tasks and in categorization experiments. A modified version of the matching-to-sample procedure (Skinner, 1950) has been used as the basic experimental preparation to study human learning and cognition. The traditional matching-to-sample situation (Cumming & Berryman, 1965) consists of a sample stimulus, varying in at least two properties (e.g., shape and colour), which has to be matched to one of two comparison stimuli according to a predetermined criterion. Some of the modifications introduced to the basic matching-to-sample procedures (see Figure 2) are the following: (1) an increase to three or four comparison stimuli, including a default option; (2) the inclusion of second-order stimuli that select, indicate, or inform about the matching criteria; (3) the use of purely observational training procedures; (4) the use of text completion as the matching response; (5) the addition of choices to describe the second-order stimuli, the sample stimuli, the comparison stimuli, the matching response, and the criteria employed for matching: (6) concurrent matching-to-sample matrices; and (7) various kinds of transfer tests (intramodal, extramodal, extrarelational, and extradimensional).

This paper will describe a set of experiments that show the complex relations taking place between human learning and linguistic factors. The basic assumption of these studies is that instructions and feedback limit human learning to variables acting within the situation, and that transfer to different

situations or to purely abstract variables depends on the occurrence of appropriate descriptions of the performance and task criteria.

Two experiments using first-order matching-to-sample with college students evaluated the effects of instructions and feedback on the acquisition and transfer of a conditional discrimination (Ribes & Martínez, 1990). In the first experiment, participants were exposed to different sequences of true, false, and self-formulated instructions informing about the correct matching response (a choice among geometric figures). At the end of every session, participants were informed about their number of correct matching responses. Correct matching consisted of choosing the comparison stimulus that differed in shape and colour from the sample stimulus. The results of this study showed that the sequence and type of instructions was important. Participants showed more correct responses under false instructions after being exposed to true instructions, but showed more incorrect responses under true instructions after being exposed to false instructions. However, in spite of the fact that feedback was delayed until the end of the session, participants initially exposed to false instructions showed some correct responding, and hence some sensitivity to the actual contingencies. In the second experiment, a matching criterion of difference was used, and participants were instructed only to choose a comparison stimulus that was related to the sample stimulus. Participants were exposed to different sequences of feedback: continuous and immediate, alternated and immediate, and delayed and cumulative at the end of the session. The lowest percentage of correct responding was found in the participants who were initially exposed to information on every trial. In contrast, the best performance was observed in those participants who began with information provided at the end of the session. In the groups with better performance and correct responding, the self-described rules reported at the end of every session corresponded to the actual matching relation employed in the task. This result suggests that reinforcing every response at the initial stage of acquisition can interfere with the verbal discrimination of the matching criterion.

In a study by Ribes, Moreno, and Martínez (1998), a second-order matching-to-sample task was used. In second-order matching-to-sample, the "informative" stimuli illustrate a special matching relation (similarity or identity). Thus, if the participants discriminate this relation, they can choose the correct stimulus even in the absence of feedback. In this case, an observational training

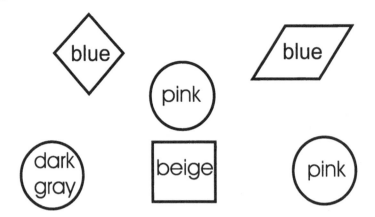

When in the upper section appear (s) ⋯ and in the middle section there is ⋯ I choose ⋯.

a) a blue rhombus and blue trapezoid
b) two figures with the same colour but different shapes
c) two figures with the same shape but different colours
d) two figures with different shapes and colours
e) two figures with the same shape and colour
f) two identical figures
g) two different figures
h) two similar figures
i) a pink circle
j) a coloured figure
k) a figure with a given shape
l) a dark gray circle
m) a beige square
n) a pink circle
ñ) the one with the same shape as the one in the middle section
o) the one with the same colour as the one in the middle section
p) the one with the same shape and colour as the one in the middle section
q) the one with a different colour from the one in the middle section
r) the one with a different shape from the one in the middle section
s) the one with a different shape and colour from the one in the middle section
t) the one identical to the one in the middle section
u) the one different to the one in the middle section
v) the one similar to the one in the middle section
w) a figure with a given shape and colour

Figure 2. Modified arrangement of a second-order matching-to-sample task using verbal responses.

procedure was used, and learning was evaluated in transfer tests. Participants were exposed for different numbers of sessions to the same sequence of three observational training procedures involving mixed trials of identity- and similarity-based matching to sample. On every trial, the procedures involved presenting the stimuli in the array one after the other, or presenting second- and first-order stimuli in successive blocks, or presenting the whole stimulus arrangement at once. A short text appeared below each comparison stimulus, indicating whether the latter was correct or not according to the matching criterion in force on a given trial. Subjects in a fourth group were exposed only to familiarization trials, in which the stimulus arrangements were presented without any instruction or information. On each session, participants were exposed after training to three types of transfer tests (intramodal, extramodal, and extrarelational); information about correct choices was provided at the end of the session. On these transfer trials, the participants chose among comparison stimuli by filling in the blanks of an incomplete text. The blanks referred to the second-order stimuli, the sample stimulus, and the correct comparison, and could be filled by choosing options that described concrete stimuli (e.g., "the green triangle"), modal properties (e.g., "the stimulus with the same colour"), or relations (e.g., "the stimulus that is different"). The results of this study showed that participants gradually increased their percentage of correct responses in the transfer tests, independently of the preceding training procedure. In fact, even the participants exposed to the familiarization procedure achieved high percentages of correct matching in the transfer tests. These findings suggest that correct responding might have been the effect of participants constructing their own verbal description of the matching relation. By forcing the participants to describe stimulus relations and their own response, the procedures used in transfer tests induced appropriate generality and abstraction of performance. Delaying feedback until the end of the session also contributed to this effect.

Finally, another study was designed to evaluate the correspondence between instructions, performance, and self-description (Ribes & Rodríguez, 2001). Three experiments were run using first-order matching-to-sample. In the first experiment, true and false instructions were used to evaluate their effects on nonverbal matching responses and the participants' own descriptions of their matching performance. Descriptions were chosen after every trial among two sets of descriptions, one correct and another incorrect, both with irrelevant and default options. Half of the participants were initially exposed to true instructions, whereas the other half was exposed to false instructions. The results of this experiment showed that participants initially exposed to true instructions showed a large percentage of correct responding and that the percentage of correct self-descriptions generally equalled that of correct matching performance. When shifted to false instructions, these participants maintained a large percentage of correct matching responses and self-descriptions, with a low degree of correspondence with the instructions. In contrast, although the participants initially exposed to false instructions achieved a large percentage of correct matching responses, their self-descriptions tended to be inaccurate, showing that in this case the instructions controlled self-descriptions but not the matching performance. In a second, otherwise identical, experiment, a verbal matching response was used: The participants chose among stimuli by filling the blanks of an incomplete text. As in the

first experiment, participants tended to neglect false instructions during matching. However, the percentage of correct self-descriptions showed positive and negative correlations with false instructions, depending on particular participants and on their sequence of exposure to the instructions. In the third experiment, feedback was added to self-descriptions, to inform participants about the correctness of the descriptions they chose. The results of this experiment showed a double effect of providing feedback after the choice of a performance description. First, self-descriptions and matching responses covaried irrespective of the instructions. Second, under correct instructions all participants showed a high level of correspondence between instructed, actual, and described performance, whereas under incorrect instructions participants showed high correspondence between actual and described performance, and low correspondence between instructions and self-descriptions.

The findings of our studies show that human learning and cognition is affected by complex interactions of linguistic and nonlinguistic variables, including performance itself. Tentatively, the results point to three possible discrimination learning processes in humans: (1) learning through instructions, with a possible insensitivity to consequences unless the correspondence between instructions and feedback breaks down; (2) learning through feedback, with an inability to describe one's own behaviour; and (3) a genuinely "abstract" "ruled-governed" behaviour comprising a successful task performance *and* explicit verbal behaviours that describe the actual contingencies effective in such performance.

Social behaviour

A third project exploring the IFT is concerned with the analysis of social interactions. Operant psychology has dealt with social behaviour as an extension of the three-term contingency that includes a second organism "sharing a common environment" with a first one (Skinner, 1953, p. 297). Although in this extension, organisms behave with respect to one another, the behaviour of each individual may be analysed separately (Skinner, 1962). I have argued (Ribes, 2001) that social behaviour involves something other than different individuals sharing common contingencies. Social organization cannot be identified with, or explained by, the extension of discriminative stimuli and reinforcers to institutions and culture conceived as shared contingencies emerging from exchanges among individuals. Thompson (1958) claims that social behaviour, as distinct from group behaviour, is the outcome of conventional practices through language: "A society is defined as a group that manifests systematic division of labor among adults of the same sex. Most social behavior of insects is genetically determined, while most social behavior of man is culturally determined through symbolic communication" (p. 331).

In division of labour, each individual performs specialized behaviours that are critical for the subsistence and survival of the entire group. In human societies, new and qualitatively different forms of labour division emerge because of language, independent of the biological endowment of the individual. This distinguishes social behaviour, exclusive of humankind, from other behaviours. Protosocial behaviour includes those kinds of inter-individual behaviours, such as motor coordination and eliciting and prompting behaviours, which are vestigial and fundamental for the emergence of any species-specific behaviour. Presocial behaviour includes only those inter-individual behaviours that are functional in the development of group hierarchies, either in feeding, mating, or territorial dominance. Parasocial behaviour consists of behaviours that occur in parallel, which look like inter-individual interactions, but which are regulated by simultaneous, individual, independent variables (as in some analogues of animal leadership, cooperation, and communication). Social behaviour may be understood only from the perspective of institutions. Institutions play the role of media of contact for social interactions. Institutions are the continuous outcomes of customs, and customs basically are the shared conventional practices of individuals. When individuals are influenced, regulated, or affected by institutions, it becomes possible to refer to interactions between different individuals with different social attributions. Thus, institutional functions may be conceived as contingencies that involve the interactions of individuals with differential social attributions in particular situations.

Social contingencies, as institutional functions, may be conceived as emerging from three basic dimensions of human social relationships: (1) power relations (traditionally studied by political science and sociology), (2) exchange relations (traditionally studied by economics), and (3) sanction relations (traditionally studied by morality and jurisprudence). Human society, as a conventional medium, is characterized by the delegation, separation, and deferring of these relations among individual members involved in particular institutional interactions. Power relations may be conceived as contingencies involving the prescription, regulation, administration, and monitoring of interactions. Exchange relations may be thought of as contingencies involved in the production, distribution, and appropriation of goods and services. Finally, sanction contingencies may be looked at as contingencies that deal with the justification, authorization, or penalization of behaviour interactions. The three sets of contingencies participate in any kind of social interaction, but from a behavioural point of view, each of them can be manipulated separately in order to conduct an experimental analysis of their relative influence and course of action. Summing up, the IFT distinguishes between animal and human societies, and stresses the conventional nature of human society as a medium of contact that enables institutional interactions among individuals, regulated by power, exchange, and sanction contingencies.

Many of the experimental situations for the behavioural analysis of social interactions have consisted of repetitive tasks without social significance (Hake & Vukelich, 1972; Lindsley, 1966; Marwell & Schmitt, 1975). An experimental preparation was designed with the dyad as a minimal unit to fulfil the following requirements, which are absent from traditional situations. (1) The experimental task should be socially significant and should not require extrinsic consequences to maintain responding. (2) Task-based responding by each participant should be independent of the others. (3) Participants should be able to respond in any of the available tasks. (4) The experimental setting should consist of a choice situation in which individual performances can be distinguished from social or shared performances. (5) Instructions about payoffs and performances should be explicit. (6) Participants should be able to track their progress on the task. (7) Participants should be able to change payoffs and contingencies. (8) Linguistic interactions should be included as part of the social performance.

The experimental task we have designed consists of a visual puzzle presented on the screen of two independent but synchronized computers (see Figure 3). Participants may be located in the same room or in separate rooms. Each of the two computers presents two displays of the same visual puzzle on its monitor. One puzzle appears in the left section of the screen, the other in the right section. The puzzle in the left section of the screen has to be completed by the participant working on the computer; the puzzle in the right section of the screen duplicates the puzzle solved by the other

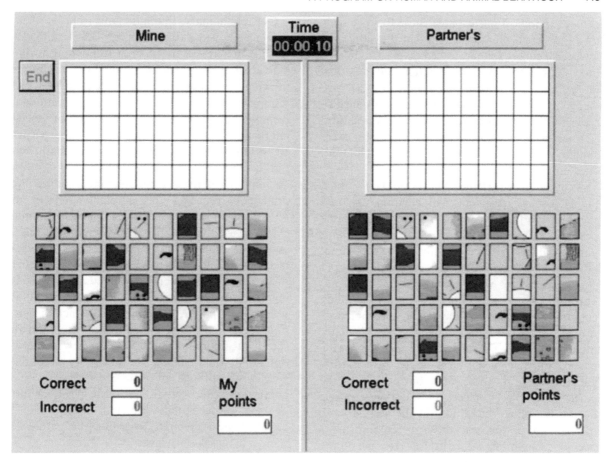

Figure 3. Typical arrangement of the computer screen at the start of a social-interaction session. [Visit the Journal website to view a colour version of the Figure.]

participant (working on the other computer). The computers are programmed synchronically in such a way that the performance of one participant, displayed on the left side of his/her monitor, is also displayed on the other participant's monitor. Therefore, each participant may track the performance of his/her peer in the process of completing the puzzle. The computer system also allows each participant to place pieces in the puzzle of his/her peer. Each time a piece is placed correctly (in any of the two puzzles), this piece automatically snaps in position, and a given amount of points may be earned and displayed on each monitor. Tracking how many points have been earned may require the activation of a special window on the screen.

Several experiments have been done to explore the exchange contingencies involved in some of the social relations traditionally studied by operant psychology: unavoidable cooperation, competition, partial altruism, and total altruism. These four social, or shared exchange, contingencies were scheduled in terms of differential earnings connected to the puzzle(s) in which pieces could be placed. In *competition*, any correct placement in any of the two puzzles provided points for the participant placing the piece. In *partial altruism*, when a participant placed a piece correctly in his/her own puzzle, points were awarded only to this participant, but when he/she correctly placed a piece in the peer's puzzle, points were awarded to both participants. In *total altruism*, when a participant placed a piece correctly in his/her own puzzle, points were awarded to this participant only, but when he/she correctly placed a piece in the peer's puzzle, points were awarded to the peer. In *unavoidable cooperation*, any correct response in any puzzle provided points for both participants.

In a study by Ribes and Rangel (2002), 24 dyads of children and college students were exposed to two sequences of experimental conditions comprising competition, partial altruism, total altruism, and unavoidable cooperation. As previously mentioned, participants could choose to solve their puzzle individually or to work on the peer's puzzle. Under competition and partial altruism contingencies, working additionally or exclusively on the peer's puzzle resulted in larger earnings. Results showed that most participants chose to solve their own puzzle, in spite of the fact that they obtained fewer earnings. Initial, forced exposure to the unavoidable cooperation condition did not promote shared performance. A second study (Ribes, Rangel, Carbajal, & Peña, 2003a) was designed to replicate the previous experiment but in a natural setting, with actual puzzles. The results were similar, and most subjects (six dyads of children) chose to solve their own puzzle.

Another study (Ribes et al., 2003c), which involved four experiments with children, explored the effects of forcing them to place pieces in the peer's puzzle. Two of the experiments dealt with partial altruism and the other two with total altruism and competition. Forced responding and choice conditions were alternated. In the partial altruism experiments, during forced-responding conditions, placing a piece in one's own puzzle was not rewarded with points, whereas placing a piece in the peer's puzzle produced earnings for the participant placing the piece or for both participants. In the first case, some, but not all, of the participants placed pieces in the peer's puzzle during the choice condition; in the second case, most of the participants chose to respond in the peer's puzzle. In the total altruism experiment, the forced-responding procedure did not have effects, and children chose to respond in their own puzzle. The participants in the competition experiment also chose to respond in their own puzzle, in spite of the fact that they earned fewer points for doing so. (Half of the dyads worked in the same room, whereas the other half worked in separate rooms. The distribution of the participants had no effects on their social interaction, however.)

An additional series of experiments (Ribes et al., 2003b) explored the effects of the inequity and asymmetry of earnings on college students' preference for individual versus social contingencies. It was assumed that different rewards for the same performance would facilitate the choice of shared contingencies when earnings were higher for one of the two members of the dyad. Inequity conditions (based on asymmetrical or symmetrical criteria for each member of the dyad) alternated with conditions in which earnings were equal and symmetrical. These manipulations were made in different experiments using competition, partial altruism, and total altruism contingencies. With the exception of one dyad in a condition of partial altruism, most participants chose to respond in the individual contingency, not taking advantage of a possible two- or three-fold increase in their earnings.

Our preliminary findings show that a social contingency with larger earnings is not sufficient to shift preferences away from responding to the individual contingency. Additionally, auditing or tracking responses did not seem related to responding in the peer's puzzle or with additional earnings. The experimental analysis of social interaction has been dominated by approaches based either on economic models and mathematical game theory (Brown & Rachlin, 1999), or on assumptions derived from operant conditioning principles regarding the automatic effects of reinforcement schedules and discriminative stimuli (Marwell & Schmitt, 1975). However, our findings, as well as other stressing the relevance of social factors (Schuster & Perelberg, 2004), suggest that these approaches are biased, limited, and misleading. In a near future we expect to explore the joint influence of power, exchange, and sanction contingencies in the development and regulation of social interactions, and to develop new preparations that could emulate the institutional contingencies constitutive of different economic and political systems. Present approaches to the study of social and economic behaviour are ill-founded on ideological premises regarding the nature of economic and social "laws."

REFERENCES

Baum, W. M., & Rachlin, H. C. (1969). Choice as time allocation. *Journal of the Experimental Analysis of Behavior, 12,* 861–874.

Brown, J., & Rachlin, H. C. (1999). Self-control and social cooperation. *Behavioral Processes, 47,* 65–72.

Burgos, J. (2003). Laudable goals, interesting experiments, unintelligible theorizing: A critical review of Hayes, Barnes, and Roche's (2001), "Relational frame theory." *Behavior and Philosophy, 31,* 19–45.

Cumming, W. W., & Berryman, R. (1965). The complex discriminated operant: Studies of matching-to-sample and related problems. In D. I. Mostofsky (Ed.), *Stimulus generalization* (pp. 284–330). Stanford, CT: Stanford University Press.

Hake, D. F., & Vukelich, R. (1972). A classification and review of cooperation procedures. *Journal of the Experimental Analysis of Behavior, 18,* 333–343.

Hayes, S. C., Barnes-Holmes, D., & Roche, B. (2001). *Relational frame theory: A post-Skinnerian account of human language and cognition.* New York: Kluwer Academic/Plenum.

Kantor, J. R. (1924–1926). *Principles of psychology.* New York: A. Knopf.

Kantor, J. R. (1959). *Interbehavioral psychology.* Chicago: Principia Press.

Kantor, J. R. (1982). *Cultural psychology.* Chicago: Principia Press.

Lindsley, O. R. (1966). Experimental analysis of cooperation and competition. In T. Verhave (Ed.),

The experimental analysis of behavior (pp. 470–501). New York: Appleton Century Crofts.

Marwell, G., & Schmitt, D. R. (1975). *Cooperation: An experimental analysis*. New York: Academic Press.

Notterman, J. M., & Mintz, D. E. (1965). *Dynamics of response*. New York: Wiley.

Ribes, E. (1982). *El conductismo: reflexiones críticas*. Barcelona, Spain: Fontanella.

Ribes, E. (1985). Human behavior as operant behavior: An empirical or conceptual issue? In C. F. Lowe, M. Richelle, D. F. Blackman, & C. D. Bradshaw (Eds.), *Behavior analysis and contemporary psychology*. Hillsdale, NJ: Lawrence Erlbaum Associates Inc.

Ribes, E. (1986). Is operant conditioning sufficient to cope with human behavior? In P. Chase & L. Parrott (Eds.), *Psychological aspects of language: The West Virginia Lectures on Psychology*. Springfield, IL: Ch. Thomas.

Ribes, E. (1992). Some thoughts on thinking and its motivation. In S. C. Hayes & L. J. Hayes (Eds.), *Understanding verbal relations* (pp. 211–224). Reno, NV: Context Press.

Ribes, E. (1993). Behavior as the functional content of language games. In S. C. Hayes, L. J. Hayes, H. W. Reese, & T. R. Sarbin (Eds.), *Varieties of scientific contextualism* (pp. 283–297). Reno, NV: Context Press.

Ribes, E. (1994). Skinner y la psicología: lo que hizo, lo que no hizo y lo que nos corresponde hacer. In E. Ribes (Ed.), *B. F. Skinner: In memoriam*. Guadalajara, Mexico: Universidad de Guadalajara.

Ribes, E. (1996). Some thoughts on the nature of a theory of behavior development. In S. W. Bijou & E. Ribes (Eds.), *New directions in the development of behavior*. Reno, NV: Context Press.

Ribes, E. (1997). Causality and contingency. *The Psychological Record*, 47, 619–639.

Ribes, E. (1999). *Teoría del condicionamiento y lenguaje: un análisis histórico y conceptual*. México: Taurus.

Ribes, E. (2000). Instructions, rules and abstraction: A misconstrued relation. *Behavior and Philosophy*, 28, 41–55.

Ribes, E. (2001). Functional dimensions of social behavior: Theoretical considerations and some preliminary data. *Mexican Journal of Behavior Analysis*, 27, monographic issue, 285–306.

Ribes, E. (2003a). What is defined in operational definitions? The case of operant psychology. *Behavior and Philosophy*, 31, 111–126.

Ribes, E. (2003b). Concepts and theories: Relations to scientific categories. In A. Lattal & P. Chase (Eds.), *Behavior theory and philosophy* (pp. 147–164). New York: Kluwer/Plenum.

Ribes, E. (2004a). Behavior is abstraction, not ostension: Conceptual and historical remarks on the nature of psychology. *Behavior and Philosophy*, 32, 55–68.

Ribes, E. (2004b). Acerca de las funciones psicológicas: un post-scriptum. *Acta Comportamentalia*, 12, 117–127.

Ribes, E. (2005). Theory, scientific research and technical applications: How related in operant psychology? In J. Burgos & E. Ribes (Eds.), *The relationships between theory, research and applications in behavior science*. Guadalajara, Mexico: Universidad de Guadalajara.

Ribes, E. (in press). Resistance to change in operant psychology: Until when? *The Behavior Analyst*.

Ribes, E., Avalos, M. L., Torres, C., Mayoral, A., & García-Leal, O. (2006a). *Spatial organization of behavior under concurrent random-time schedules of water delivery*. Manuscript in preparation.

Ribes, E., Cortés, A., & Romero, P. (1992). Quizá el lenguaje no es un proceso o tipo especial de comportamiento: algunas reflexiones basadas en Wittgenstein. *Revista Latina de Pensamiento y Lenguaje*, 1, 58–74.

Ribes, E., & López, F. (1985). *Teoría de la conducta: un análisis de campo y paramétrico*. México: Trillas.

Ribes, E., & Martínez, H. (1990). Interaction of contingencies and rule instructions in the performance of human subjects in conditional discrimination. *The Psychological Record*, 40, 565–586.

Ribes, E., Moreno, D., & Martínez, C. (1998). Second-order discrimination in humans: the roles of explicit instructions and constructed verbal responding. *Behavioral Processes*, 42, 1–18.

Ribes, E., & Rangel, N. (2002). A comparison of choice between individual and share contingencies in children and young adults. *European Journal of Behavior Analysis*, 3, 61–73.

Ribes, E., Rangel, N., Carbajal, G., & Peña, E. (2003a). Choice between individual and share social contingencies in children: An experimental replication in a natural setting. *European Journal of Behavior Analysis*, 4, 105–114.

Ribes, E., Rangel, N., Casillas, J. R., Alvarez, A., Gudiño, M., Zaragoza, A., & Hernández, H. (2003b). Inequidad y asimetría de las consecuencias en la elección entre contingencias individuales y sociales. *Revista Mexicana de Análisis de la Conducta*, 29, 131–168.

Ribes, E., Rangel, N., Juárez, A., Contreras, S., Abreu, A., Alvarez, A., Gudiño, M., & Casillas, J. R. (2003c). Respuestas "sociales" forzadas y cambio de preferencias entre contingencias individuales y sociales en niños y adultos. *Acta Comportamentalia*, 11, 197–234.

Ribes, E., & Rodríguez, M. E. (2001). The effects of feedback and type of matching response in the correspondence between instructions, performance, and self-descriptions in a conditional discrimination with humans. *The Psychological Record*, 51, 309–333.

Ribes, E., & Torres, C. (2000). The spatial distribution of behavior under varying frequencies of temporally scheduled water delivery. *Journal of the Experimental Analysis of Behavior*, 73, 195–209.

Ribes, E., Torres, C., García-Leal, O., & Isiordia, R. I. (2006b). *Concurrent fixed-time schedules of water delivery effects on the spatial organization of behavior in the rat*. Manuscript in preparation.

Ribes, E., Torres, C., Montes, E., & Correa, L. (2006c). *Effects of concurrent random-time schedules on the spatial distribution of behavior in rats*. Manuscript submitted for publication.

Ryle, G. (1949). *The concept of mind*. New York: Barnes & Noble.

Schoenfeld, W. N. (1976). The "response" in behavior theory. *Pavlovian Journal of Biological Science*, 11, 129–149.

Schoenfeld, W. N., & Farmer, J. (1970). Reinforcement schedules and the "behavior stream". In

W. N. Schoenfeld (Ed.), *The theory of reinforcement schedules* (pp. 215–245). New York: Appleton Century Crofts.

Schuster, R., & Perelberg, A. (2004). Why cooperate? An economic perspective is not enough. *Behavioral Processes*, *66*, 261–277.

Sidman, M. (1994). *Equivalence relations and behavior: A research history*. Boston: Author Cooperative.

Silva, K. M., & Timberlake, W. (1998). The organization and temporal properties of appetitive behavior in rats. *Animal Learning and Behavior*, *26*, 182–195.

Skinner, B. F. (1938). *The behavior of organisms*. New York: Appleton Century Crofts.

Skinner, B. F. (1950). Are theories of learning necessary? *Psychological Review*, *57*, 193–216.

Skinner, B. F. (1953). *Science and human behavior*. New York: MacMillan.

Skinner, B. F. (1957). *Verbal behavior*. New York: Appleton Century Crofts.

Skinner, B. F. (1962). Two "synthetic social relations". *Journal of the Experimental Analysis of Behavior*, *5*, 531–533.

Staddon, J. E. R., & Simmelhag, V. (1971). The superstition experiment: A reexamination of its implications for the principles of adaptive behavior. *Psychological Review*, *78*, 30–43.

Thompson, W. R. (1958). Social behavior. In A. Roe & G. G. Simpson (Eds.), *Behavior and evolution* (pp. 291–310). New Haven, CT: Yale University Press.

Tonneau, F. (2001). Equivalence relations: A reply. *European Journal of Behavior Analysis*, *2*, 99–128.

INTERNATIONAL JOURNAL OF PSYCHOLOGY, 2006, 41 (6), 449–461

Person, behaviour, and contingencies (an aesthetic view of behaviourism)

Marino Pérez-Álvarez

University of Oviedo, Spain

José Manuel García-Montes

University of Almería, Spain

*T*he concept of person is a fundamental one in any psychology worthy of the name, yet it is not among the technical terms of behaviourism. Indeed, behaviourism was reticent, not surprisingly, about the concept of person, given its traditional substantiality and intrapsychic sense. But behaviourism, particularly the Skinnerian variety, has the ideas to develop a perfectly acceptable conception of the person. Notable among these would be the idea of operant subject (author and actor). With regard precisely to the person as subject-actor of the behaviour, it is worth underlining the affinity of behaviourism with person in its radical (etymological) sense, derived from the theatre (persona=mask=role=behavioural repertoires). In fact, in its original dramaturgical sense, the person gives a face to others and according to socially organized contingencies (scripts, norms, rules). Thus, person is a term correlative to the stage, or, in other words, to contingencies. The present work sets out to develop this affinity between the original sense of person and radical behaviourism. In this line we include the aesthetic view of behaviourism. In order to understand its meaning, we begin by considering art as behaviour, and thus, the person as a work of art (Pérez-Álvarez & García-Montes, 2004). We advocate a poetic statute of the person, which is none other than the operant constructivist sense that characterizes behaviourism (seen from a new perspective). The most decisive aspect of this reappraisal is that it includes the experience of the self at its deepest level: the skin. Not the world under the skin, as Skinner would say, but *on* the skin.

*L*e concept de personne est fondamental dans toute psychologie digne de ce nom, quoiqu'il ne fasse pas partie des termes techniques du behaviorisme. En effet, le behaviorisme est réticent, ce qui n'est pas surprenant, à propos du concept de personne compte tenu de son substantialisme traditionnel et de son sens intrapsychique. Mais le behaviorisme, particulièrement celui de tendance skinnerienne, propose de développer une conception parfaitement acceptable de la personne. Notamment, parmi les idées proposées se retrouve celle de sujet opérant (auteur et acteur). Concernant plus précisément la personne en tant que sujet acteur du comportement, il vaut la peine de souligner l'affinité du behaviorisme avec la personne dans son sens radical (étymologique), dérivé du théâtre (personne=masque=rôle=répertoires comportementaux). En fait, dans son sens dramatique original, la personne donne un visage aux autres en accord avec les contingences socialement organisées (les scripts, normes et règles). Ainsi, le terme personne est associé au scénario, ou, en d'autres mots, aux contingences. Le présent travail vise à développer cette affinité entre le sens original du terme personne et le behaviorisme radical. Dans cette perspective, nous incluons la vision esthétique du behaviorisme. Afin de comprendre sa signification, nous commençons par considérer l'art en tant que comportement, puis la personne en tant qu'oeuvre d'art (Pérez-Álvarez & Garcia-Montes, 2004). Nous préconisons le statut poétique de la personne, lequel est nul autre que le sens constructiviste opérant qui caractérise le behaviorisme (vu d'une nouvelle perspective). L'aspect le plus décisif de cette réévaluation est qu'elle inclut l'expérience du soi à son niveau le plus profond : la peau. Il ne s'agit donc pas du monde en dessous de la peau mais, comme Skinner aurait dit, sur la peau.

*E*l concepto de persona es fundamental en cualquier psicología digna de tal nombre, pero no se encuentra entre los principales términos técnicos del conductismo. De hecho el conductismo fue reticente y eso no debe sorprendernos, acerca del concepto de persona, dado su sentido tradicionalmente substancialista e intrapsíquico. Pero el conductismo, en particular la versión Skinneriana, posee las ideas para desarrollar una conceptuación perfectamente aceptable de persona. Entre estas se destaca la idea de sujeto operante (autor y actor). En relación precisamente con la persona como sujeto-actor del comportamiento, vale la pena señalar la

Correspondence should be addressed to Marino Pérez-Álvarez, Departamento de Psicología, Universidad de Oviedo, Plaza Feijóo, s/n, 33003-Oviedo, Spain (E-mail: marino@uniovi.es).

This study was supported by Research Grant SEJ2005-00455.

DOI: 10.1080/00207590500491585

afinidad del conductismo con el concepto de persona en su sentido radical (etimológico), derivado del teatro (persona=máscara=rol=repertorios comportamentales). De hecho en su sentido dramatúrgico original la persona se da cara a los demás de acuerdo a contingencias socialmente organizadas (guión, normas, reglas). En esta forma la persona es un término que se correlaciona con el escenario o en otras palabras con las contingencias. El presente trabajo busca relacionar la afinidad existente entre el sentido original de persona y el conductismo radical. En esta línea de pensamiento incluimos el punto de vista estético del conductismo. Con el fin de entender su significado comenzamos considerando el arte como comportamiento y por lo tanto la persona como una obra de arte (Pérez-Álvarez y García-Montes, 2004). Abogamos por el estatuto poético de la persona que no es otro nada más que el sentido constructivista operante que caracteriza el conductismo (visto desde una perspectiva nueva). El aspecto más decisivo de esta reconceptuación es que incluye la experiencia del yo en su sentido más profundo: la piel, no el mundo debajo de la piel, como diría Skinner, sino sobre la piel.

EXPOSITION OF THE TOPIC

Importance of the person

The person is a fundamental concept for psychology as a science, for society in general and for people in particular.

Psychology studies behaviour, but behaviour is always the behaviour of someone. So psychology also studies that someone. This it does through a variety of concepts, such as organism, self, subject, character, personality, and so on. Although all of these concepts have their own meaning, they all revolve around the concept of person. Indeed, psychology is increasingly using the notion of person, instead of, or at least in conjunction with, these terms (e.g., Fierro, 2002; Mischel, 2004). In any case, as considered here, the person would be a basic concept for psychology. In relation to society, it is sufficient to bear in mind that institutions such as the law, morals, and civil liberties are based on the notion of person. Moreover, people ask themselves who they are and, indeed, personal identity has become a question of great importance in today's constantly changing society, with so many different functional contexts. Few are able to say, as did Don Quixote four centuries ago: "I know who I am" (Pérez-Álvarez, 2005).

But in spite of its importance, the person is not conceptualized within behaviourism, nor in the analysis of behaviour, as would befit philosophy and the science of psychology that they respectively represent. In this regard, we might say that behaviourism as philosophy and the analysis of behaviour as experimental and applied science probably represent the most rigorous system of psychology. This is despite the fact that it is not currently the dominant approach in the discipline, and notwithstanding the developments it may yet undergo (among which would be the required conceptualization of the person). In truth, behaviourism and behaviour analysis have been, in general, reticent about the idea of person, and understandably so, given its traditionally substantialist and intrapsychic meaning. But however we look at it, the concept of person is fundamental for any kind of psychology worthy of the name.

Radical behaviourism as a reference

Nevertheless, behaviourism, and Skinnerian behaviourism in particular, is equipped with ideas for developing a sound conception of person, and one not only coherent with its own system, but valid for society in general and people in particular. The behaviourism of reference here is, indeed, Skinner's radical behaviourism, whose approach (along with a clarification of the customary misunderstandings) we need not deal with here (Skinner, 1974). It becomes clear why Skinner's radical behaviourism should serve as a reference when we consider that it establishes the decisive criterion, distinguishing precisely between radical and methodological, on the basis of which the different existing behaviourisms must be measured (Pérez-Álvarez, 2004). It also marks a turning point in the very history of psychology (Fuentes & Quiroga, 2004; Moore, 1995). As regards the existence of different behaviourisms, it is ironic that not only has behaviourism not died (as prematurely announced) but, at the height of the "cognitive era," there is more of it than ever—some 14 varieties in all (O'Donohue & Kitchener, 1999).

Thus, behaviour analysis around the world would do well to take Skinner as a reference, without ignoring, of course, the value of subsequent contributions, even as footnotes to his work. In any case, as Ardila (2004) argues, Skinner is the most influential psychologist in the entire history of psychology, as shown by studies on the subject (Haggbloom et al., 2002).

The ideas referred to for developing the concept of person in accordance with the coordinates of behaviourism and behaviour analysis derive precisely from the work of Skinner, from diverse texts and contexts.

BEHAVIOURIST IDEAS FOR A CONCEPTION OF THE PERSON

Three broad ideas can be found in the work of Skinner on which to develop the concept of person, and to which, indeed, have been added important footnotes. These are: (1) the organized system of responses, (2) the *locus* of behaviour, and (3) self-control.

Organized system of responses

The organized system of responses is the definition given by Skinner (1953) for the self. Of course, the whole idea of self implies a functionally unified system of responses, but, as Skinner himself points out, this is assuming a great deal, since one often has more than one system of responses, including some that may even be incompatible with one another. In any case, this would be explained according to functional analysis, determining the different contexts on which the response systems depend, so that it could no longer be said that they depend on the supposed unitary entity of the self.

In the case of incompatible systems, the incompatibility would not be important if the relevant variables were never present at the same time. Thus, following Skinner's example, an individual's system of behaviours or personality (as he also says) in the context of his family may be quite different from that he shows in the presence of close friends. The problem would occur if one day the friends go to his home or the family goes to the place where he meets up with his friends.

Thus, the concept of self, as Skinner says, may have an initial advantage on representing a relatively coherent system of responses, but fails, first on assuming a unity where there is none, and second because there is a need to explain the variety of systems in which it consists through functional analysis of behaviour.

The durability and success of the concept of self, however, in spite of any possible weaknesses, is explained by the fact that it allows the construction of discourse about one's story, giving a narrative sense to what would often be no more than disparate systems of behaviour dependent on certain contingencies (not to say random events). In any case, it can be seen as a poetics of identity (Sarbin, 1997), to which we shall return later.

The idea of an organized system of responses persists in the tradition of behaviourism as "behavioural repertoires," this term even becoming practically distinctive of the behaviourist (just as "oedipal sphere" is of the psychoanalyst, or "mental scheme" is of the cognitivist). Indeed, the idea of repertoire has formed the basis for an entire theory of personality, such as that of Staats (1996), distinguishing three broad systems (emotive-motivational, linguistic-cognitive, and imitative-instrumental). Even so, Staats' model is not particularly committed to the Skinnerian idea, so that his insistence on cumulative learning would conflict with the contingential analysis stressed by Skinner. In the face of such analysis, Staats' "systems of personality" would be too general.

As Skinner (1974) argues, complex contingencies create complex repertoires, and different contingencies create different persons, "under the same skin." So-called multiple personalities would be no more than extreme forms of this type. In this regard, the question would not be how many personalities one has, but rather how many behavioural repertoires one is capable of performing or exhibiting (Phelps, 2000).

In any case, the notion of repertoire does not resolve the problem (insofar as it is a problem) of functional unity, which was equally unresolved by the self, unless it be in narrative terms (which would be quite another story).

Locus of behaviour

The "*locus* of behaviour" is the response given by Skinner (1972) in his analysis of what it means to "have a poem." This was an opportune occasion for considering the issue of creativity, in this case in relation to poetry. Creativity suggests a consideration of the person as a self-originating source of productions for which he or she becomes admired. It is certainly true that people are more likely to admire the "author" the less they know about the conditions of the "creation." The author tends not to give a high profile to his or her influences, and at the same time leads the audience to understand that the creation results from an inspiration, which in the times of the muses came supposedly from Olympus, but today is universally assumed to come from within the person. The effect is, on the one hand, the admiration of others and one's own vainglory, and on the other, total obscurantism about the meaning of "having a poem" or having (done) anything else, regardless of how admirable it may be.

As we might suppose, Skinner's analysis is revealing. It rests on the notion of *locus*, which designates the point of confluence of variables from the past (history of reinforcement) and the present (current contingencies) on which the behaviour and, where applicable, the resulting *oeuvre*, depends. This point or place is none other than the organism or person that has emitted such behaviours. It is interesting to note that the past is contemporaneous with the present. It is not in any *topos* of the unconscious, or in any cognition store, nor even in the hippocampus of the brain. The past forms part of the present, incorporated in the organisms or persons themselves, changed and continually changing through the actions taken at each moment. Quite another thing is how notable these changes are from one moment to the next.

The notion of *locus* repudiates the person as the claimed creative source and, at the same time, affirms it as the "sole place," even if only because nobody else, without exception, has this same personal history. The creator thus becomes the point of confluence of a series of current and past influences, which result in the work produced, but this was not inside its author, but was rather operated and made, or composed, by doing things with words (poem) or through other media. In this regard it is interesting to recall the "method of composition" of the poem *The Crow* revealed by its author, Edgar Allen Poe (1846), the perfect behaviour analyst *avant la lettre*.

The idea of *locus* has been developed in two relatively different ways: as host and as context. The idea of host was proposed by Baer (1976) to specify the role of the organism in relation to behaviour. The organism would be the host, and behaviours would be the guests. The reasoning behind this is that contingencies of reinforcement operate on behaviours, rather than on the organism itself. The organism would also depend on the environment, but the latter actually reinforces behaviours. The organism would therefore act as host to a series of behaviours (guests), which could have different functions according to places and times (like the repertoires mentioned above). Thus, behaviours would have to be analysed not only in relation to environmental conditions, but also with respect to their consequences for the host and other guests.

As regards the idea of context, it was introduced by Relational Frame Theory (Hayes, Barnes-Holmes, & Roche, 2001) to specify the role of private events, particularly in therapy. The context here is above all the one given by language in educational practices. It is shown how language comes to constitute the texture of the self or the person, forming a whole verbal social context, within which private events occur, including those of clinical relevance (traumatic memories, fears, obsessions, voices). Thus, the therapy developed in this line, Acceptance and Commitment Therapy (ACT; Hayes, Strosahl, & Wilson, 1999; Wilson & Luciano, 2002), distinguishes between the self as context (verbal social) and the self as content (behaviours and private events). This distinction has also, and more generally, been formulated in terms of person/behaviour.

The advantage of this distinction opened up by the idea of context is twofold: On the one hand, it permits a conception of self-distancing (making possible the perspective of the person with respect to one's own private events and behaviours). On the other, it links in with a whole tradition that has already distinguished this dual aspect of the self or person and that it should be acknowledged—beginning with the I/me of W. James (1890) and G. H. Mead (1934), and continuing with the self and identity of K. E. Scheibe (1995).

Self-control

Self-control represents a classic chapter of human behaviour (Skinner, 1953). Note that the self of self-control is oneself in the task of managing the conditions upon which one's own behaviour depends. It assumes, therefore, the self-distancing referred to above. Apart from this, self-control would be one's capacity to direct one's own life, which includes the will, freedom, and responsibility traditionally attributed to the person. The difference is that behaviour analysis studies these human attributes in relation to the contextual conditions that make them possible, rather than considering them as inherent to the person, as traditional humanist conceptions are content to assume.

The point is that self-control is a particular case of behaviour control. One does for oneself what one would do to control the behaviour of others, and what others would do and probably did do in the past with respect to it. Self-control is learned, then, in social practice, as one also learns the will that it actually involves. Self-control implies wanting something and striving for it (will). Thus, willpower consists of *resistance* to temptation from objects of desire that give immediate gratification but that may be disadvantageous in the long term, and *persistence* towards actions whose gratification is deferred and that may bring unpleasant immediate effects. We need hardly add that this derives from particular reinforcement contingencies (Rachlin, 2000).

In addition to what has been said about self-control, the idea of operant subject would also have to be taken on board. This notion of operant subject involves two aspects that should be highlighted here. On the one hand, there is the consideration of the individual as an indivisible whole, as opposed to its customary dismemberment by other psychologies into a jumble of internal mechanisms. On the other, there is the notion of the subject as essentially active, in a practical, effective, and constructive sense; as a creator of culture and a promoter of social change (Glenn, 2004). This is in contrast to the mental activity arrogated by traditional psychology, and also quite different from the idea this psychology has of the behaviourist subject as passive and merely reactive. This idea that psychology—and subsequently the public at large—has formed of the behaviourist subject is just one of the many misunderstandings and distortions that have been disseminated in relation to the work of Skinner, as Ardila (2004) points out.

The idea of the operant subject involves his situation *in* the world, based on which and in relation to which he acts, operating effects that in turn work back on his own behaviour and on the subject himself, changing him (as already stated). Note that it is the subject that is in the world (the *being-in-the-world* of the existentialists), not the world that is in the subject, as maintained by mentalism (see Fallon, 1992; Woolfolk & Sass, 1988).

In this context, we would have to consider the issue of *freedom*, which, by the way, is by no means at odds with behaviourism (yet another misunderstanding). True, Skinner (1971) was critical of the concept of freedom derived from a homunculist

humanism that speaks of the internal man and the autonomous man, as though the human being were exempt from the conditions of the world. However, Skinner is not anti-humanist, but rather anti-homunculist. We might say, paraphrasing Sartre, that behaviourism is a type of humanism. Indeed, Ardila (2003) defends behavioural humanism precisely on a Skinnerian basis.

What Skinner argues is that the ultimate origin of control is environmental, but his very notion of control, including self-control (operant subject), introduces variations within the "causal chain." Indeed, the overabundance of environmental control, far from impeding control, obliges a decision between some possible actions and others. It is the contingent condition of behaviour and ultimately of the human being that establishes and obliges freedom (Pérez-Álvarez, 2004). As Sartre would say, we are obliged to be free, and we might add here, "because of contingencies" (see Morf, 1998). Insofar as something is possible rather than necessary or impossible, doing something has meaning. Of course, the consequences of behaviours condition successive actions, thus closing off some possibilities and opening up others. But one is always faced with some or other contingencies, and this situation, as the reader will recall, defines the "free operant," a technical concept of behaviour analysis (Ferster, 1953).

Nor should it be forgotten that the conditionality of the stimuli involved suggests probability more than determinism. However, it must also be borne in mind that one is always in the world, not beyond its conditions. The question here is perceiving freedom within determinism. The universe may be determinist but the person has his or her degrees of freedom.

If contingency establishes freedom, freedom establishes responsibility for one's own actions and omissions. And this is how society sets things out, and what it expects. Although control arises ultimately from the environment, as Skinner would say, and especially from socially organized contingencies and metacontingencies (Glenn, 2004; Skinner, 1969), society relies on the fact that the subject of the behaviour is capable of responding in a controlled way according to circumstances. As Skinner (1989) says, "Cultures thus hold their members responsible for what they have done, and members 'feel responsible'" (p. 31). Society's control operates, so to speak, through the self-control of individuals themselves, as operant subjects, who operate freely and at the same time are subject to norms. On the question of norms or rules we would have to mention rule-governed behaviour, a specification of behaviour control introduced by Skinner (1957, 1969) and extensively developed in subsequent work (Hayes, 1989).

In sum, it has been shown that behaviourism is equipped with ideas on which to develop the concept of person. We have reviewed notions such as the *organized system of responses* (and in this line behavioural repertoires), the *locus of behaviour* (and with it the organism as host and the verbal social context), and finally, *self-control and the operant subject*, which might well be installed as the notion of person we were seeking. Nevertheless, and based on these ideas, we shall propose a bolder conception of person, unfettered by the technical terms of behaviour analysis, even if still within the coordinates of its basic philosophy, which is none other than radical behaviourism. This proposal can be dubbed dramatic or aesthetic, the meanings of which will become clear in the course of its development.

DRAMATURGY OF THE PERSON

First of all, we should consider an essential affinity between person and behaviourism. As the reader will recall, the word "person" has its origins in the Greek *prosopon*, meaning "mask," the mask by which classical Greek actors were recognized and made themselves heard. Through synecdoche, in a case of extended tact, as Skinner (1957) would say, the mask came to designate the actor, and thus, "person" would in principle mean actor. Note that the etymology of person also implies presentation to others and recognition by others of what one represents. In theatre, the others are the rest of the actors and the audience.

The next step was to take the word person from theatre to refer now to individuals in real life (as actors), which would occur in times of Roman Law. This metaphorical extension, another case of extended tact, is undoubtedly due to the similarity between theatre and life, even though it is not clear what imitates what. The point here is also that the person in real life has a radically social origin. The root of the person, like the etymology of the word "person" itself, is in his or her social character. As the Spanish philosopher Ortega y Gasset (1958)

would say, man is an etymological animal, explained by his history.

But the person is correlative of the stage. As Bruner (1990) suggests, on entering life it is as though we stepped onto a stage to take part in a play already well under way, a play whose somewhat open plot determines what roles we can play and which dénouements we can set off. Other characters on the stage already have some idea of what the play is about; this is a sufficiently elaborated idea for negotiation with the new arrival to be possible.

This means that in order to understand and explain people's "performances" we have to look at the stage on which their actions take place, and not into their brain, psyche, or mind (if that were possible). If the conditions on which people's behaviours depend are internal, it would be more than difficult to understand what they were doing. The audience in a theatre understands the drama played out by the characters not because they penetrate their minds, but precisely because of what they see happening on the stage. It is no coincidence that the word "theatre" comes from *theorein*, which means to see comprehensively, and is whence we derive "theory." A theatrical or dramaturgic theory would in fact be akin to behaviourism. Indeed, behaviour analysis consists of analysing behaviour according to contingencies (the stage or situation) and metacontingencies (the context of the play or the social frame of reference).

What happens in the theatre of life is that the stages on which people's behaviour unfolds are multiple. This means that the person has many faces or masks, or, as mentioned earlier, systems or repertoires of behaviours; we might even say that there are different persons *on* the same skin. Skinner (1989) himself establishes the similarity between masks and the behavioural repertoires called persons. The key would lie, in any case, in contingencies of reinforcement. The notion of person involves the multiplicity of masks (repertoires), but, of course, these masks, rather than disguising or "masking," show the person as he or she actually is. In this sense the person is multifaceted, so that, depending on the stage or situation (contingencies of reinforcement), one mask or another may come into play.

The different masks or ways of being cannot coexist. Certain forms of being characteristic of oneself always remain offstage. From the others' point of view, there are always sides of a person that remain unseen. But that does not mean we can say that they are inside oneself. Where is the form of behaving with one's friends in the pub when one is at home with the family? The person–behaviour–contingencies articulation makes the interior/exterior distinction unnecessary.

The person is the behaviour he or she emits. *Ye shall know them by their fruits*, it is written in the Gospels. The person is always behaving in some way. In fact, it would be impossible not to behave. Mere presence, even in silence, says something. The stream of consciousness of which W. James speaks would be better described as a stream of behaviours. Behaviours make one's life, and thus write one's story. The behaviours of life are acts of meaning (Bruner, 1990), whose sense is conferred by the culture that envelops and constitutes all human action. In this regard, we could speak of life as the development of a drama (after all, "drama" means action). Remember that to enter life is actually to set foot on a stage (to exist, from *exit*).

The meaning of existence opens up a horizon of possibilities, and thus possible worlds also become reality (Bruner, 1986). Life can without doubt be seen as a drama (Burke, 1945; Goffman, 1959; Scheibe, 2000), in line, moreover, with a long tradition (going back to the Greeks). This is also in agreement with popular psychology (Bruner, 1990). In any case, more than the development of this dramatic sense of life, what we are considering here is the construction of the person and, as we shall see, of the person as a work of art.

AESTHETICS OF THE PERSON

Aesthetics and behaviour analysis

It has been said that the person is the behaviour he or she emits, but behaviour is also what makes the person. The person makes him- or herself, obviously, according to the conditions of possibility offered by the world (historical, social, family circumstances, and so on). So he or she does not come from inside, nor grow like a plant. Nor is this self-construction constituted merely by self-control, even though it starts out from it. In this line, we might say that among the objects on which the subject operates is him- or herself as an object. The subject him- or herself is the object of his or her own behaviours, in line with Skinner's (1989) distinction between controlling and controlled selves.

This realization of oneself, in the dual sense of being aware of one's presence and of arranging the image presented, is due above all to the fact that one is an object for others. Bear in mind that the world is already functioning when one enters the stage. One begins to be a person and to take on roles on a stage that recognizes individuals precisely as persons, as subject-actors. And this coincides, indeed, with the meaning of person previously proposed. What we are trying to stress here is the meaning taken on by person as the construction and *oeuvre* resulting from one's own behaviours and, more especially, as the stimulus and presence with a view to producing certain impressions and effects in others, which would include being recognized as what one is or wants to be.

The person, however, is not a static work (a statue), but rather a moving one, a performing one, defined by his or her masks (a character). Not just any character, but rather a character with a style of his or her own. "One thing is needful," says Nietzsche (2001), with evangelical solemnity, "to 'give style' to one's character—a great and rare art" (*The Gay Science*, p. 290).

This inscription of the person in the domain of aesthetics, far from being surprising in the context of behaviour analysis, should really be seen as endorsing it. For a start, "aesthetics," from the Greek *aesthesis*, refers in principle to stimulation and sense-perception, and in sum to the impression of things, and hence to its correlative emotional effect, be it pleasing or frightening or provocative of compassion, as in the contemplation of a tragedy (according to Aristotle). With time, this etymological sense will give way to a sense that stresses the subject's judgement and experience. In any case, both sides (stimulative and experiential) form part of aesthetics and of the person. To better understand the person as a work of art we would do well to begin by seeing art as behaviour.

Art as behaviour

In order to see art as behaviour, we must start out from an evolutionist or biobehavioural perspective (Dissanayake, 1998, 1992), which should be fitted into a specifically human perspective, in accordance with a constructivist (Sánchez, 2005) and pragmatist (Shusterman, 2002) aesthetics. Art as behaviour refers not to a specific artistic activity, such as painting or dancing, but rather to a general behavioural complex (Dissanayake, 1988, p. 37), that is, to a "class of behaviour," as the behaviourist would say, which this author refers to as "a behaviour of art." Note the emphasis placed on the behaviour or activity itself, more than on the finished work, now converted into object. Thus, the behaviour of art can be situated in the perspective of its evolutionary function. Specifically, Dissanayake's (1988) theory emphasizes play and ritual as a starting point (reservoir) "from which other, potentially 'artistic' behaviours might be derived" (p. 130).

What would be the evolutionary function of the behaviour of art? It would be a sort of "making special or extra-ordinary," a means of enhancement, "inseparable from and intrinsically necessary to the control of the material conditions of subsistence that allowed humans to survive" (Dissanayake, 1992, p. 92). Among means of enhancement as forms of control would be visual display (including the decoration of one's own body), shaping and embellishing one's surroundings, poetic language, song and music, dance, ritual and dramatic performance—in sum, aesthetic experience. "Throughout human history," says Dissanayake (1992), "the arts have arisen as enhancements, special behaviours shaping and embellishing the things we care about. Without extravagant and extraordinary ways to mark the significant and serious events of our lives, we relinquish not our hypocrisy so much as our humanity" (p. 139).

But this "need" to make things special has its specifically human configuration. In this regard, constructivist aesthetics (Sánchez, 2005), distinguishing itself from evolutionary aesthetics and at the same time correcting it (though that of Dissanayake would not be one of those most needful of such correction), offers two contributions of relevance to what is being discussed here. One would be its consideration of the problem of "what to do with life," given human awareness of its finite nature, as a condition that reorganizes the utilities, values, and functions (no longer merely at the service of survival). Aesthetic objects and experiences would thus be situated on the horizon of the meaning of life, which changes everything.

The other contribution of constructivist aesthetics would be precisely its operant and constructivist nature, by which we understand the production of what was not there before (artistic creation) and the transformation of experience, giving rise to different forms of being-in-the-world (new possible realities and worlds). This means that aesthetic objects and experiences are not limited nor pre-formed in accordance with a supposed genetic catalogue; rather, they would be, and we stress this expression, *contingent* upon human praxis (needless to say, in relation to the historico-cultural conditions of reference). Thus constructivist aesthetics resituates the behaviour of art on the open horizon of social practice, more as a function of cultural contingencies than of genetic predisposition.

For its part, pragmatist aesthetics (Shusterman, 2002), questioning the traditional practical/aesthetic dichotomy, extends the concept of art, beyond its "muse-based" conception (in Dewey's terms), to popular art. Thus, it recognizes popular aesthetics in its own right, and not in contrast to or as a negative reference for "highbrow aesthetics." Pragmatist aesthetics also endorses the operant nature (corporeal, not mental) of constructivist aesthetics, highlighting the involvement of the body as an object of transformation and a locus of experience, which has led pragmatist aesthetics to propose an entire discipline called "somaesthetics."

In this line, pragmatist aesthetics allows itself to reproach "highbrow aesthetics" for its dispassionate detachment. Consider a rock concert compared to a classical music event. "The much more energetic and kinaesthetic response provoked by the rock shows up the fundamental passiveness of the traditional aesthetic attitude of disinterested and detached contemplation; a contemplative attitude with its roots in the pursuit of philosophical and theological knowledge and not of pleasure, of individual enlightenment and not of communal interaction or social change" (Shusterman, 2002, p. 243).

It should also be borne in mind that the classical aesthetic categories are above all existential issues. As Kundera (2005) points out, both simple folk and the refined classes constantly come into contact with the beautiful, the ugly, the sublime, the comic, the tragic, the lyrical and sudden changes, with catharsis, and, to speak of less philosophical concepts, with lack of sense of humour, with kitsch, and with vulgarity.

The person as a work of art

In order now to consider the person as a work of art, we might begin by recalling its nature as radically committed to presentation and representation in relation to others. Thus, in the context of

Western culture, we can trace a long "chain of personality," reflecting this preoccupation with oneself in relation to others, and stretching from the heroes of the *Iliad*, through medieval knights, the courtier of the baroque, and the *gentleman* of the bourgeois era, not forgetting the *dandy*, up to the consumer age, where we find, characterized in this case by his frivolity, the *metrosexual* (Pérez-Álvarez & García-Montes, 2004). Naturally, the term "work of art" would apply equally to the aristocratic style and to that of, for example, the punk (Hebdige, 1979).

The above refers to a historico-cultural scale, but entering the stage involves a learning process in which the person one is going to be is formed. In this regard, it is interesting to note that one is an object for others before being an object for oneself, and we might even say an aesthetic object, constructed according to the tastes of others (mainly one's parents), and in correspondence with the image they want to project through *their* child. One is a "you" (or he/she) for others before the "I" one eventually becomes. In this line, one develops the social character that establishes personal identity, notwithstanding developmental metamorphoses, including possible rebellions against what "they" did to us. Whatever the case, it is once more a question of a kind of "chain of being" corresponding to a preoccupation with oneself vis-à-vis others. The task, clearly dramatic in nature, would thus consist of being who you appear to be (corresponding to what is expected in different contexts), without failing to be who you are, and trying to be yourself at all times (Pérez-Álvarez & García-Montes, 2004); in other words, in juggling different behavioural repertoires.

What is formed, then, is an entire style that includes even body kinematics, as an indication of the "depth" to which persons are shaped and moulded. If even the way we walk can be considered a signature of personal identity (Richardson & Johnston, 2005), then imagine the implications for our way of being, whose shaping begins in the "intimacy" of the rearing process (Dissanayake, 2000). It is worth highlighting, all the same, the constitutively mimetic nature of the human being (Pérez-Álvarez, 2005). In this line we would have to return to the concept of "making special" this time in relation to forming a personality for oneself. Even so, this eagerness to make oneself special should perhaps be qualified in relation to societies more oriented to the feeling of community, where the stylized construction of the

subject may consist more in fulfilling the norms of group membership than in competing with the group (Creighton, 1990). Indeed, even in our own Western culture we are not free of this dual tendency: on the one hand towards uniqueness and on the other towards conformity and belonging. It is in such a social context that we would be faced with "the problem of style" (Simmel, 1991). According to Simmel, "style" is that form of artistic artifice by means of which, giving the appearance of a work of art, one's unique and special character is negated.

In sum, we can speak of the person as work of art for three reasons: because it is the work of behaviours themselves (first of others, but finally one's own), because it is a discriminative stimulus of certain behaviours of others (the "impression" produced), and because it is the subject-actor of the drama of life. Consequently, we must acknowledge a poetic statute of the person.

The poetics of subjective experience

Up to now the person has been presented as an aesthetic object, but is of course also an experiential subject, the subject of aesthetic experience. Here we shall touch on experience only in relation to perceiving oneself as the aesthetic object that one is for others and for oneself (subjective experience). The subjective experience fits perfectly the sense of "poetics" (from *poiesis*, construction) as verbal and even literary construction (Bruner, 1997; Sarbin, 1997). The identity of oneself has a narrative form: It is not something previously constituted that develops, nor is it a cumulative process; rather, it is a narrative identity constituted in time, which reconfigures the past as the future presents itself and, in turn, projects the future in accordance with the past.

The general idea is that experience, far from springing or emanating from a supposed self-originating interior, has its origin in a whole series of social practices. The source of experience is culture, assuming, therefore, the cultivation or ploughing of an otherwise inexistent piece of "land." It is no coincidence that the classic thinkers, such as Luís Vives (1492–1540), for many the father of modern psychology, speak of a "culture of the soul." The notion of "culture" is clearly imbued with an agrarian sense, related to ploughing and cultivation. But in reference to the soul, we should not assume a pre-existing plot on which to plough, but rather something with a wholly poetic character, created, not out of nothing (enter the historical-social context), but giving rise to the emergence of something that was not previously given nor even prefigured; this would correspond to the sense of *poiesis*.

Naturally, there is the body as a sense organ, but the body is, from the moment of its birth, inscribed in the culture, so that there would not even be a natural "clean slate" in the sense of the outdated concept of "noble savage." Culture would be the condition of possibility and at the same time the limit of the creation of oneself or the poetics of identity. In this regard, and in reference to Western culture in particular, we should highlight the "care of thyself" even over and above the "know thyself," as stressed by Foucault (2001)—a "care of thyself" that would give rise to the inflation of subjectivity that characterizes Western culture (and which is so carefully cultivated today by the consumer society). The point is that this subjective experience is constructed, and assumes therefore an operant process of construction, of poetic construction. As such construction it is a reality that forms part of the world.

But its peculiarity is that it is given only to an observer. As Skinner (1945) puts it, each person who speaks is in contact with a part of the world that is peculiar to him or her. The "world under the skin," as he would often say. Thus, Skinner diverts the question to the operations through which society teaches individuals to take account of that part of the world that is their own. Note that Skinner's approach does not consist, as does that of methodological behaviourism (today's cognitive psychology), of inferring the "internal world" ("mental states", "cognitive processes"), because it would be unobservable; instead he studies the operations by virtue of which it becomes observable and relevant for people. Skinner's behaviourism is radical because it goes to the root of psychological phenomena. Remember that it is in the context of this problem that Skinner (1945) establishes the fundamental distinction between methodological behaviourism and radical behaviourism, of which it might well be said, in a Nietzschean fashion, that it splits the history of psychology in two (see Fuentes & Quiroga, 2004; Moore, 1995).

In that 1945 work, Skinner describes four means by which the verbal community, without access to a private stimulus, can nevertheless generate a verbal behaviour in response to it. Regardless of whether there are four means or more, the important thing is that the problem of the "internal world" is proposed and solved in terms of the constructive process that makes it possible. What is involved is a process of ploughing (cultivation, *cultura animi*) that forges its path in the performance of verbal operations. What we are talking about, then, is a poetic process, regardless of its greater or lesser poetry. It might be said that Skinner beats Wittgenstein to solving the question of private language, but it is of little import that he gets there first: What is relevant is that it is a neater solution.

An important aspect of the poetics of experience is, undoubtedly, the experience of the self. In this regard it is appropriate to turn to the theory of the self developed in the Skinnerian line by Kohlenberg and Tsai (1991). The experience of oneself results from an entire verbal social practice, described in three stages, through which the "I" emerges as a functional unit, common to the different activities in which the reference "I" is present (*I* see this and that, *I* have this or that, *I* am like this or like that, I). Undoubtedly, the body is the basis and the axis of reference, but the speaker-I establishes the narrative construction or the poetics of identity. Kohlenberg and Tsai's formula (1995) "I speak, therefore I am" is valid.

Nevertheless, it is necessary to consider the experience of oneself at an even deeper level, as rooted in pride and shame, the feelings of the self par excellence. Pride involves the experience of oneself as being responsible for socially valued achievements and, ultimately, as a socially valued person, so that one is committed to living up to one's own expectations. *Shame*, in turn, involves the experience of having failed to reach one's own standards according to one's social commitment (with respect to the group of reference). Shame is a feeling that affects the whole person (in contrast to guilt), moving us to disappear from view, in the same way as pride leads us to stress our presence. Pride, like its counterpart shame, is learned from action–result contingencies occurring in early development (Mascolo & Fisher, 1995). This process of contingencies gives rise to the generalized feeling of oneself as a responsible and self-conscious agent of what one does. This experience of oneself is especially notable in the case of shame. In this sense, shame, more than a basic and universal emotion, as it is claimed to be now (Kemeny, Gruenewald, & Dickerson, 2004), could be said to be co-founder, together with pride, of the person, as understood here.

In any case, note that the organ of shame is the skin, represented by the face. Thus, the self would be embodied in the skin, which would be the most profound organ of the human being (with Skinner's permission).

FINAL CONSIDERATIONS

After an exposition of the behaviourist ideas of the person, we have shown the affinity of the person with behaviourism, adopting for this purpose a dramaturgic and aesthetic perspective. The dramaturgic perspective permits us to understand the way in which the person develops in accordance with the stage on which he or she lives his or her life. Indeed, we have reaffirmed the theatrical view as a theory that would be quite appropriate for the analysis, or better still, the *synthesis* of behaviour (Ardila, 1988). For its part, the aesthetic perspective permits us to see the poetic (constructive, creative) nature of operant behaviour, among whose constructions is personal identity itself, both in its objective aspect (impression for others) and in the subjective one (feelings of oneself). In this regard, we have situated the sensitive organ of the person *in* the skin.

We have brought art and aesthetics into the equation so as to provide a new view of behaviourism, but the contributions would be bidirectional. Art and aesthetics can benefit from the behaviourist view as much as this view benefits from them. In particular, the constructivist and pragmatist character of behaviourism could serve to rescue art from its creative obscurantism and from disinterested contemplation. In this regard, art has been extended beyond its muse-based conception, and aesthetics even further beyond art. Even so, it remains to establish more precise criteria in relation to where the prose of life begins to be poetic creation. For the time being, the criteria of "making special and enhancement" (Dissanayake, 1988) can suffice for defining art. For its part, the aesthetic would be seen in all, be it art or not, that is "well made" or "well done" and, in turn, the "aesthetic experience" would involve some form of emotion significant for life (not merely fun or unease), so that even melancholy, for example, could have an aesthetic sense instead of simply being sad depression (Brady & Haapala, 2003).

Person, behaviour, and contingencies: Note that they actually make up the field of psychology. Psychology studies behaviour, but the behaviour is someone's (a person's), and takes place in some situation or context or on some stage (contingencies). In this sense, behaviour constitutes the articulation of the field of psychology, and therefore, its centre and object of analysis. Behaviourism has certainly consolidated itself in the *analysis*—both experimental and applied—of behaviour. However, this analysis may have led "the analysis of behaviour" to remain too locked inside its own technical terms (in any case originally related to the laboratory animal), thus losing impact with people, society, and psychology itself, despite probably being the soundest and most honest psychological system. In this context there would be a need for a *synthesis* that, without losing sight of behaviour as a reference, would study human behaviour in all its complexity. This would incorporate other types of knowledge not developed in its own behaviourist terms (though not at odds with its approach), which may in fact contribute new perspectives and fields of interest. And indeed, such a synthesis has already been proposed by Ardila (1988, 2003), under the title "experimental synthesis of behaviour," as a unifying paradigm for psychology, and it is in this line that the present work is situated.

REFERENCES

Ardila, R. (1988). *Síntesis experimental del comportamiento [Experimental synthesis of behaviour]*. Madrid, Spain: Alambra.

Ardila, R. (2003). La necesidad de unificar la psicología: el paradigma de la síntesis experimental del comportamiento [The need to unify psychology. The paradigm of the experimental síntesis of behaviour]. *Revista Colombiana de Psicología, 12,* 28–37.

Ardila, R. (2004). Entrevista al Dr. Rubén Ardila [Interview with Dr. Rubén Ardila]. Retrieved June 2005 from http://www.metapsicologia.com/index.php?page=entrevistaardila).

Baer, D. M. (1976). The organism as host. *Human Development, 19,* 87–98.

Brady, E., & Haapala, A. (2003). Melancholy as an aesthetic emotion. *Contemporary Aesthetics, 1.* Retrieved June 2005 from http://www.contempaesthetics.org/pages/article.php?articleID=214).

Bruner, J. (1986). *Actual minds, possible selves*. Cambridge, MA: Harvard University Press.

Bruner, J. (1990). *Acts of meaning*. Cambridge, MA: Harvard University Press.

Bruner, J. (1997). A narrative model of self-construction. *Annals of the New York Academy of Sciences, 818,* 145–161.

Burke, K. (1945). *A grammar of motives*. New York: Prentice-Hall.

Creighton, M. R. (1990). Revisiting shame and guilt cultures: A forty-year pilgrimage. *Ethos, 18,* 279–307.

Dissanayake, E. (1988). *What is art for?* Seattle, WA: University of Washington Press.

Disasanayake, E. (1992). *Homo aestheticus: Where art comes from and why.* Seattle, WA: University of Washington Press.

Dissanayake, E. (2000). *Art and intimacy. How the arts began.* Seattle, WA: University of Washington Press.

Fallon, D. (1992). An existential look at B. F. Skinner. *American Psychologist, 47,* 1433–1440.

Ferster, C. B. (1953). The use of the free operant in the analysis of behavior. *Psychological Bulletin, 50,* 263–274.

Fierro, A. (2002). *Personalidad, persona, acción: un tratado de psicología [Personality, person, action: A treatise of psychology].* Madrid, Spain: Alianza.

Foucault, M. (2001). *L'herméneutique du sujet. Course au Collage de France, 1982 [The hermeneutics of the subject: Lectures at the College de France 1982].* Paris: Seuil/Gallimard.

Fuentes, J. B., & Quiroga, E. (2004). Los dos principios irrenunciables del análisis funcional de la conducta y del conductismo radical [The two non-renunciable principles of functional analysis of behaviour and radical behaviourism]. *Psicothema, 16,* 555–562.

Glenn, S. S. (2004). Individual behavior, culture, and social change. *The Behavior Analyst, 27,* 133–151.

Goffman, E. (1959). *The presentation of the self in everyday life.* Garden City, NY: Doubleday Anchor.

Haagbloom, S. J., Warnick, R., Warnick, J. E., Jones, V. K., Yarbrough, G. L., Russell, T. M., Borecky, C. M., McGahhey, R., Powell, J. L. III, Beavers, J., & Monte, E. (2002). The 100 most eminent psychologists of the 20th century. *Review of General Psychology, 6,* 139–152.

Hayes, S. C., (Ed.). (1989). *Rule-governed behavior: Cognition, contingencies, and instructional control.* New York: Plenum Press.

Hayes, S. C., Barnes-Holmes, D., & Roche, B. (Eds.). (2001). *Relational Frame Theory: A post-Skinnerian account of human language and cognition.* New York: Plenum Press.

Hayes, S. C., Strosahl, K. D., & Wilson, K. G. (1999). *Acceptance and Commitment Therapy: An experiential approach to behavior change.* New York: Guilford Press.

Hebdige, D. (1979). *Subculture: The meaning of style.* London: Methuen.

James, W. (1890). *Principles of psychology* (2 vols). New York: Henry Holt.

Kemeny, M. E., Gruenewald, T. L., & Dickerson, S. L. (2004). Shame as the emotional response to threat to the social self: Implications for behavior, physiology, and health. *Psychological Inquirer, 15,* 153–160.

Kohlenberg, R. J., & Tsai, M. (1991). *Functional analytic psychotherapy: Creating intense and curative therapeutic relationship.* New York: Guilford Press.

Kohlenberg, R. J., & Tsai, M. (1995). I speak, therefore I am. A behavioral approach to understanding problems of the self. *The Behavior Therapist, 18,* 113–116.

Kundera, M. (2005). *Le rideau. Essai en sept parties [The curtain. Essays in seven parts].* Paris: Gallimard.

Mascolo, M. F., & Fisher, K. W. (1995). Developmental transformations in appraisals for pride, shame, and guilt. In J. P. Tangney & K. W. Fisher (Eds.), *Self-conscious emotions. The psychology of shame, guilt, embarrassment, and pride* (pp. 64–113). New York: Guilford Press.

Mead, G. H. (1934). *Mind, self, and society from the standpoint of a social behaviorist.* Chicago: University of Chicago Press.

Mischel, W. (2004). Toward an integrative science of the person. *Annual Review of Psychology, 55,* 1–22.

Moore, J. (1995). Some historical and conceptual relations among logical positivism, behaviorism and cognitive psychology. In J. T. Todd & E. K. Morris (Eds.), *Modern perspectives on B. F. Skinner and contemporary behaviorism* (pp. 51–74). New York: Greenwood.

Morf, M. E. (1998). Sartre, Skinner, and the compatibilist freedom to be authentic. *Behavior and Philosophy, 26,* 29–43.

Nietzsche, F. (2001). *La ciencia jovial [The gay science]* (Ed. G. Cano). Madrid, Spain: Biblioteca Nueva.

O'Donohue, W., & Kitchener, R. (1999). *Handbook of behaviorism.* New York: Academic Press.

Ortega y Gasset, J. (1958). *El hombre y la gente [Man and people].* Madrid, Spain: Revista de Occidente.

Pérez-Álvarez, M. (2004). *Contingencia y drama. La psicología según el conductismo [Contingency and drama. Psychology according to behaviourism].* Madrid, Spain: Minerva.

Pérez-Álvarez, M. (2005). Psicología del Quijote [Psychology of Don Quixote]. *Psicothema, 17,* 303–310.

Pérez-Álvarez, M., & García-Montes, J. M. (2004). Personality as a work of art. *New Ideas in Psychology, 22,* 157–173.

Phelps, B. J. (2000). Dissociative identity disorder: The relevance of behavior analysis. *The Psychological Record, 50,* 235–249.

Poe, E. A. (1846). The philosophy of composition. *Graham's magazine.* April 1846, pp. 163–167. Retrieved June 2005 from http://www.eapoe.org/works/essays/philcomp.htm).

Rachlin, H. (2000). *The science of self-control.* Cambridge, MA: Harvard University Press.

Richardson, M. J., & Johnston, L. (2005). Person recognition from dynamic events: The kinematic specification of individual identity in walking style. *Journal of Nonverbal Behavior, 29,* 25–44.

Sánchez, J. C. (2005). Estética y constructivismo: filogenia, historia y vida humana [Aesthetics and constructivism: Phylogeny, history and human life]. *Estudios de Psicología, 26,* 173–193.

Sarbin, T. R. (1997). Poetics of identity. *Theory and Psychology, 7,* 67–82.

Scheibe, K. E. (1995). *Self studies. The psychology of self and identity.* Westport, CT: Praeger.

Scheibe, K. E. (2000). *The drama of everyday life.* Cambridge, MA: Harvard University Press.

Shusterman, R. (2002). *Estética pragmatista. Viviendo la belleza, repensando el arte [Pragmatist aesthetics. Living beauty, rethinking art].* Barcelona, Spain: Idea Books.

Simmel, G. (1991). The problem of style. *Theory, Culture and Society, 8,* 63–71 (Original work published 1908).

Skinner, B. F. (1945). The operational analysis of psychological terms. *Psychological Review, 52,* 270–277.

Skinner, B. F. (1953). *Science and human behavior.* New York: Macmillan.

Skinner, B. F. (1957). *Verbal behavior*. New York: Appleton-Century-Crofts.

Skinner, B. F. (1969). *Contingencies of reinforcement: A theoretical analysis*. New York: Appleton-Century-Crofts.

Skinner, B. F. (1971). *Beyond freedom and dignity*. New York: Knopf.

Skinner, B. F. (1972). A lecture on "having a poem". In B. F. Skinner (Ed.), *Cumulative record* (pp. 345–355). New York: Appleton-Century-Crofts.

Skinner, B. F. (1974). *About behaviorism*. New York: Knopf.

Skinner, B. F. (1989). The initiating self. In B. F. Skinner (Ed.), *Issues in the analysis of behavior* (pp. 27–33). Columbus, OH: Merrill.

Staats, A. W. (1996). *Behavior and personality: Psychological behaviorism*. New York: Springer.

Wilson, K. G., & Luciano, M. C. (2002). *Terapia de Aceptación y Compromiso (ACT) [Acceptance and Commitment Therapy (ACT)]*. Madrid, Spain: Pirámide.

Woolfolk, R. L., & Sass, L. A. (1988). Behaviorism and existentialism revisited. *Journal of Humanisict Psychology, 28*, 108–119.

INTERNATIONAL JOURNAL OF PSYCHOLOGY, 2006, 41 (6), 462–467

Psychology Press
Taylor & Francis Group

The experimental synthesis of behaviour

Rubén Ardila

National University of Colombia, Bogota, Colombia

*T*he experimental synthesis of behaviour is a programme for the unification of psychology. The central core of the theory is behaviour analysis, and its aim is to explain the findings of contemporary psychology in behavioural concepts. The experimental synthesis of behaviour is not "eclectic." Following a post-Kuhnian description, the author states that psychological schools were analogous to paradigms, and that a state of normal science (in Kuhn's terms) could be reached. The main characteristics of the experimental synthesis of behaviour, as a programme for the unification of psychology, are as follows. (1) A behavioural level of explanation; psychology has its own level, which includes the behaviour of organisms and their varied relations to the environment; behaviour is not reducible, in strict sense, to biology or to social science. (2) The method is experimentation, but in the initial stages importance is given to observational and correlational procedures. (3) Emphasis is on learning: Human behaviour is primarily learned, with a biological (genetic) basis. (4) The wide range of phenomena that are to be explained include all the traditional fields of scientific psychological research. (5) Emphasis is also on the environment, both social and physical. (6) Importance is given to the basic technology derived from behavioural research.

*L*a synthèse expérimentale du comportement est un programme pour l'unification de la psychologie. Le cœur central de la théorie est l'analyse comportementale et son but est d'expliquer les résultats de la psychologie contemporaine dans des concepts comportementaux. La synthèse expérimentale du comportement n'est pas éclectique. A la suite d'une description post-kuhnienne, l'auteur affirme que les courants psychologiques étaient analogues aux paradigmes et qu'un état de science normal (en utilisant les termes de Kuhn) pourrait être atteint. Les principaux caractéristiques de la synthèse expérimentale du comportement, tel que le programme d'unification de la psychologie sont: (1) Un niveau d'explication comportemental; la psychologie a son propre niveau qui inclut le comportement des organismes et leurs diverses relations à l'environnement; le comportement ne peut être réduit, au sens stricte du terme, à la biologie ou à la science sociale. (2) la méthode est l'expérimentation mais, dans les stades initiaux, une importance est donnée aux procédures observationnelle et corrélationnelle. (3) L'emphase est sur l'apprentissage: le comportement humain est essentiellement appris, avec une base biologique (génétique). (4) Le large éventail de phénomènes à expliquer inclut tous les domaines de la recherche psychologique scientifique. (5) L'emphase est aussi sur l'environnement, à la fois social et physique. (6) Une importance est donnée à la technologie de base dérivée de la recherche comportementale.

*L*a síntesis experimental del comportamiento es una propuesta programática para la unificación de la psicología. El núcleo central de la teoría es el análisis del comportamiento, y su objetivo es explicar los hallazgos de la psicología contemporánea en conceptos comportamentales. La síntesis experimental del comportamiento no es "ecléctica". Siguiendo una descripción post-kuhniana el autor afirma que las escuelas psicológicas pueden considerarse análogas a los paradigmas y que la psicología puede alcanzar un estado de ciencia normal (en los términos de Kuhn). Las principales características de la síntesis experimental del comportamiento como programa para la unificación de la psicología son las siguientes: (1) El nivel comportamental de explicación; la psicología tiene su propio nivel de acción que incluye la conducta de los organismos y sus relaciones con el ambiente; la conducta no es reducible en sentido estricto a la biología ni a la ciencia social. (2) El método es la experimentación, pero en los estados iniciales se le da importancia a los procedimientos observacionales y correlacionales. (3) El énfasis en el aprendizaje; la conducta humana básicamente es aprendida con un fundamento biológico (genético). (4) El amplio rango de fenómenos que se explican, que incluye todos los campos tradicionales de la investigación científica en psicología. (5) El énfasis en el ambiente, tanto social como físico. (6) La importancia que se le otorga a la tecnología derivada de la investigación conductual.

Correspondence should be addressed to Ruben Ardila, PO Box 88754, Bogotá, Colombia (E-mail: psycholo@aolpremium.com).

http://www.psypress.com/ijp
DOI: 10.1080/00207590500491593

INTRODUCTION

The disunity of psychology is considered to be one of the problems of greatest concern faced by the discipline. A number of authors have referred to this topic as one of the main problems facing psychology at the beginning of the 21st century (see Sternberg, 2005). This is also a very relevant issue in behaviour analysis, when referring to the "different behaviorisms" (see Baum, 2005; O'Donohue & Kitchener, 1999).

The present author has proposed a unifying paradigm for psychology called the experimental synthesis of behaviour. It has its roots in the experimental analysis of behaviour (Skinner) but goes beyond it, and its main objective is to obtain consensus in relation to the basic issues of psychology as a discipline. This paradigm follows Kuhn's (1970) analysis of the development of science in terms of paradigms. The experimental synthesis of behaviour considers that the "schools" of psychology are analogous to the paradigms proposed by Kuhn in his analysis of the historical development of the scientific disciplines.

The disunity of psychology has not been good for the discipline, and has produced much confusion and controversy. The nature of psychology has been discussed for many decades, and psychology has been defined as the study of the "soul," of the mind, and of behaviour. Probably at the present time the great majority of psychologists define the discipline as the study of the behaviour of organisms.

In spite of the controversies that gave origin to "schools," to systems, and to the present concern for the problems of unification of psychology, the facts found in a given investigation are recognized by all specialists. However, the scientific findings that do not fit in our particular theory are not taken into consideration when a comprehensive explanation of the phenomena is proposed. In this sense, theory orients scientific research and also influences the analysis of the results.

The experimental synthesis of behaviour (Ardila, 1993) is an effort in the direction of unification of psychology. Its name derives from the experimental analysis of behaviour, and it can be considered a post-Skinnerian development. Since its original presentation, a large number of groups have been formed in different countries (Spain, Chile, Puerto Rico) that are working in this paradigm and have produced important results.

ORIGINS

As with all sciences, psychology had many births. The "official" one was that at Leipzig, in the fall of 1879, when Wundt founded the first laboratory of experimental psychology. Investigations were conducted using the methods of natural sciences— especially those of physiology—and psychology formally became a branch of science and not of philosophy. There were other parallel "births" more or less at the same time. Boring's (1950) version, which is the "official" one, has been confronted with other versions that place the origins at different times. But all versions began in Europe at around the same time—the last part of the 19th century. A total of eight schools of psychology emerged from this time. They are as follows.

Wundt's psychology was called *voluntarism*, but as time passed, and because of Titchener's influence, it became known as *structuralism*. Science chroniclers consider it the first psychological school. The second was *functionalism*, which was "born" in Chicago in 1896. Its main practitioners were Angell, Carr, Dewey, and Woodworth, all of whom were restless with Wundt's psychology, it being too static for the United States spirit.

Reflexology has its origins in Pavlov's and Bechterev's Russia. It is a laboratory science that was intended to give a physiological basis to the propositions of the British associationists. However, it was somewhat reductionist and too physiological. Dogs, but also humans, were studied and, under Darwin's influence, were considered members of life's kingdom.

Behaviourism cannot be understood without studying the work of Watson, a man who was very interested in impacting the world. His life and work were directly related to the time and place in which he lived: the United States during the first decades of the 20th century. Wundt had insisted that psychology was the study of consciousness. Watson, however, insisted that it was the study of behaviour and that it did not need to make any reference to consciousness, just as physics and chemistry did not need to. Watson changed the way we look at psychology today. Now, everybody defines it as the science of behaviour or conduct.

Gestalt was the product of three Germans: Wertheimer, Kohler, and Koffka, intellectual descendents of the most traditional way of thinking of their country, who felt uncomfortable with the analytic emphasis placed on psychology at the time. For gestaltists, the "structured whole" was to be studied, instead of the analysis of the elements of consciousness, or behaviour.

Lewin's *topology* has much to do with gestalt theory, although its structure is very different. It is the application to social and child behaviour of the ideas of a man who was too creative and original to be restricted to other schools of thought. Lewin's topology has had many applications, i.e., to industry, conflict theory, and human development.

Meanwhile, Freud was working in Vienna, treating patients with functional nervous problems that other physicians were not able to treat. His experiences helped him to develop a psychological school, *psychoanalysis*, which was very different from the rest, and which the public found more acceptable than structuralism, functionalism, reflexology, behaviourism, gestalt, and topology. Psychoanalysis was interested in sexuality, aggression, the early infancy, dreams, myths, literature and anthropology. Initially, Freud was ignored, then deified, and finally, given the recognition he deserved.

Finally, there is Binswanger's school of *existential psychology*. Much is owed to Kierkegaard, Husserl, and other philosophers of existentialism for the formation of this school of thought.

These eight psychological schools—structuralism, functionalism, reflexology, behaviourism, gestalt, topology, psychoanalysis, and existential psychology—belong to the past. Today, there are no psychological schools in existence. A school implies a global conceptualization of a particular work field. This is somewhat similar to Kuhn's (1970) paradigms, although he could not completely agree with our analysis of the concept of paradigm and its application to the development of psychology. The creators of these schools considered that they had the explanation for all psychological phenomena, that they had adequate methodology, and also that they could ignore all that was done by other schools. On the other hand, a school of thought neatly centres on one person (Wundt, Carr, Watson, Freud, etc.), both

geographically and conceptually, and is one way of confronting phenomena.

There were schools in all sciences, and not only in psychology. They represent an adolescent stage of development, a dogmatic and simplistic way of studying phenomena. Initially, there were schools in physics, chemistry, astronomy, and biology; now they exist in economics, anthropology, linguistics, sociology, and other behavioural sciences. However, with the development of knowledge, all schools die a natural death. Thus, I believe that, just as chemists no longer believe in flogism, nor biologists in vitalism, so, there are no structuralists, classical behaviourists, or reflexologists to be found in psychology today.

Today, nevertheless, psychologists still differ in methodology, working fields, and worldviews. But today we do not have psychological schools; we have psychological systems. The difference is that systems are not as dogmatic as schools; they depend less on a working style, a single exponent, and a geographical area.

Nowadays, we have five psychological systems: neo-behaviourism, neo-psychoanalysis, cultural psychology, humanistic psychology, and cognitive psychology (see Table 1).

Neo-behaviourism can be linked to Hull and Skinner's highly refined systems. It places great importance on the philosophy of science. However, Hull considered hypothetic-deductive methodology to be of most importance, whereas Skinner suggested that inductive methodology should take priority. Skinner's greatest advantage over Hull is that his work involves laboratory studies and practical applications. Any science cannot be considered so without technology, and Skinner's radical behaviourism originated a technology that is not found in Hull's work. Skinner calls his system the "experimental analysis of behaviour," and it is a psychology that is still in force today.

TABLE 1

"Schools" of psychology, systems of psychology and the unifying paradigm

"Schools" of psychology	*Systems of psychology*	*Unifying paradigm*
Structuralism		
Functionalism	Neo-behaviourism	
Reflexology	Neo-psychoanalysis	
Behaviourism	Humanistic psychology	Experimental
Psychoanalysis	Cultural psychology	synthesis of behaviour
Gestalt	Cognitive psychology	
Topology		
Existential psychology		

Neo-psychoanalysis incorporates the ideas of Freud, the "ego" analysis, and the importance of social factors. Erick Fromm, Karen Horney, and other neo-psychoanalysts have a conceptualization of man that basically depends on psychoanalysis, but which has moved away from Freud in many important areas.

Cultural or dialectic-materialistic psychology began with Vygotsky and structured itself through Leontiev, Luria, and other thinkers interested in creating a dialectic, historic, and Marxist psychology. For them the mind is the result of history; man reflects natural reality, transforms the world, and is transformed dialectically by such a world. Social structure is a macrosystem within which human actions make sense. Consciousness is a product of history. Today the term "cultural psychology" is preferred to name this system.

The fourth system in force today, *humanistic psychology*, owes much to Maslow and May. Its origins are in what they termed here and now, and its roots are in existentialism—as are the techniques required to understand and help humans.

Cognitive psychology is a general approach to psychology that emphasizes the internal mental processes. For cognitive psychology, behaviour is not specifiable simply in terms of its overt properties but requires explanations at the level of mental events, mental representations, intentions, beliefs, and so forth. Cognitivists are not necessarily anti-behaviourists but consider that behaviourism fails to provide a coherent characterization of cognitive processes (thinking, language, decision-making).

These five systems—neo-behaviourism, neo-psychoanalysis, cultural psychology, humanistic psychology, and cognitive psychology—are less dogmatic than the schools already described. They do not attempt to answer all the questions. They centre less on one person's ideas in a single geographical area, and more on a philosophical conceptualization.

Where are we heading? From schools we have passed to systems. We are heading towards a unified concept of psychology—in its philosophy and praxis—as a science and a profession. This is a unifying paradigm in the way that Kuhn conceived it. However, it is not an eclectic system, but a paradigmatic conceptualization that could unify psychology.

I have called this conceptualization the *experimental synthesis of behaviour*. It comes from neo-behaviourism, as its name indicates, but goes beyond this.

In the new paradigm, consciousness is integrated with behaviour and is considered a social-historical product. Some elements of psychoanalysis are thought of as having relevance for a new psychology. Humanistic values and psychology within an existential framework are emphasized, and the term *behavioural humanism* is used. And all this is integrated to a neo-behaviourism that is less dogmatic, more integrative, and far-reaching.

For some writers, unification of psychology is not possible. Some even think that there are no laws in psychology. Others consider that neither computers nor rats have anything to do with psychological work. There is no scientific knowledge in psychology and, subsequently, a technology has never been developed, since a technology presupposes the existence of a science. It is also said that no converging points can be found between the ideas of Kornilov, Leontiev, Staats, Piaget, and Freud, and that speaking of unification of psychology is just a proposition of a new psychological school.

The experimental synthesis of behaviour intends to study the behavioural level of explanation. It places great importance on learning, and considers that complex problems are to be studied precisely, and more adequate mathematic models employed. It wishes to go beyond dogmatism and "schools," which only fragmented psychology.

In the search for this paradigm, onto- and filogenetic factors have a central position. Work is done within a behavioural humanism that gives sense to what psychologists are trying to do in understanding and modifying the world. The model of the experimental synthesis of behaviour should be sufficiently integrated and flexible at the same time, so as to embrace all fields of *scientific* psychology without becoming eclectic.

THE DISAPPEARANCE OF PSYCHOLOGICAL SCHOOLS

As we said earlier, since Wundt's time a series of psychological schools have been proposed to explain human behaviour. They were usually centred around authors, such as Wundt, Dewey, Pavlov, Freud, Watson, Werthelmer, Lewin, and Maslow, a set of beliefs, and methods. Each school attempted to define psychology and start from the beginning. The founders of each school knew what the other schools were doing, but did not acknowledge them: Freud knew of Wundt's work, Pavlov was aware of what the gestalt psychologists were doing, and so on. But every one of them began with different assumptions, had different models of man, and different definitions concerning what psychology was about. Each school was a closed world, impermeable to outside influence and findings that opposed its conceptual frame.

Although there are no psychological schools today, there are several approaches to psychology. The five major approaches already described are neo-behaviourism, neo-psychoanalysis, humanistic psychology, cultural psychology, and cognitive psychology. The approaches began with different conceptual frameworks and conceptions of human beings. Psychology was defined in relatively different terms (even though there are many common elements), and different methodologies were used by each. In fact, we still do not have a unifying paradigm. The concepts of "school" and of "system," which have caused so much harm to the development of our discipline, have not entirely disappeared, although there is a clear trend in that direction.

The application of Kuhn's analysis of the history of sciences to the case of psychology has been critically discussed by several authors (see Driver-Linn, 2003). In our case, we are using Kuhn's ideas in a way that is different from his original formulation; the classical schools of psychology are considered analogous to Kuhn's paradigms (see also Staats, 1983).

CHARACTERISTICS OF THE EXPERIMENTAL SYNTHESIS OF BEHAVIOUR

The main characteristics of the experimental synthesis of behaviour are as follows.

1. *The level of explanation is behaviour.* Psychological phenomena do not need to be reduced to physiology or to sociology. Psychology is the science that studies the behaviour of organisms; it is not the science of mind.

2. *The method.* Experimentation has many advantages that the alternative methods do not have. However, in the initial stages of an area or in the investigation of a problem, many methods could be used: correlational, observational, field studies, case studies, qualitative methodologies. The experimental analysis of behaviour uses multiple methods depending on the problem under investigation. For different problems, different methods should be used.

3. *The emphasis on learning.* The large majority of behaviour is based on learning, particularly in the case of complex human behaviour. Our learning capabilities are based on our genetic predispositions, of course. But the patterns that the organisms present—and this is very clear in the case of human behaviour—are based on learning.

Because of that, learning is considered a basic process for psychological explanations.

4. *The range of behaviour to be explained.* The experimental synthesis of behaviour has its research program to explain the whole range of facts of scientific psychology. Some of the findings are clearly described in the context of specific "schools" or specific "methodologies," but others are more general, for instance the issues of social psychology. The experimental synthesis of behaviour as a comprehensive explanation of behaviour should account for all the psychological facts, regardless of the frame of reference in which they were originally investigated.

5. *Emphasis on the environment.* The events that are observed and analysed in psychology are the interactions of the organism with the events and objects that constitute the stimulus factors in the environment. The relations are observable and measurable, and occur in time and space. Environment is both physical and social, external and internal.

6. *Technology.* A science from which no technology is derived will never have the social impact of one that gives origin to technology. Science and its applications sometimes go hand in hand. In many other cases technology precedes science and it is instigated by social demands.

At the international level, we can make a contribution to the understanding and possible solution of one of the greatest concerns of contemporary psychology, that is, current disunity. In this age of globalization, the search for communalities, and interest in points of convergence, this paradigm for the unification of psychology can be a step in the direction that psychology is taking in the new century.

REQUIREMENTS

The experimental synthesis of behaviour might become a unifying paradigm for psychology, and put an end to many of the problems currently faced by psychology at the conceptual level. In order to do so, the experimental synthesis of behaviour would need to do the following.

1. *The study of more complex problems.* This includes those related to cognitive processes, language, social behaviour, emotions, etc. This is already happening and there is an increasing tendency in this direction.

2. *The use, in an initial stage, of observational and correlational data.* It is clear that such data provide only general guidelines, and only

experimental data can provide the essence of science. But observational and correlational data provide useful information for future experimental work. It is not a question of making the method more flexible, but of not sacrificing important events due to the lack of methodological resources with which to study them experimentally.

3. *The use of mathematics and formulation of theoretical structures to integrate facts.* Experimental analysis of behaviour as a nontheoretical system is very close to facts, and this is highly important in the initial stages of a science. But with current developments we believe it is time to formulate theories—or at least micro-theories—and develop more comprehensive explanatory systems. Formulations are more adequate when mathematics is used.

4. *The eradication of dogmatism.* This was characteristics of "schools."

5. *Emphasis on behavioural humanism.* Science has goals and objectives; it is a human activity. As such, science is ethically and politically neutral. However, the activity of a scientist—as human behaviour—has ethical and political implications. Science emerges in a specific social context. Its applications have several ideological and social implications. Experimental synthesis and its applications should serve humans. This principle has been named behavioural humanism, and is part of classical humanism, which states that "humans are the measure of all things." However, it does not stop at words but searches for facts. It seeks to modify humans in an adaptive way—not to serve a political system but to serve human beings themselves. It assumes that, ultimately, there is an effective technology in psychology. Therefore, it can be applied for the betterment of human beings, and attempts to remedy the traditional problems of our species such as poverty, exploitation, mental illness, social dysfunction, tensions between groups, prejudice, negative attitudes, and many others.

IN CONCLUSION

The present time is heading toward convergence, globalization, points of unity, synthetic theories, cross-disciplinary bridges, etc. In the specific case of psychology a consensus has been obtained in certain basic aspects such as the subject matter of the discipline, some methodological issues, philosophical frame of reference, etc. Maybe the unity is still far in the future, but some recent developments point in that direction.

A unifying paradigm implies the existence of a group of specialists who are united by an education and a common practice, and are aware of the work of other members of the group. It implies broad intra-professional communication, deep involvement in problems derived from the paradigm, and consensus concerning technical aspects of the discipline. This experimental synthesis aims to explain all the findings of scientific psychology in behavioural terms (defining "behaviour" in broad terms and including in that concept cognition, emotion, individual differences, and so forth); to utilize data from diverse origins (observational, correlational, to be used in controlled experimental research); to grant special importance to theory construction and mathematical modelling; to try to emphasize a humanistic frame of reference based on human behaviour—behavioural humanism. This integrative paradigm could help to make psychology a "normal" science: an established science that would be beyond the polemics and dogmatism that are characteristics of the initial stages in the development of all disciplines.

As Sternberg (2005, p. 5) pointed out, "Unity rather than fragmentation is the sensible path for psychology to take."

REFERENCES

Ardila, R. (1993). *Síntesis experimental del comportamiento* [The experimental synthesis of behaviour]. Bogotá, Colombia: Planeta.

Baum, W. M. (2005). *Understanding behaviorism.* (2nd ed.). Malden, MA: Blackwell.

Boring, E. G. (1950). *A history of experimental psychology.* New York: Appleton-Century-Crofts.

Driver-Linn, E. (2003). Where is psychology going? Structural fault lines revealed by psychologists' use of Kuhn. *American Psychologist, 58,* 269–278.

Kuhn, T. S. (1970). *The structure of scientific revolutions.* Chicago: University of Chicago Press.

O'Donohue, W., & Kitchener, R. F. (Eds.). (1999). *Handbook of behaviorism.* San Diego, CA: Academic Press.

Staats, A. W. (1983). *Psychology's crisis of disunity.* New York: Praeger.

Sternberg, R. J. (Ed.). (2005). *Unity in psychology.* Washington, DC: American Psychological Association.

INTERNATIONAL JOURNAL OF PSYCHOLOGY, 2006, 41 (6), 468–479

Experimental analysis of behaviour in the European French-speaking area

Marc N. Richelle

Université de Liège, Liège, Belgium

Esteve Freixa i Baqué

Université de Picardie, Amiens, France

Jean-Luc Lambert

Université de Fribourg, Fribourg, Switzerland

Valentino Pomini

Université de Lausanne, Lausanne, Switzerland

*T*he influence and development of behaviour analysis in French-speaking Europe has been different in the different countries, as can be seen when comparing developments in France and in the French-speaking parts of Belgium and Switzerland. French psychology has shown persistent reluctance towards behaviour analysis, except for a few individuals in a few institutional circles. On the other hand, Belgium has been the main centre from which behaviour analysis has propagated to the French-speaking area as a whole. Territorial specificities both in experimental analysis and in applied behaviour analysis are described and placed in context. In general, French-speaking Europe has not been especially receptive to Skinner's radical analysis of behaviour. Few of Skinner's books have been translated into French, as compared with other major Western languages. In none of the geographical areas being considered was psychology prepared to integrate radical behaviourism, in spite of its having important experimental developments in learning, perception, cognition, and other basic processes. By the time some faint echoes of Skinner's work reached France and its neighbours, cognitivism had already invaded. In spite of the lack of experimental and conceptual developments, applications mainly in behaviour therapy and in special and normal education did take place in all French-speaking countries.

L'influence et le développement de l'analyse comportementale dans l'Europe francophone a été différente dans les différents pays, comme on peut le constater en comparant les développements en France et dans les parties francophones de la Belgique et de la Suisse. La psychologie française a manifesté une réticence persistante par rapport à l'analyse comportementale, à l'exception de quelques individus dans quelques cercles institutionnels. D'autre part, la Belgique a été le centre principal à partir duquel l'analyse comportementale s'est propagée à L'Europe francophone en entier. Les spécifiés territoriales, tant dans l'analyse expérimentale que dans l'analyse comportementale appliquée, sont décrites et placées en contexte. En général, l'Europe francophone n'a pas été particulièrement réceptive à l'analyse comportementale radicale de Skinner. Peu des livres de Skinner ont été traduits en français, en comparaison à d'autres langues occidentales principales. Dans aucune des régions géographiques considérées, la psychologie n'a été préparée pour intégrer le behaviourisme radical, malgré les importants développements expérimentaux au niveau de l'apprentissage, de la perception, de la cognition et d'autres processus de base. Lorsque certains faibles échos des travaux de Skinner sont arrivés en France et ses voisins, le cognitivisme avait déjà envahi la place. Malgré le manque de développements expérimentaux et théoriques, des applications principalement dans la thérapie comportementale, dans l'éducation normale et spéciale ont bel et bien eu lieu dans tous les pays francophones.

*L*a influencia y el desarrollo del análisis del comportamiento en los países francófonos de Europa han sido diferentes de los desarrollos en otras partes del mundo. Esto puede verse comparando los desarrollos en Francia y en las partes francófonas de Bélgica y Suiza. La psicología francesa ha mostrado una renuencia persistente al análisis del comportamiento, excepto en el caso de unos pocos individuos y unos pocos círculos institucionales. Por otra parte Bélgica ha sido el principal centro desde el cual se ha propagado el análisis del

Correspondence should be addressed to Marc N. Richelle, Professur émerite de l'Université de Liège, Sart-Doneux, 29, B-5353 Goesnes, Belgium (E-mail: marc.richelle@ulg.ac.be).

DOI: 10.1080/00207590500492021

comportamiento al área de los países francófonos como un todo. El artículo describe y coloca en contexto las especificaciones territoriales tanto en el análisis del comportamiento como en el análisis conductual aplicado. En general la Europa de habla francesa no ha sido especialmente receptiva al análisis radical del comportamiento de Skinner. Pocos de los libros de Skinner han sido traducidos al francés, en comparación con los otros idiomas occidentales importantes. En ninguna de las áreas geográficas que estamos considerando, la psicología estaba preparada para integrar el conductismo radical, a pesar de importantes desarrollos en aprendizaje, percepción, cognición y otros procesos básicos. En la época en que algunos débiles ecos de la obra de Skinner llegaron a Francia y a sus países vecinos, el congnitivismo ya había ocupado su lugar. A pesar de la carencia de desarrollos experimentales y conceptuales las aplicaciones, especialmente en terapia del comportamiento y en educación tanto especial como normal, se desarrollaron en todos los países de habla francesa.

INTRODUCTION

A survey of experimental analysis of behaviour (EAB) research and applications in the French-speaking European territories provides a striking example of the fact that psychology, although a scientific and therefore universal field, shows national or regional peculiarities that can be explained to some extent by its local specific history, but also by the persistence of ambiguous attitudes as to the scientific approach to human behaviour.

On the whole, French-speaking Europe has not been especially receptive to Skinner's radical behaviourism, which generated about half a century ago the so-called experimental analysis of behaviour (EAB). One piece of evidence for this is the limited number of Skinner's books that have been translated into French, as compared with other major (and sometimes minor) Western languages. The first two titles offered to French readers were *The Technology of Teaching* (1969/1968) and *Contingencies of Reinforcement* (1971/1969), both published by a Belgian publisher, the first author (Marc N. Richelle) being his scientific adviser for books in psychology. *Beyond Freedom and Dignity* (1971) was published in Paris in 1972 by a big publishing company, but with minimal publicity and few, almost unanimously negative, press reviews; one of them, written by a reputed social psychologist, captured the French intelligentsia feeling in its title "Sommes-nous des rats?" and in his self-satisfaction argument that French people fortunately escaped the influence of what appeared essentially to be stuff for Americans (meaning USA citizens). The same publisher also translated *Enjoy Old Age* (1983), curiously enough with an equal lack of publicity, though that pragmatic small book contains little behaviouristic theorizing. *About Behaviourism* (1974/1979) was published in French by a Swiss publisher in 1974 and it was not until spring 2005 that *Walden Two* (1948/2005b) and *Science and Human Behaviour*

(1953/2005a) were published by a freelance publisher in Paris, after years of efforts and the goodwill of unpaid translators. This sets up the stage for the description that follows of EAB in France and its close neighbours that share the French language.

However, language is not such a unifying factor as to erase differences between France on one hand and French-speaking regions of Switzerland and Belgium on the other. The latter did not share globally the French attitude towards EAB; their respective approaches had their specific features.

EAB can be considered at various levels. One refers to the experimental methods originally developed in Skinner's laboratory, based on operant techniques. These can be put to work to a number of purposes, with little or no reference to theoretical ideas elaborated by Skinner and his followers. At another level, EAB implies such theoretical elaborations, basically a monist conception of (human) behaviour, the rejection of mentalism as explanatory fiction, a selectionist view of the shaping and emergence of new behaviour. At a third level, EAB is essentially a field of applications, to a large extent rooted in the experimental approach characterizing the first level, and to a variable extent sharing the theoretical tenets qualifying the second level (as shown in the compromise between cognitive and behavioural approaches in cognitivo-behavioural therapies, a somewhat chimaeric, self-contradictory expression to the view of some radical behaviourists). The terms "applied behaviour analysis" (ABA) will cover hereafter applications in various contexts—education, therapy, management, etc.—related with or inspired by EAB level I or II or both.

THE CASE OF FRANCE

Level 2: EAB as a theoretical position

At first sight, having the legacy of its famous philosophers and scientists of the 18th century,

France would appear to be appropriately prepared to welcome the behaviourist approach to psychology at the beginning of the 20th century. In some sense, it was, and some French psychologists have even claimed primacy of Piéron over Watson. In fact, the former, in his inaugural lecture at the Collège de France in 1907 (Piéron, 1908), advocated the view that the subject matter of psychology is behaviour, rather than mental life. His lecture in some way anticipated Watson's manifesto. However his position was closer to methodological behaviourism than to radical behaviourism as Skinner would define it later in the century. As Parot (1995) showed, Piéron remained basically a dualist, as most French psychologists of his time and subsequently. The conception of psychology as the science of behaviour (*comportement*) was, at least superficially, widely accepted in introductory textbooks, but very few of those who shaped French scientific psychology in the century could be called behaviourists. Pierre Naville was the only person with in-depth knowledge of behaviourism and openly in favour of its tenets, but he was a philosopher and sociologist, not a psychologist (Freixa i Baqué, 1985; Naville, 1946).

The French reluctance towards behaviourism did not change in the second half of the century when Skinner's influence was growing in North America and in many other countries; we have pointed in the Introduction to the lack of interest on the part of publishers in translating his books, and the negative response of critics. These completely missed some major differences in Skinner's ideas as compared with traditional behaviourist schools of thought, namely the interest in verbal behaviour, thought, and private events. In these respects, Skinner's views would appear closer to Pierre Janet's influential *psychologie des conduites* (the word *conduite*—also used by Piaget—being a quasi-equivalent to *comportement*, but including indirectly observable behaviours, which were explicitly taken into account by Skinner). To sum up, French psychology ignored the theoretical and epistemological contributions of radical behaviourism, with a few exceptions in the last quarter of the century, which will be presented hereafter. It remained, on the whole, completely closed to EAB second level. Of course, some elements of Skinner's contributions were part of traditional courses in experimental psychology, under the headings of "Learning and Conditioning." The field had its experts, such as Jean-François Le Ny—originally a specialist of Pavlovian psychology—and Christian Georges, among others; but significantly they both became prominent figures of the cognitivist movement as soon as it developed.

In the 1980s, a handful of behaviourally oriented psychologists appeared on the university stage in France. One was of Catalan origin, E. Freixa i Baqué, who had been deeply influenced during his studies in Barcelona by two behaviourally oriented teachers, namely Pere Julià and Ramon Bayés. He worked for some time on his doctoral research—on a purely psychophysiological topic—in the psychiatry department headed by P. Pichot in Paris, where behaviour therapy was beginning to be part of the treatment approaches. He moved to the University of Lille, first hosted by the psychophysiology laboratory headed by Vincent Bloch, where he continued to develop his interests in radical behaviourism. The department of psychology in Lille was by no means a centre of Skinnerian studies, but it offered a context favourable to the opening of new avenues by young people. Such intellectual tolerance was unusual in those days in French psychology departments, where the cognitivist movement was clearly dominant. Lille was an exception, due to individual personalities then responsible for the development of teaching and research, such as P. Lecocq, an expert in human memory closer to cognitive psychology than to radical behaviourism, or Jacqueline Bideaud, a reputed Piagetian. One student of the latter, Jean-Claude Darcheville, working in developmental psychology, moved from the Piagetian approach to behaviourism, and engaged in experimental research using the operant paradigm on young children. By the same time, Marc Hautekette had started to teach behaviour modification and to train students in the practice of behavioural methods, pioneering what eventually led to the organization of a specialized degree for professional psychologists, who were soon recognized for their competence, especially by associations of parents of autistic children, or child victims of other behavioural problems. The small initial nucleus expanded by the training of new Phd's in the field, among whom were Vinca Rivière, Yanic Miossec, François Tonneau, Michel Sokolowski, Alain Madelein, Bruno Facon, and Samuel Delepoule. Some of these moved to other universities, in France or abroad. Freixa i Baqué himself moved to the University of Picardie in Amiens, starting, with his former student Sokolovski, a second EAB nucleus in the North of France. He is presently in charge of the first teaching facility explicity labelled as EAB, in a department with a strong psychoanalytic influence. The new small group organized the fourth European

Meeting on the Experimental Analysis of Behaviour in Amiens in 2000 (see below in the section on Belgium).

We have described the case of Lille in some detail, because it is the first and a unique place on the French university map where EAB could develop and gain some credentials, both in basic research and theory and in applied fields of behaviour modification and therapy. Why was it unique? And why did it happen there only, rather than in some other university? To the first question, the answer is to be found in two factors: one is the dominant wave of cognitivism that has been propagated all over French psychology since the early 1960s, such that behaviourism was proclaimed a blind alley; the other is the dominance of the psychoanalytic approach in the clinical psychology part of French departments. We shall see later to what extent that factor is still crucial today, and is the source of a crisis of unexpected dimensions. To the second question, the answer is also twofold: first, for some local reasons, psychoanalysts had less weight in the Lille department, and second, as already pointed out, the human context was more favourable than elsewhere to the exploration of new alleyways—even if they be of behaviouristic orientation—by young members of the staff. This is not to say that there has not been, on French territory, any individual psychologist interested in the EAB, but in no case have such pioneers seemed to find the conditions that existed in Lille to escape isolation.

As well as Freixa i Baqué, and at about the same time, two other young psychologists with a radical behaviourist background, Fanny Muldman and Alexandre Dorna, settled down in Paris, flying from Chile after Pinochet's *coup d'etat*. Dorna, a social psychologist, developed a research group in the field of political psychology. Recently, after many efforts, and together with Freixa i Baqué, he was successful in having *Walden Two* and *Science and Human Behaviour* published in Paris.

Level 1: The use of Skinnerian techniques for various laboratory purposes

Operant conditioning techniques were put to work independently of adherence of the user to Skinner's theory of behaviour, just because they were most efficient in a variety of contexts. If we want to trace the history of that aspect of EAB, we shall have to turn to the section on French-speaking Belgium below. From the 1950s on, a number of French researchers took advantage of operant methods, mainly in psychopharmacological and psychophysiological studies with animal subjects. To name but a few: Cardo, in Bordeaux, used them in self-stimulation studies; Simon and his group at the Paris VI medical school, in behavioural pharmacology; Delacour at Institut Marey in Paris, in psychophysiological work. The techniques were also used in sophisticated research on the neurobiology of motor control in monkeys, at the CNRS Institute of neurophysiology, established in Marseille in the mid-1960s and headed by Jacques Paillard. They also became routine in the last decades of the century in many university laboratories at medical school and sciences faculties, as well as in private companies' research centres, especially in the pharmaceutical industry, sometimes hiring behaviourally trained psychologists from abroad. Animal laboratories were few in departments of psychology, so those who used Skinnerian techniques did so on human subjects. A typical case was Viviane Pouthas, then a member of Fraisse's laboratory in Paris, who was interested in the psychology of time, an area in which the prominent French experimental psychologist had been a pioneer and had gained international recognition. She engaged in the study of very young children using operant methods. She eventually trained PhDs along the same lines, and they applied these methods expertly, without any commitment to behaviourist theory (Pouthas, 1985, 1995).

Level 3: Applied behaviour analysis

As can be understood from the two preceding sections, applied behaviour analysis in France, with a few exceptions such as Lille, did not derive from theoretical or experimental research inspired by radical behaviourism. It grew mainly from the concern of some psychiatric departments that the array of treatments should be widened. Rejecting the dichotomic view of psychiatric treatments, which opposed the psychoanalytic approach and the biological approach, with its high reliance on drugs, some prominent psychiatrists in charge of leading university clinics promoted an eclectic approach. In this they were open to new treatments if these were useful in improving patients' conditions. Two examples, in Paris, were Pierre Pichot at Saint Anne Hospital and Daniel Widlöcher at La Salpêtrière. The latter is an open-minded psychoanalyst, who encouraged his collaborators to engage in new practices as these were made available by various orientations in psychiatry and psychopathology. Pichot had already been pioneering by introducing psycho-metric techniques for evaluation of personality, normal and pathological, in the psychiatry depart-ment; he encouraged a research psychologist in his group, Mélinée Agathon, familiar with Pavlovian work, to explore the new behavioural treatments, in which Pavlovian conditioning merged with behaviour modification derived from American behaviourism. She contributed to the training of young psychiatrists by teaching the principles of behaviour therapy from the early 1970s. This seems to have been the origin of behaviour therapy in France.

A French Association of Behaviour Therapy was founded in 1972 (Agathon, 1982), which was eventually changed into an association of cognitivo-behavioural therapy (AFTCC for *Association Française de Thérapie Cognitivo-Comportementale*). This followed a general trend all around the world to reconcile two schools of thought in the field of application, which had been (and still are in many cases) opposing each other, sometimes aggressively, in academic circles. This might be one case, among others in the history of psychology, where practitioners confronted with real-life problems wisely go beyond exacerbated conflicts of theories. Curiously enough, while France, as we have seen, was not particularly prepared to accept the behavioural approach, a number of both psychiatrists and psychologists showed interest in the newly created association, perhaps because of a general need for alternate and diversified approaches to treatment, based on a scientific analysis. People like Pichot, Widlöcher, and Zazzo were members and/or Presidents. However, the most active centres from which applied behaviour analysis was to develop were not in Paris, where it had timidly originated, but in the provinces. In Lyon, a young psy-chiatrist, Jean Cottraux, acquired expertise in cognitivo-behavioural practices, founded a highly specialized group, and soon became the leading figure in the field (Cottraux, 1979). He was active in propagating cognitive-behaviour therapy (CBT) in psychiatric circles, both through the AFTCC platform and by participating in professional meetings for psychiatrists and psychologists at large. One can estimate at about 1000 the number of recognized practitioners of CBT. This is a large number, considering the French context, but it is small compared with equivalent professional societies in other European countries of compar-able size, such as Germany or Spain.

In spite of its progresses, the behavioural approach is far from having gained its place in the teaching and practice of clinical psychology and psychiatry. As already alluded to, psycho-analysis is still the dominant school of thought at the institutional level (although more so in psychology departments than in psychiatry, where the tough biological approach has to some extent counterbalanced Freudian influence), and the most popularized through the media.

At this point, it seems appropriate to provide the reader with a brief account of recent events that illustrate the present highly conflicted rela-tions between cognitivo-behavioural approaches and psychoanalysis, making France a *unique case* on the international scene. The special evolution of psychoanalysis in France should be remembered. Having received Freudian theories somewhat later than other countries—including the USA—France soon developed its original brand of psycho-analysis, elaborated by Jacques Lacan. He made his reputation on claiming to restore the true meaning of Freud's writings, consequently sepa-rated from the existing society of French psycho-analysts, and built his enormous success on hermetic abstruse discourse that would give free rein to infinite games of interpretation. Looked at from outside, such success appears rather strange in a culture that defines itself by the clarity of ideas and style, inherited from Montaigne, Voltaire, Diderot, Montesquieu, and many others. Not the whole world has been receptive to Lacan's message: For reasons we leave to historians to explain, it found an echo in Argentina, and some audience in the USA post-modern circles, affiliated with humanities departments rather than psychological or medical sciences. His superficial misuse of tough sciences such as mathematics and physics, just to impress, has been brilliantly denounced by Sokal and Bricmont (1997). However, Lacan, who was never offered a position in a French university, managed to attract many devotees and to exert unexpected influence on clinical psychology and psychiatry. His son-in-law, Jacques Alain Miller, has taken over the propaga-tion of his ideas in an even more militant style. He is the central figure in the following story. To make it clear, the reader should know that in France, the title of psychologist, designating a profession, is protected by the law, like the title of medical doctor, and requires defined conditions in terms of university training and degrees. It is not the case of the title "psychotherapist," which anyone can advertise on his/her door. In fact, many individuals who do not fulfil the require-ments for practising psychology or medicine are practising one or another form of the numerous kinds of psychotherapies now available on the market.

Recently, a Minister of Health, having to consider funding of psychotherapeutic treatments by the health security system, ordered a study on comparative outcomes of various kinds of psychotherapies from the prestigious National Medical Research Institute (INSERM), while a project of law was submitted to the parliament aiming at defining the conditions (in terms of university degrees) to practise psychotherapy. The INSERM report, based on a survey of about 1000 studies evaluating different kinds of psychotherapies, was released early in 2005. It showed a very poor record for psychoanalytic treatments, somewhat better for family treatment of various orientations, and much better (yet far from perfect!) for cognitive-behavioural approaches. This, together with the legal requirements for practising, provoked a violent reaction from psychoanalytic circles that took on a political dimension. Some political leaders, including the new Minister of Health, now in charge of foreign affairs, attended a meeting chaired by Miller, the leader of the Lacanian group. The Minister declared publicly his adherence to the psychoanalytic credo, as formulated by Miller, that psychological interventions are not amenable to any scientific evaluation. He added that the INSERM report, although ordered by a former member of the government, and paid for, of course, with public money, was withdrawn from the website of the Ministry of Health. A violent campaign was organized with the support of the media, stigmatizing non-psychoanalytic therapists, especially those of the cognitivo-behavioural orientation, accused of sharing Nazi-like ideology at work in the American forces in Guantanamo Bay and in Iraq. Here is only one short quotation from the arguments propagated by that psychoanalytic party: "*Criminal inclinations of the United States are clearly illustrated by what occurred at the prison of Abou-Graïb. One must know that tortures, psychological and physical alike, which have disgusted the whole world are applications of methods that have a name: these are exactly the behavioural methods*" (Miller, 2005).

What is at stake here, of course, is the scientific status of psychology applied to human psychological problems, and the right of patients and clients to know in advance where they are being taken to by their therapist. Discarding the use of scientific criteria in some areas of psychological theory or practice is very much like claiming a religious alternate to the theory of biological evolution. The Lacanian psychoanalysts with whom French scientific psychologists are confronted today might be compared to creationists challenging scientific biology. They appeal to the magical concept of individual freedom and respect of the person in order to escape any questioning as to the outcomes of their practice, and to maintain their power and their economic advantages.

EAB IN SUISSE ROMANDE (FRENCH-SPEAKING SWITZERLAND)

There are four universities where psychological and educational sciences are taught in French in Switzerland: Geneva, Lausanne, and Neuchatel, located in French-speaking "cantons" proper, and the Catholic University in Freiburg, where teaching is offered in French and in German—the population of the canton being distributed between the two languages, with dominance for German. Geneva has a strong tradition of developmental psychology, going back to the founders of Institut Rousseau, among whom Claparède and Bovet had a prominent position and international prestige. Piaget was the major figure in the next generation, experimental psychology being practically identified with his own research programme. His creative genius was also very exclusive: Piaget had little inclination to attract around him psychologists not sharing his theory and methodology. It was no wonder, therefore, that EAB was not represented in the Faculty of Psychology and Education that eventually succeeded the Institut Rousseau. Other universities developed specialties having little or no place in Geneva, but mainly in applied fields such as social psychology, work and organization psychology, etc. They did not show more interest than Geneva in having EAB at level 1, involving theoretical and laboratory research. One should point also to the fact that, except for the efforts made by André Rey between 1940 and 1965 in Geneva, with little institutional support, animal research was not in favour in Swiss university departments of psychology. When it was given a (limited) place in Geneva, it was in the ethological area. To sum up, Suisse romande did not have fertile soil to grow behaviourist ideas and experiments, at least at the institutional level. There might have been a few persons interested in Skinner's thinking at an individual level. At least two of them can be mentioned here: André and Anne-Marie Gonthier-Werren. They worked for a quarter of a century in the field of technology of education, within the Skinnerian framework, pioneering in applied behaviour analysis, which will be discussed below. They have been fighting to have Skinner's book *Science and Human Behaviour* translated and published. They put a lot of energy, time and generosity into that project, which finally was achieved after two decades (Skinner, 1956/2005a).

Fortunately, applications of EAB in education, psychological treatment, and health psychology developed better than fundamental research, although they were slow in gaining audience. In a scanning survey of the Swiss scientific literature for the years 1980–1990, hardly a dozen of papers were found, mainly in the late '80s, dealing with ABA. These focused essentially on one of three domains: (1) behaviour modification in some aspects of psychopathology, initiated by Jean-Pierre Dauwalder, professor at the University of Lausanne; (2) school and educational context, more specifically computer-assisted learning, as a modern version of programmed instruction, and the use of classroom observation and techniques of reinforcement; and (3) special education, a field mainly developed in Freiburg by the group headed by Lambert.

From then on, applications did develop and were increasingly given institutional attention. As far as behaviour therapies are concerned, one has to emphasize, here as in most other places, that they have been associated with cognitive therapies. EAB is now a subject matter of teaching at various levels of the curricula. In Freiburg, a specific course is devoted to it in the first year of the BA degree at the Department of Remedial and Specialized Pedagogy. It is a part, of varying importance, of courses on learning processes in the curricula of students in psychology and in education at the universities of Geneva, Lausanne, and Freiburg. It is a component in specialized training in behaviour therapy as offered in the Lausanne University Institute for Psychotherapy, in the section of behavioural and cognitive therapies headed by Valentino Pomini. It is included in the continuous training of psychotherapists at the Geneva Medical School, Department of Psychiatry, which delivers a degree (3 years) in cognitivo-behavioural psychotherapies.

As a rule, behavioural and cognitive approaches have been developing mainly within the psychiatric institutions in Lausanne and Geneva, and to a more modest extent in psychiatric institutions in the cantons of Freiburg, Valais, and Neuchatel. A number of specialized units are active in various domains such as the treatment of anxiety and mood problems, of schizophrenia, of addictions (toxicomania, alcoholism, gambling), as well as in psychiatric rehabilitation, or treatment of feeding problems, for which cognitivo-behavioural approaches are well established, if not given preference. As another evidence of the progress of the approach, one can mention the recent opening at the Prangins Hospital (the West Psychiatric Sector) of the first treatment unit specializing in cognitivo-behavioural treatment, headed by Dominique Page. This is not to say that other units do not also apply that kind of treatment; what is significant is that it is the first explicitly labelled as such, emphasizing the therapeutic practice orientation rather than the pathological category of patients to be treated.

An increasing number of day-care psychiatric units, aiming at rehabilitation of patients in normal social life, also include cognitivo-behavioural programmes in their therapeutic offerings.

Applications to education have equally been developing in various institutions specializing in mental retardation, in children and adolescents with behavioural problems, and in family education. Many of these applications are backed by the Department of Remedial Pedagogy at the University of Freiburg, where practicum training in behaviour modification is offered. Several programmes inspired by Lovaas are also applied to autistic children.

Contrasting with the institutional environment, behavioural approaches are far less in favour among *private practitioners*, be they psychiatrists or psychologists. In Lausanne, a medium-sized city, they can be counted on the fingers of one hand, about the same number as in Freiburg, a smaller place. Geneva might have a few more. Behavioural prctitioners are clearly outnumbered by those using other approaches, such as psychoanalysis.

Three professional associations are currently active in French-speaking Switzerland. One is the Swiss Association for Cognitive Therapy, the second the Swiss Society for Behavioural and Cognitive Therapy, and the third the French-Speaking International Interdisciplinary Association for Training and Research in Behavioural and Cognitive Therapy. The first two, in spite of their different labels, do indeed cover the same domain, largely defined as behavioural and cognitive therapies. Most of their members are medical doctors and psychologists, grouped together in the first case, or distributed in two sections as in the second.

All three associations organize seminars and workshops, complementing the teaching offered in universities, and the first two have established collaboration with universities—Geneva for the first, Lausanne and Freiburg for the second—in the implementation of courses towards specialized certificates and diplomas. It can be concluded that in the last few years training in applied analysis of behaviour has been seriously strengthened in Suisse romande (French-speaking Switzerland) and the times are gone when those persons wanting to receive training in the area had to go to Lyon to obtain the diploma organized there by Jean Cottraux. All the training programmes briefly described above attract a number of motivated persons. They obviously meet a demand from physicians and psychologists as well as from nurses and other people taking part in mental health programmes.

EAB IN FRENCH-SPEAKING BELGIUM

Belgium is a small country, but complex because of its linguistic problems, which eventually resulted in 1980 in a federalist structure, with some consequences on university and scientific affairs. The following account is limited to the French-speaking part of Belgium, and should not be extrapolated to the Flemish-speaking part, where the development of EAB has been somewhat different (for a survey of psychology in Belgium, see Richelle, Janssen, & Brédart, 1992). As in Switzerland, the common language has naturally favoured close relations with French psychology, although it has not eliminated the specific features of French-speaking Belgian psychology, as derived from different university traditions, shaped by different influences, and not constrained by such administrative and cultural centralization as is the case in France. One could say that within a small territory, the psychological landscape was more diversified. Although teaching of and research in psychology had been developed from the end of the 19th century, especially at the University of Louvain (a Flemish city where the French-speaking Catholic University was then located), the expansion of the field took place after the Second World War. Because of the individuals in charge of experimental psychology, each of the three universities, Brussels, Louvain, and Liège, would develop its own style and orientation with respect to main areas of research and theoretical emphasis. In Brussels, Paul Bertelson, who had been trained in the UK at the Broadbent laboratory, worked on reaction times and later developed a research group in cognitive human psychology. In Louvain, Georges Thinès, a former assistant of Michotte, perpetuated his master's interest in perception, but developed studies of animal behaviour along Lorenz's lines. At the University of Liège, Marc Richelle, who trained in Geneva and at Harvard, and was an unusual hybrid of

Piaget and Skinner, started an operant laboratory in 1959, hosted by the pharmacology department at the Medical School. Operant chambers were homemade, and the control circuits were built after the model then in use at Skinner's laboratory, from electromechanical relays wired onto the external face as needed for running the schedules of reinforcement. Presumably, these were the first operant conditioning chambers on the European continent (maybe including the UK and Ireland). As a return for the hospitality of pharmacologists, research was partly devoted to behavioural pharmacology in animals (the story of the beginnings of the Liège laboratory and of related behavioural research in psychopharmacology has been told in Richelle, 1991). The laboratory was soon integrated into a newly created psychology department and became the core of the Chair of Experimental Psychology, where all psychology students had to take their practicum, taking part in one of the research projects being run at that time. Most of these projects involved EAB *stricto sensu* using animal subjects; others were genuine approaches to problems not traditionally considered by behaviour analysts in Anglo-Saxon countries, and still others were outside the Skinnerian framework, as Richelle made a point of not limiting the perspective of his students to one exclusive approach.

In the first category, behavioural pharmacology studies continued, using mainly schedules involving temporal regulations of behaviour (such as fixed interval, or differential reinforcement of low rates of responding). From the early 1960s, behavioural time in its own right became the major and most permanent theme of operant research. Helga Lejeune devoted her career to time estimation and timing behaviour and is an internationally reputed expert in the field; she contributed a number of original findings and theoretical elaborations, especially on cross-species and cross-schedule comparisons (Lejeune, Richelle, & Wearden, in press; Richelle & Lejeune, 1980). Engaged in time studies also, Françoise Macar moved soon after her Masters degree to the CNRS neurophysiology laboratory in Marseille— headed by the French psychophysiologist Jacques Paillard—where she continued along the same tracks, using human subjects. Both have maintained collaboration, joined by Pouthas, in Paris (see above). A third line of research in the 1970s is worth mentioning: The attempt to replicate Neal Miller's experiments on operant control of visceral responses, with the purpose of applying the technique to explore psychosomatic problems. A member of the staff, Ovide Fontaine, a psychiatrist, had been attracted by the techniques developed in Miller's laboratory, which he visited. His work was, unfortunately, doomed to failure, as Miller himself had to admit his incapacity to replicate his own results (giving the scientific community an exceptional example of intellectual honesty by publishing a paper on the issue; Dworkin & Miller, 1986). Fontaine then concentrated on his second field of interest, the development of behaviour therapy, which will be discussed below. A fourth line of research, closely related to the issue of selectionism as a major tenet of radical behaviourism, was aimed at exploring behavioural variability as the source of novel behaviour and creative production. Experiments on animals and humans were carried out and several theoretical papers published (Boulanger, 1990; Richelle, 1987, 1992, 1995; Richelle & Botson, 1974).

In the second category, two domains of research should be mentioned that exemplify cross-fertilization between approaches traditionally kept separate. One is the use of Skinnerian methodology, especially progressive errorless learning, in the study of cognitive development as described by Piaget. This research was initiated by Claude Botson and run by her and Michèle Deliège in a series of original experiments, which showed how mastery of concepts and logical relations in development could be boosted to some extent by adequate learning conditions, but to some extent only, as some crucial acquisitions in Piaget's description appeared to be strongly dependent upon developmental constraints (Botson & Deliège, 1975). The second domain was innovative in merging EAB and the ethological approach to animal behaviour. A close collaboration with a colleague in ethology, Jean-Claude Ruwet (psychology students had to take an introductory course in ethology in their second year), was put to concrete form in joint seminars, the organization of a small international symposium (Richelle & Ruwet, 1972), and research putting together methods and hypotheses from both fields. The best of this collaboration has been a study by a master student on hoarding in the Syrian hamster, using operant conditioning in a semi-natural environment, with recording 24 hours per day over a period of several months and systematic observation of natural behaviour. For reasons explained in Richelle (1991), the study remained unpublished. A third domain is worth mentioning here, although it resulted more in theoretical than experimental contributions, i.e., psycholinguistics. They bore upon the relations between Skinner's analysis of verbal behaviour and linguistic approaches, especially Chomsky's theory

(Richelle, 1972, 1993a, b). Anecdotally, it should be mentioned here that the first seminar on generative grammar ever held in French-speaking Europe, freely organized by Richelle and Nicolas Ruwet, took place, for local reasons, in the operant animal laboratory. Ruwet had been a student of Chomsky, and had just obtained his PhD with a remarkable thesis on generative grammar, as it was formulated at that time.

In the third category, one can mention research in visual perception, led by Roger Genicot, or much later—from the early 1980s—in musical perception, launched by Irène Delège in collaboration with the Music Conservatory in Liège. Her dynamism eventually led her to found the European Society for Cognitive Sciences and Music (ESCOM), to start a new journal in sciences of music, and to attract several international meetings in the field to Liège. It might seem rather curious to some external behaviour analysts that a laboratory with a behaviourist orientation would host and support cognitivist psychologists. It was the philosophy of the laboratory to welcome people who had a project, and allow them full freedom to develop it.

Although the laboratory was essentially devoted to *experimental work*, some advanced students and researchers became interested in applications. Behaviour therapy became the main field of O. Fontaine, who founded the Belgian Association for Behaviour Therapy, and was active in the creation of the European Society; he contributed to developing collaborations with clinicians in various specialties at the Medical Faculty (Fontaine, 1979; Fontaine, Cottraux, & Ladouceur, 1984). Jean-Luc Lambert, Xavier Seron, and Martial Van Der Linden acquired expertise in behaviour modification (Seron, Lambert, & Van Der Linden, 1977). Lambert specialized in mental retardation and since 1980 has been professor at the University of Freiburg, in Switzerland (see above). The other two became reputed neuropsychologists, Seron leading a group in Louvain-la-Neuve, and Van der Linden one in Liège, and later in Geneva. As neuropsychology was a branch of psychology that had developed for some years in the cognitive orientation, none of these practitioners would identify himself with EAB, although behaviour modification methods are integrated in practices towards the re-education of brain-damaged patients.

Richelle and his group undoubtedly formed the main centre of EAB in French-speaking Europe, and the point of origin of the diffusion of Skinner's work and thinking in the French area. Richelle's book *Le Conditionnement Operant* was published in 1966, followed by *Skinner ou le Péril Behaviouriste* (1978) and a number of papers on various issues, such as verbal behaviour, the relation between Piaget's constructivism and Skinner's theory, EAB, and ethology, reprinted in French in Richelle (1993a), and the substance of which is part of *B. F. Skinner: A Reappraisal* (Richelle, 1993b). The first three books of Skinner published in French were translated by Richelle, as mentioned in the Introduction. The Liège laboratory organized the first two European Meetings on the Experimental Analysis of Behaviour (EMEAB) in 1983 and 1988. Skinner was present at the first of these meetings, attended by more than 300 participants, and delivered an invited lecture entitled "The Evolution of Behaviour" (see Lowe, Richelle, Blackman, & Bradshaw, 1985). The 1988 meeting was no less successful and, as the first, was an encounter between behaviour analysts from Europe and other continents and psychologists or other scientists working with different approaches on the topics selected, such as the psychology of time, reasoning, language, and behavioural medicine (see Blackman & Lejeune, 1990). The third EMAB took place in Dublin in 1997, and the fourth in French-speaking Europe again, in Amiens in 2000.

One has to say that Liège is no longer the EAB centre it had been for more than three decades. Shortly after Richelle retired in 1995, the label of the "experimental psychology" laboratory changed to "cognitive psychology," the new generation having adopted other epistemological frames of reference.

At the level of applied analysis of behaviour, behavioural therapy in French-speaking Belgium developed largely better than in France, but not as well as in the Flemish part of Belgium, where psychoanalysis was less dominant and where clinical psychologists were more open to Anglo-Saxon influences. Besides the decisive impulse given by Fontaine from Liège, at the Catholic University of Louvain, a stronghold of Freud, Lacan, and Szondi disciples, two psychoanalysts questioned the exclusivity of the psychoanalytic stance. Winfrid Huber wrote his Doctor's thesis on the comparative study of psychoanalytic vs behavioural hypotheses on therapeutic processes in the treatment of phobias (Huber, 1967). He soon introduced information on behaviour therapies into his teaching of clinical psychology and psychological treatments (Huber, 1987). Jacques Van Rillaer made a complete break with psychoanalysis and became a champion of behaviour

therapies and of the demystification of Freudian claims to superiority in theory and treatment efficiency (Van Rillaer, 1981). At the University of Mons-Hainaut, Ghislain Magerotte introduced behaviour modification in the field of special education. On the whole, as in most other places, the behaviour therapy label was changed to cognitivo-behavioural therapy. This now has its place, varying in extent from one university to the other, in the *teaching and training* of clinical psychology everywhere and in the *practice* of an increasing number of practitioners. The behavioural approach has also been increasingly adopted in *special education* for physically or mentally handicapped children, or more widely in *general education*. We cannot possibly mention here all individuals or teams that make use, more or less intensively, of EAB principles in their educational or clinical practice. Let us limit ourselves to one example, probably unique in its style in French-speaking countries: the Institute for Child and Family Development established in Auvelais by Christian Lalière.

CONCLUSION

This survey of EAB in French-speaking Europe is admittedly far from complete. In the time allocated, the authors could not possibly enquire into all the historical details and other ramifications. They apologize for omissions of persons or groups that were deserving of mention. It is hoped that, as it is, this paper provides a reasonably accurate picture of the EAB movement in the territories bounded by their common language, but distinct in their receptiveness—or lack of receptiveness—to the last important phase of American behaviourism. The picture can be characterized briefly in the following points.

1. In none of the three geographical areas being considered could psychology be said to be prepared to integrate radical behaviourism, for reasons linked to the past—while everyone would pay lip-service to the definition of psychology as the science of behaviour, few were willing to endorse the implications of behaviourism, not to speak of radical behaviourism; or to the present—by the time some faint echoes of Skinner's work reached France and its neighbours, cognitivism had already invaded the place. Many endorsed Chomsky's peremptory judgment on *Verbal Behaviour* and took this as a pretext to dispense with reading Skinner's original work for themselves.

2. Although in all three areas, some laboratories adopted the operant techniques that were especially appropriate in their research, usually in animal studies in psychopharmacology, psychophysiology, and the like, interest in the theoretical aspects of radical behaviourism was quite limited. The few exceptions, notably in Liège, and later in Lille, were the result of the peculiar trajectory of individuals who did work at the propagation of Skinner's ideas.

3. On the contrary, *applications*, mainly in behaviour therapy and in special and normal education, did develop in all French-speaking countries or regions, at different times and rates, from the 1970s on. On the whole, Belgium was first, followed by France and then Switzerland. In France, progress was confronted with the reactions from psychoanalytic circles, which became highly polemical and conflictual. This was especially so in the last 2 years, when psychoanalysts felt threatened by legal dispositions aimed at controlling the formation of all psychotherapists and by scientific reports questioning the efficiency of psychoanalytic treatment. Although some polemics occurred in Belgium and Switzerland as well, they remained more urbane and never reached the violent tone that has characterized the French situation.

4. To the question: How is it that applications, especially to treatment, had so much more success than the theory from which they were derived? A partial answer is: Because behavioural approaches have merged with cognitive approaches, which have, so to speak, exorcized them. Another answer would go like this: Practitioners are pragmatic people, and if they observe that two kinds of therapy seem complementary rather than opposite, they see no sense in rejecting one in favour of the other; they use both. Would people in practice have gone beyond theoretical debates, and reconciled behaviourism and cognitivism? Who knows?

REFERENCES

Agathon, M. (1982). Behaviour therapy in France, 1976–1981. *Journal of Behaviour Therapy and Experimental Psychiatry, 13*, 271–277.

Blackman, D. E., & Lejeune, H. (Eds.). (1990). *Behaviour analysis in theory and practice. Contributions and controversies.* Hove, UK: Lawrence Erlbaum Associates Ltd.

Botson, C., & Deliège, M. (1975). *Le développement intellectuel de l'enfant. Une méthode d'approch: les apprentissage sans erreurs.* Brussels, Belgium: Direction générale des études, Ministry of National Education.

Boulanger, B. (1990). *La variabilité comportementale. Une approche développementale chez l'humain.* Unpublished Doctoral thesis, University of Liège.

Cottraux, J. (1979). *Les therapies comportementales.* Paris: Masson.

Dworkin, B. R., & Miller, N. E. (1986). Failure to replicate visceral learning in the acute curarized rat preparation. *Behavioural Neurosciences, 3*, 299–314.

Fontaine, O. (1979). *Introduction aux thérapies comportementales.* Brussels, Belgium: Mardaga.

Fontaine, O., Cottraux, J., & Ladouceur, R. (Eds.). (1984). *Cliniques de thérapie comportementale.* Liège, Belgium: Mardaga.

Freixa i Baqué, E. (1985). El conductismo y el marxismo en Francia: el conductismo, Skinner, la izquierda, y los otros. *Revista Mexicana de Análisis de la Conducta, 11*, 175–237.

Huber, W. (1967). *Interprétation ou déconditionnement. Etude comparative des hypothèses formulées par la psychanalyse et la "behaviour therapy" sur les processus thérapeutiques dans le traitement des phobies.* Unpublished Doctoral thesis, University of Louvain.

Huber, W. (1987). *La psychologie clinique aujourd'hui.* Brussels, Belgium: Mardaga.

Lejeune, H., Macar, F., & Pouthas, V. (1995). *Des animaux et des hommes, hommage à Marc Richelle.* Paris: Presses Universitaires de France.

Lejeune, H., Richelle, M., & Wearden, J. H. (in press). About Skinner and time: Behaviour: Analytic contributions to research on animal timing. *Journal of the Experimental Analysis of Behaviour.*

Lowe, C. E., Richelle, M., Blackman, D. E., & Bradshaw, C. M. (Eds.). (1985). *Behaviour analysis and contemporary psychology.* Hove, UK: Lawrence Erlbaum Associates Ltd.

Miller, J. A. (2005) Agence Lacanienne de Presse, Nouvelle série, n° 46 - Paris, le samedi 19 mars 2005 (www.forumpsy.org)).

Naville, P. (1946). *Psychologie, marxisme, matérialisme.* Paris: Marcel Rivière.

Parot, F. (1995). Le behaviourisme, une révolution américaine. *Acta Comportamentalia, 3*, 8–19.

Piéron, H. (1908). L'évolution du psychisme et l'étude objective du comportement. *Revue du Mois.* March 1908, 291–310. Reprinted (1958) in *De l'actinie à l'homme* (pp. 3–22). Paris: Presses Universitaires de France.

Pouthas, V. (1985). Timing behaviour in young children, a developmental approach to conditioned spaced responding (pp. 100–109). In J. Michon & J. Jackson (Eds.), *Time, mind and behaviour.* Heidelberg, Germany: Springer.

Pouthas, V. (1995). Apprentissage operant chez le jeune enfant: analyse expérimentale du comportement et développement cognitive (pp. 85–104). In H. Lejeune, F. Macar, & V. Pouthas (Eds.), *Des animaux et des hommes, hommage à Marc Richelle.* Paris: Preses Universitaires de France.

Richelle, M. (1966). *Le conditionnement operant.* Neuchatel, Switzerland, & Paris: Delachaux & Niestlé.

Richelle, M. (1972). Analyse formelle et analyse fonctionnelle du comportement verbal. *Bulletin de Psychologie, 26*, 252–259.

Richelle, M. (1978). *Skinner ou le péril behaviouriste.* Brussels, Belgium: Mardaga.

Richelle, M. (1987). Variation and selection, the evolutionary analogy in Skinner's theory. In S. Modgil & C. Modgil (Eds.), *B. F. Skinner, consensus and controversy* (pp. 127–137). New York/London: Falmer Press.

Richelle, M. (1991). Behavioural pharmacology in Continental Europe: A personal account of its origins and development. *Journal of the Experimental Analysis of Behaviour, 56,* 415–423.

Richelle, M. (1992). La analogía evolucionista en el pensamiento de B. F. Skinner. In J. Gil Roales-Nieto, C. Luciano Soriano, & M. Perez Alvarez (Eds.), *Vigencia de la obra de Skinner* (pp. 115–124). Granada, Spain: Universidad de Granada.

Richelle, M. (1993a). *Du nouveau sur l'Esprit? Et autres questions en suspens.* Paris: Presses Universitaires de France.

Richelle, M. (1993b). *B. F. Skinner: A reappraisal.* Hove, UK: Lawrence Erlbaum Associates Ltd.

Richelle, M. (1995). Eloge des variations. In J. Lautrey (Ed.), *Universel et différentiel en psychologie* (pp. 35–50). Paris: Presses Universitaires de France.

Richelle, M., & Botson, C. (1974). *Les conduites créatives. Essai d'exploration expérimentale.* Brussels, Belgium: Ministry of National Education.

Richelle, M., Janssen, P. J., & Brédart, S. (1992). Psychology in Belgium. *Annual Review of Psychology, 43,* 505–529.

Richelle, M., & Lejeune, H. (1980). *Time in animal behaviour.* Oxford, UK: Pergamon.

Richelle, M., & Ruwet, J.-C. (Eds.). (1972). *Problèmes de méthode en psychologie comparée.* Paris: Masson.

Seron, X., Lambert, J-L., & Van Der Linden, M. (1977). *La modification du comportement.* Brussels, Belgium: Mardaga.

Skinner, B. F. (1969). *La Révolution scientifique de l'Enseignement* (trans. M. Richelle, *The technology of teaching* [1968]). Brussels, Belgium: Dessart/Mardaga.

Skinner, B. F. (1971). *L'Analyse experimentale du Comportement* (trans. A.-M. & M. Richelle, *Contingencies of reinforcement* [1969]). Brussels, Belgium: Dessart/Mardaga.

Skinner, B. F. (1972). *Par-delà la Liberté et la Dignité* (trans. A.-M. & M. Richelle, *Beyond freedom and dignity* [1971]). Paris: Robert Laffont.

Skinner, B. F. (1979). *Pour une Science du Comportement: le Behaviourisme* (trans. F. Parot, *About behaviourism* [1974]). Neuchatel, Switzerland, and Paris: Delachaux & Niestlé.

Skinner, B. F. (2005a). *Science et Comportement humain* (trans. A. & R.-M. Gonthier-Werren, *Science and human behaviour* [1953]). Paris: In Press.

Skinner, B. F. (2005b). *Walden 2, Communauté expérimentale* (trans. A. & R.-M. Gonthier-Werren & F. Lemaire, *Walden Two* [1948]). Paris: In Press.

Sokal, A., & Bricmont, J. (1997). *Impostures intellectuelles.* Paris: Odile Jacob.

Van Rillaer, J. (1981). *Les illusions de la psychanalyse.* Brussels, Belgium: Mardaga.

INTERNATIONAL JOURNAL OF PSYCHOLOGY, 2006, 41 (6), 480–485

Behaviourism and the science of behaviour: Its development in Italy

Paolo Moderato

IULM University, Milan, Italy

Giovambattista Presti

University of Parma, Parma, Italy

*T*he development of behaviourism in Italy is presented, beginning with Virgilio Lazzeroni, who in 1942 published a paper in which he claimed that behaviour was the subject matter of psychology. The behaviourist tradition is relatively young in Italy, due to the influence of the cultural environment centred on idealistic philosophy. The tree of Italian behaviourism has two roots, which can be labelled Pavlovian-reflexiological-psychiatric, and Skinnerian-operant-psychological. The founding of the Italian Association for Behaviour Analysis and Modification (AIAMC, for its initials in Italian) in 1977 was particularly influential. The first ABA International Convention was held in Venice in 2001 and the first Conference of the European Association of Behaviour Analysis was held in Parma in 2003. Other national and international scientific meetings have been organized, and also 4-year postgraduate courses in behaviour analysis and therapy. Almost all of the main books of the behavioural literature have been translated into Italian, and a number of original books by native authors have been published. At the present time behaviourism has reached a fairly good critical mass within psychology in Italy, though it is still a minority if compared with the psychoanalytic approach or to the systemic approach. There is research and practical work on theoretical, clinical, educational, and organizational topics.

*L*e développement du behaviourisme en Italie a commencé en 1942 lorsque Virgilio Lazzeroni publia un article dans lequel il affirmait que le comportement était un sujet appartenant au domaine de la psychologie. La tradition behaviouriste est relativement jeune en Italie, du à l'influence de l'environnement culturel centré sur la philosophie idéaliste. L'arbre du behaviourisme italien présente deux racines qui peuvent être identifiées comme pavlovienne-réflexologiste-psychiatrique et skinnerienne-opérante-psychologique. La fondation de l'Association italienne pour l'Analyse et la Modification du Comportement (AIAMC) était particulièrement influente en 1977. Le premier congrès international de l'Association pour l'analyse du comportement fut tenu à Venise en 2001 et la première conférence de l'Association européenne d'analyse du comportement a eu lieu à Parma en 2003. D'autres rencontres scientifiques nationales et internationales ont été organisées, ainsi que des cours universitaires de niveau supérieure de 4 années en analyse et thérapie du comportement. Par ailleurs, la plupart des principaux livres portant sur le behaviourisme ont été traduits en italien et plusieurs livres rédigés par des auteurs italiens ont été publiés. De nos jours, le behaviourisme a atteint une masse critique considérable dans le domaine de la psychologie en Italie, quoiqu'il s'agisse encore d'une minorité en comparaison à l'approche psychanalytique ou à l'approche systémique. Nous retrouvons à la fois de la recherche et du travail pratique, autant sur les plans théorique, clinique, académique et organisationnel.

*S*e presenta el desarrollo del conductismo en Italia comenzando por Virgilio Lazzeroni quién en 1942 publicó un artículo en el cual afirmaba que el comportamiento era el campo de trabajo de la psicología. La tradición conductista es relativamente joven en Italia, debido a la influencia del ambiente cultural centrado en la filosofía idealista. El árbol del conductismo italiano tiene dos raíces que pueden denominarse Pavloviana-reflexiológica-psiquiátrica, y Skinneriana-operante-psicológica. La fundación en 1977 de la Asociación Italiana de Análisis y Modificación del Comportamiento (AIAMC, por sus iniciales en italiano) tuvo especial influencia. La primera Convención Internacional de ABA tuvo lugar en Venecia en 2001, y la primera Conferencia de la European Association of Behaviour Analysis se llevó a cabo en Parma en 2003. Se han organizado otros encuentros nacionales e internacionales y cursos de postgrado de 4 años en análisis y terapia del comportamiento. Casi todos los principales libros de la literatura conductual se han traducido al italiano y se ha publicado un cierto número

Correspondence should be addressed to Paolo Moderato, Institute of Behaviour, Consumers and Communication, IULM University, Via Carlo Bo 8, Milan 20143, Italy (E-mail: paolo.moderato@iulm.it).

http://www.psypress.com/ijp   DOI: 10.1080/00207590500492419 de libros originales de autores nativos. En el momento actual el conductismo ha alcanzado en Italia una masa crítica aceptablemente buena dentro de la psicología, aunque todavía es minoritaria si la comparamos con el enfoque psicoanalítico o el enfoque sistémico. Existe investigación y trabajo práctico en temas teóricos, clínicos, educativos y organizacionales.

THE HISTORICAL CONTEXT

The development of behavioural psychology in Italy cannot be fully understood without glancing briefly at the birth and development of Italian psychology *tout court*, which, in turn, needs to be located in the history of late 18th century. Following this perspective it is also worth comparing what was happening in Italy in the second half of the 19th century with what was happening in the rest of Europe.

Many readers might not know that Italy only became a unified nation in 1861, after two wars of independence: However, "unity" was more on paper than in actuality. First of all, many regions that are part of Italy today did not belong at that time to the Italian State (for example, Rome and surroundings and some parts of the Venice area towards the north-east), and were annexed to the Kingdom of Italy after the First World War. Rome became the capital of our country after a war against the Pope in 1870.

At that time Italy was a divided country: different languages, different cultures, different economic conditions, different foods and habits, different political traditions, and no plans to integrate and dissolve all these diversities (many traces of which still can be found today).

Italian psychology was born in this climate, basically in the same period as in the rest of Europe. In 1870 Roberto Ardigò published *Psychology as a Positive Science*, and in 1873 Giuseppe Sergi published *Principles of Psychology*, just one year before the publication of *Gründzuge der Physiologischen Psychologie* by W. Wundt, the man who is celebrated as the father of scientific psychology. Actually Sergi was not a psychologist; he was a teacher of philosophy in high school.

It is remarkable that psychology was born in Italy with very different cultural premises to those in Germany, Great Britain, and France. The hot dispute, originated in those countries by the associationist view, materialistic philosophy, and Darwinian evolutionary theory, reached Italy only as a soft reflection of the debate and did not mark or change at all the traditional spiritualistic attitude of Italian philosophers.

The positivist philosopher R. Ardigò (1828–1920) is looked upon as the father of Italian psychology. Even though he had a theoretical attitude more than an experimental one, he led some interesting research in the field of perception. Though his starting point of view was a positivistic one, it is important to underline that he refused the reduction of psychology to physiology.

At the beginning of the 20th century, psychology was progressively expanding in Italy: In 1905 the journal *Rivista di Psicologia* was founded and the Vth International Congress of Psychology took place in Rome. In the same year three positions of professor of psychology were available for the first time in Italian universities.

After the First World War, Italy went through a political period called "fascism," which lasted for 20 years. The Fascist Party obtained power in a nondemocratic way, with no elections, and imposed its new standards in all the fields, including culture. The cultural climate became hostile to psychology, particularly because the "official" philosophy of fascism had a strong attitude against science and stated the primacy of philosophy over science. Furthermore, it should be remembered that, because of the cultural isolation that characterized Italy during that time, the circulation of ideas was strongly hampered, including whatever material originated from foreign countries—particularly from the Anglo-Saxon ones. But fascism was ambivalent toward psychology: It showed criticism against psychology as a science and against its basic research, but attention to all possible applications, especially in the field of industry and war.

At the beginning of the fascist age, there were many professors and lecturers of psychology in several universities, but at its end there was only one in Rome, Ponzo, and one in Milan, Gemelli, a Franciscan friar who founded the Università Cattolica del Sacro Cuore in the 1920s and who in 1927 established a laboratory of psychology. The Catholic University, being a private university, was very powerful and independent from political power; therefore Gemelli could keep on working both in basic and applied fields, counterbalancing the negative effects of isolation that Italian academic psychology suffered, because it lacked exchange of scientific ideas with foreign research centres.

Two other things cannot be neglected: First, due to racial persecution many Jewish professors were forced to resign, to abandon their research work, and to escape abroad (see, for example, the famous physics group of Via Panisperna, who went to the USA). Second, some professors refused to take the oath of allegiance to the fascist government and consequently were stripped of their positions.

All these factors should make clear that it is not unusual that behaviourist psychology remained unknown until 1942, when Virginio Lazzeroni introduced the term "psychology of behaviour," referring for the first time in Italy to behaviour as the main topic of psychology.

THE BEGINNINGS

In 1992 in Siena, the homeland of Virginio Lazzeroni, the 50th birthday of Italian behaviourism was celebrated with a congress entitled: "Behaviourism at fifty in Italy." To tell the truth, Italian behavioural psychology started to develop in a significant way sometime later, in the second half of the 1960s, fed by two different roots. However, for many years the Institute of General and Clinical Psychology of Siena represented a point of reference for theoretical and research work on behaviour theory and therapy.

In the same years the psychiatrist Gastone Canziani went to Sicily from the "mitteleuropean" Trieste, and started teaching psychology at the University of Palermo, where he founded the Institute of Psychology and a laboratory in which experimental research on Pavlovian conditioning was carried on. Curiously, his position of Professor of Psychology was created under the Allied administration and was called Am-chair, since the money that circulated in occupied Italy was called Am-Lire.

As has been mentioned previously, Italian behaviourism has two main roots: one can be defined as *Pavlovian-reflexological-psychiatric*, a group in Milan; the other *Skinnerian-operant-psychological*, shared by three groups in Milan, Padua, and Rome. These groups followed independent routes until the end of the 1970s, when three of them joined in a common path. The residual one followed a cognitive course.

The Pavlovian-reflexological-psychiatric group was formed and developed around some constitutive appointments: In 1965, at the XV Congress of the Italian Society of Neurology, a whole symposium on "Conditioned reflexes: Update on the theoretical experimental and clinical problems of the higher nervous activity" was held. The Soviet Sokolov and the Italians Arian, Bisiach, De Franco, and Goldwurm participated among the others in the debate. In 1968, in Milan, Goldwurm and Cazzullo organized the International Congress of "*Collegium Internationale Activitatis Nervosae Superioris*" (*CIANS*). Gelder, Rachman, and Wolpe, among others, attended the congress and presented clinical applications of systematic desensitization. In 1970, in Milan, inside the congress of psychiatry and neurology of Italian and French societies, a section devoted to "Therapies of counter-conditioning of neuroses" was held.

At the end of the 1960s the Brazilian behaviourist Isaia Pessotti came to Italy to hold a series of seminars for the internship activities of the Institute of Psychology of the Medical School of the University of Milan, and contributed to the establishment of a laboratory to conduct research in the experimental analysis of behaviour. In 1970 the volume by Pessotti, *Introduction to the Study of the Operant Behaviour*, was translated and published in Italian. After his retirement in Brazil Pessotti came several times to Italy, and he held a position of Professor of Psychology at the University of Urbino.

The following year two pivotal books were translated and published in Italian: Skinner's *Science and Human Behaviour* and Eysenck and Rachman's *The Causes and Cures of Neuroses*, which represent the first official introduction of behaviour therapy into Italy. In 1972 Victor Meyer taught behaviour therapy at the Postgraduate School of Psychology of the University of Milan and Ettore Caracciolo organized, at the European Centre of Education of Villa Falconieri in Frascati, an International Conference on "Recent trends in psychology of learning". This was the first time an Italian audience had attended Fred Keller's lectures. Many other distinguished scholars in the field of learning attended the conference: H. J. Eysenck, Gregory Kimble, Barbel Inhelder, Victor Meyer, Jean-Francois LeNy, Joseph Nuttin, Pierre and Geneviève Oléron, Isaia Pessotti, Leo Postman, Marc Richelle, and Slama-Cazacu.

As a consequence of these cultural stimulations, a behaviourist group was constituted in Rome around the "Skinner Institute," chaired by Antonio Tamburello, and another one gathered in Milan at the Institute of Psychology of the School of Medicine around Ettore Caracciolo. The scientific work of this group, in the following years, focused on theoretical issues and applications of the analysis of behaviour, especially in the field of experimental research and intervention in normal and special education.

In the middle of the 1970s another group of radical behaviourists joined together at the University of Padua: Roberto Anchisi, Beatrice Bauer, Aldo Galeazzi, Paolo Meazzini, Ezio Sanavio, and Salvatore Soresi. Through meetings and congresses they disseminated behaviour modification in north-east Italy. In 1977, within the XXVIIth Congress of the Italian Society of Psychology (SIPs), which took place in Viareggio, for the first time a session on behavioural psychology was held and chaired by Virgilio Lazzeroni.

THE TAKE-OFF

At the end of the 1977 in Verona, the two groups, the Pavlovian-reflexological-psychiatric and the Skinnerian-operant-psychological, joined and melded together to represent the first and constitutive nucleus of the Italian Association for Behaviour Analysis and Modification (AIAMC). Roberto Anchisi was the first president: Paolo Meazzini, Gian Franco Goldwurm, Paolo Moderato, Ezio Sanavio, Anna Meneghelli, Daniela Sacchi, Paolo Moderato again, Davide Dettore, and Aldo Galeazzi were presidents of the association in the following years.

In June 1978, in Venice, the International Congress "Learning: theory, experimentation, applications in clinical, educational, social setting" was organized by Paolo Meazzini. Many international scholars attended the congress: H. J. Eysenck, Daniel K. and Susan O' Leary, S. Rachman, Arthur Staats, and Travis Thompson among others.

In 1980 the First Congress of AIAMC took place in Rome: special guests were H. J. Eysenck and Brenda Milner. In 1981 the IInd Congress took place in Turin and Joseph Wolpe was the guest.

In July 1983 the first meeting of the European Group of Experimental Analysis of Behaviour was organized in Liège by Marc Richelle. Many behaviour analysts joined there from all over the world: B. F. Skinner, L. V. Baker, Derek Blackman, Robert Boakes, Arne Brekstad, Charles Catania, Steve Hayes, Fergus Lowe, Linda Parrott Hayes, Ullin Place, Emilio Ribes, Roberto Ruiz, and Terje Sagvolden, among others. For the very first time an Italian group of behaviourists, the historical nucleus of the Institute of Psychology of the University of Messina (Caracciolo, Perini, Moderato, Gentile and Presti), went abroad to discuss their research

and had the chance to meet B. F. Skinner and share their vision with scholars from all over the world.

THE AGE OF MATURITY

In autumn 1983 the III Congress of AIAMC had as special guests Sidney W. Bijou and Marc Richelle. The proceedings were published in a homonym volume. In 1986 the IV Congress of AIAMC was held in Milan. The theme was "Behaviour therapy and modification in the 80s." Special guests were C. Dostalek, R. P. Liberman, and P. V. Simonov. The proceedings were also published in the homonym volume.

In July 1988 Marc Richelle organized, once again in Liège, the second European meeting of the European Group of Experimental Analysis of Behaviour, the most important European meeting for behaviour analysts who operate in the "Old Continent" and who could meet distinguished overseas colleagues: among these were Charles Catania, Philip Hineline, H. S. Pennypaker, Morris Sidman, Emilio Ribes, Roberto Ruiz, and Joao Claudio Todorov. The usual group of Italian behaviourist scholars (Caracciolo, Perini, Moderato, Pino, Presti, and Gentile) attended the conference.

In 1989 Latini Dies, the Association of Behavioural Psychotherapy of Latin language countries, was founded following an idea of G. F. Goldwurm, and held its first congress in Rome. Ramon Bayes, Leonidas Castro-Camacho, J. Cottraux, O. Fontaine, J. Miguel-Tobal, Emilio Ribes, and many Italian scholars from behavioural and cognitive areas attended this first conference of a biennial series. Further conferences took place in the following years in Sitges, Spain (1991), in Toulouse, France (1993), in Guadalajara, Mexico (1995), and in Cascais, Portugal (1997).

In 1992 the AIAMC changed its constitution and its denomination, becoming the "Italian Association of Behaviour Analysis and Modification and Behaviour and Cognitive Therapy." In the same year, thanks to the contribution of the University of Guadalajara, *Acta Comportamentalia*, a Latin languages journal of behaviour analysis, was founded and presented during the first Congress on Behaviourism and Behaviour Sciences, which took place in Guadalajara (Mexico). *Acta Comportamentalia* is edited by Emilio Ribes and co-edited, for the Italian section, by Paolo Moderato.

In December 1992, in Siena, the VIIth Congress of the Italian Association of Behaviour Analysis and Modification celebrated Virgilio Lazzeroni and 50 years of behaviourism in Italy.

The VIII Congress of the AIAMC took place in Palermo in 1994, within the *Second Congress on Behaviourism and Behaviour Sciences*, a series ideated by Peter Harzem to bring discussion on behavioural issues around the world, with meetings held every 2 years. The maturity of Italian behavioural psychology was testified to by the presence of so many international scholars such as P. Andronis, R. Arrington, S. W. Bijou, C. Bruner, P. N. Chase, C. Goyos, D. Greer, P. Harzem, L. Hayes, P. Hineline, B. Hopkins, T. V. J. Laying, F. Lowe, F. Mechner, T. C. McWhinney, J. Moore, E. K. Morris, G. Novak, M. Pelaez, U. Place, H. Reese, E. Ribes, M. Sato, M. D. Zeiler, and W. Verplanck. Not all the international participants have been mentioned, but nobody will forget the day when Fred Keller gave his very last lecture in a congress before his death the following spring.

In 1995 a new journal was started, *Psicoterapia Cognitiva e Comportamentale*, edited by E. Sanavio.

In 1997, 20 years after the foundation of the AIAMC, the Congress of EABCT (the European Association for Behaviour and Cognitive Therapy) was held in Venice. In view of the fact that people from 39 different countries went to Venice it could be said that it was much more than a simple "European" Congress.

Another important landmark in the spreading of behavioural culture in Italy was the establishment in the second half of the 1990s of a series in psychology published by McGraw-Hill Italy and edited by Paolo Moderato and Francesco Rovetto. This series, which in 8 years has now published more than 90 books, is probably the most behaviourally oriented series in Italy and covers topics in different areas including clinical and developmental psychology, verbal behaviour, and OBM.

Two other important milestones marked the maturity "phase" of the Italian behaviouristic history: the First ABA International Convention, held in Venice in 2001, and the First Conference of the European Association for Behaviour Analysis, held in Parma in 2003. We were particularly honoured when the organizing committees chose Italy for these two founding events, implicitly recognizing the difficult job done in the former 30 years in disseminating the behaviouristic culture and in pursuing original research by Italian scholars.

A formal recognition of this hard work has been the SABA award for international dissemination, given to Paolo Moderato in Toronto in 2002, but actually deserved by all his Italian group of researchers and collaborators.

TODAY

In these first 60 years since Lazzeroni's pivotal lessons, behaviourism has reached a fairly good critical mass within psychology in Italy, though still a minority if compared to the psychoanalytic or even the systemic approach. On the other hand, in some areas like anxiety disorder therapies, special education, organizational behaviour, and ergonomics we might say that behaviour analysis is the mainstream.

In addition to these traditional fields, new and exciting ones, like the analysis of human interaction in the emergent virtual worlds, pursued by the *ePsychology* research group at the University of Parma, have been opened by behavioural-oriented researchers in Italy in these last years. The web experience is part of everyday social life, especially for the youth generations, who have not seen a world without computers. Although this is an area mostly neglected by mainstream behaviourism, it is almost impossible not to agree with Skinner's visionary words that "...the discrepancy between man's technical power and the wisdom with which he uses it has grown conspicuously wider year by year..." (Skinner, 1948/1976, p. 59). Computer-mediated interaction is behaviour, and thus the domain of a science of behaviour. Basic and applied issues can be investigated, such as analysis of textual utterances under different conditions, online social behaviour, anonymity, distance-learning, e-therapy, Internet-related behavioural disorders, and teleworking, just to cite a few. Obviously the issues to be faced are many, since computer-mediated communication might lack some of the features of real-life verbal interactions, while it is characterized by interesting features, like the use of emoticons or avatars in virtual environments. However, we think that these are issues to be addressed by experimental studies, rather than relying on a priori assertions on what is effective and what is not. In our view, answers to these issues cannot come from computer scientists or cognitive-oriented people: Neither focus on the "interaction," which is the central point in analysing and giving answers to the above-mentioned issues (Presti, 2001; Presti & Moderato, 2001). Thus, the main goal of the research group in Parma is to understand and implement the new digital society, extending into such fields as web interfaces, online learning, online communities, *e-therapy*, and verbal behaviour.

THE FUTURE

The Italian Association of Behaviour Analysis and Modification and Behaviour and Cognitive Therapy (AIAMC) today is a pretty large association (about 600 members), in which there are different branches: cognitive, behavioural, behavioural-cognitive, and so on. In the Association, behaviour analysts are in a minority, but this did not prevented us organizing successful behaviour-analytic meetings, as in Palermo, in Venice and in Parma, to carry on research in the emergent fields of behaviour analysis and to apply effective procedures in different areas.

Shifting away from behaviour analysis issues, the AIAMC has progressively become a clinical professional association, with little interest in research and its applications, and small interest in fields other than psychotherapy. Thus a group of us decided to establish a new parallel organization, committed to developing behaviour analysis and its applications in Italy. This organization, born at the end of 2004, is called IESCUM, an Italian acronym which stands for European Institute for the Study of Human Behaviour (a no-profit organization). It is based in Parma with a nationwide breadth. It will pursue its actions along these main directions: searching and providing funds for basic and applied research and promoting behavioural culture and application in different fields in Italy. The main tool to reach this last goal will be an online journal, which will publish commentaries and digests on the most recent advancement in behavioural studies (www.iescum. org).

If we were to describe a characterizing feature of the Italian method of behaviourism we would say that it is humanistic. The term defines the work of Leonardo Da Vinci, master of arts, fine painter, engineer, and inventor of amazing machines and apparatus, as well as defining the attitude and personality of B. F. Skinner, too often misrepresented as a man who was not a scientist.

REFERENCES

Anchisi, R., & Gambotto Dessy, M. (1992). *Non solo comunicare*. Torino, Italy: Cortina.

Ballanti, G. (1975). *Il comportamento insegnante*. Roma, Italy: A. Armando.

Caracciolo, E., & Rovetto, F. (1988). *Handicap: nuove metodologie per il ritardo mentale*. Milano: Angeli.

Di Nuovo, S. (1992). *La sperimentazione in psicologia applicata*. Milano: F. Angeli.

Larcan, R., Moderato, P., & Perini, S. (1984). *Nuove prospettive nelle scienze del comportamento: normalità e patologia dell'apprendimento*. Messina, Italy: Carboneditore.

Lazzeroni, V. (1942). Su alcuni orientamenti della psicologia moderna. *Rivista di Psicologia, XXXVIII*, 1–2.

Lazzeroni, V. (1966). *Le origini della psicologia contemporanea*. Firenze, Italy: Giunti.

Lazzeroni, V. (1985). *L'interpretazione del comportamento normale e patologico*. Milano: F. Angeli.

Mainardi Peron, E. (1988). *Ansia e dolore: la prospettiva comportamentista*. Pordenone, Italy: Erip.

Meazzini, P. (1980). *Il comportamentismo: una storia culturale*. Pordenone, Italy: Erip.

Meazzini, P. (1978). *La conduzione della classe*. Firenze, Italy: Giunti.

Meazzini, P., & Corao, A. (1978). *Apprendimento ed emozioni*. Firenze, Italy: Giunti.

Meazzini, P., & Galeazzi, A. (1978). *Paure e fobie*. Firenze, Italy: Giunti.

Meneghelli, A., & Sacchi, D. (1989). *Terapia e modificazione del comportamento negli anni '80*. Milano: Ghedini.

Moderato, P. (1989). *Apprendimento e memoria*. Milano: Angeli.

Moderato, P. (1995). Apprendimento. In S. Sirigatti (Ed.), *Manuale di psicologia generale*. Torino, Italy: UTET.

Moderato, P. (1997). *Apprendimento e organizzazione dell'esperienza*. Milano: F. Angeli.

Perini, S., & Bijou, S. W. (1993). *Lo sviluppo del bambino ritardato*. Milano: F. Angeli.

Presti, G. (2001). *Lo psicologo nella rete*. Milan: McGraw-Hill.

Presti, G., & Moderato, P. (2001). *Life on the Internet: A new field for experimental and applied behaviour analysis?* Paper presented at the Association for Behaviour Analysis' First International Conference, Venice (Italy), 28–30 November.

Rovetto, F. (1990). *Elementi di psicofarmacologia per psicologi*. Milano: F. Angeli.

Sanavio, E. (1978). *Le nevrosi apprese*. Milano: F. Angeli.

Sanavio, E. (1978). *I comportamenti ossessivi e la loro terapia*. Firenze, Italy: Giunti.

Sanavio, E. (1991). *Psicoterapia cognitiva e comportamentale*. Firenze, Italy: NIS.

Sanavio, E., Bertolotti, G., Michielin, P., Vidotto, G., & Zotti, A. (1986). *CBA 2.0 scale primarie. Una batteria a vasto spettro l'assessment psicologico*. Firenze, Italy: OS.

Skinner, B. F. (1948). *Walden two*. New York: Macmillan (Paperback ed. 1976. New York: Prentice Hall.).

INTERNATIONAL JOURNAL OF PSYCHOLOGY, 2006, 41 (6), 486–499

Observational learning

R. Douglas Greer

Columbia University Teachers College and Graduate School of Arts and Sciences, New York, NY, USA

Jessica Dudek-Singer

St John's University, New York, NY, USA

Grant Gautreaux

Columbia University Teachers College and Graduate School of Arts and Sciences, New York, NY, USA

*I*nconsistencies in the use of terms such as "modelling," "copying," "imitation," and "observational learning" impede progress in studies of natural, behavioural, and cultural selection. Recent evidence suggests distinctions between the effects of observation on: (a) emission of previously acquired repertoires, (b) acquisition of new repertoires, (c) acquisition of conditioned reinforcers, and (d) acquisition of observational learning as a new repertoire. Prior research failed to identify whether changes in behaviour after observation constituted *learning* because tests were not done for the presence or absence of the repertoires prior to observation. Changing one's queue because of the potential of receiving faster service constitutes a performance task and is quite different from learning a language by observation. We describe new investigations reporting procedures leading to: acquisition of observational learning, acquisition of operants and higher-order operants by observation, and the acquisition of conditioned reinforcers as a function of observation. The conditioned reinforcement effects after observation are related to the "copying" effects on reversal of sexual selection in some species. An observational effect on performance constitutes a different function from learning new repertoires. Acquiring new reinforcers is still another function. We propose empirically derived distinctions between these that are important in the analyses of the roles of natural selection, behavioural selection, and cultural selection in adaptation, changes in performance, learning, and the spread of cultural practices.

*L*es inconstances dans l'utilisation de termes tels que «modelage», «copiage», «imitation» et «apprentissage observationnel» nuisent au progrès dans les études de sélection naturelle, comportementale et culturelle. Des données récentes suggèrent des distinctions entre les effets de l'observation sur: (a) l'émission de répertoires acquis antérieurement, (b) l'acquisition de nouveaux répertoires, (c) l'acquisition de renforcements conditionnés et (d) l'acquisition d'apprentissage observationnel comme un nouveau répertoire. Une recherche antérieure n'a pas permis d'identifier dans quelle mesure les changements dans le comportement après l'observation constituaient un apprentissage parce que les tests ne permettaient pas d'identifier la présence ou l'absence de répertoires avant l'observation. Changer de file afin de potentiellement recevoir un service plus rapide constitue une tâche de performance et est assez différente d'un l'apprentissage du langage par observation. Nous décrivons de nouvelles études rapportant des procédures menant à: l'acquisition d'apprentissage observationnel, l'acquisition d'opérants et d'opérants d'ordre supérieur par l'observation et l'acquisition de renforcements conditionnés en tant que fonction de l'observation. Les effets du renforcement conditionné après l'observation sont associés aux effets du copiage sur le renversement de la sélection sexuelle chez certaines espèces. Un effet observationnel sur la performance constitue une fonction différente comparativement à l'apprentissage de nouveaux répertoires. Acquérir de nouveaux renforcements est aussi une autre fonction. Nous proposons des distinctions appuyées empiriquement entre ces termes, lesquelles sont importantes dans les analyses des rôles de la sélection naturelle, de la sélection comportementale et de la sélection culturelle dans l'adaptation, les changements de performance, l'apprentissage et la progression des pratiques culturelles.

Correspondence should be addressed to R. Douglas Greer, PhD, Teachers College Columbia University, Box 76, New York, NY 10027, USA (E-mail: dgreer3872@aol.com).

© 2006 International Union of Psychological Science

DOI: 10.1080/00207590500492435

*L*as inconsistencias en el uso de términos como "modelamiento", "copiado", "imitación" y "aprendizaje observacional" impiden el progreso en los estudios acerca de la selección natural, conductual y cultural. La evidencia reciente sugiere que existen diferencias entre los efectos de la observación acerca de: (a) la emisión de repertorios adquiridos previamente, (b) la adquisición de nuevos repertorios, (c) la adquisición de reforzadores condicionados, y (d) la adquisición de aprendizaje observacional como un repertorio nuevo. La investigación previa no pudo identificar si los cambios de conducta que ocurrían después de la observación eran *aprendizaje*, debido a que las pruebas no se hacían para la presencia o ausencia de los repertorios anteriores a la observación. Cambiarse uno de fila debido a la posibilidad de recibir un servicio más rápido constituye una tarea de ejecución y es muy diferente de aprender un lenguaje por observación. En el presenta artículo describimos nuevas investigaciones que reportan procedimientos conducentes a la adquisición de aprendizaje observacional, a la adquisición de operantes y de operantes de orden superior por observación. Los efectos reforzantes condicionados después de la observación se relacionan con los efectos de "copiado", acerca de la inversión de la selección sexual en algunas especies. Un efecto observacional sobre la ejecución constituye una función diferente que el aprendizaje de repertorios nuevos. Adquirir nuevos reforzadores es también otra función diferente. Proponemos distinciones derivadas empíricamente, entre estos que son importantes en los análisis de los papeles que juega la selección natural, conductual y cultural en la adaptación, en los cambios de ejecución, en el aprendizaje y en la extensión de las prácticas culturales.

INTRODUCTION

There is amazing unanimity on the distinctions between: (a) behaviour change that is attributed to direct contact by the organism with the contingencies of reinforcement and punishment, as differentiated from (b) behaviour change that occurs through indirect contact that is attributed to observation (Catania, 1998; Skinner, 1938). However, there is little consistency in the use of terms for behaviour change that occurs through observation. These include terms such as "modelling," "copying," "imitation," "echoing," "parroting," and "observational learning." The lack of precision and consistency in the usage of these terms impedes progress in investigations of complex human behaviour either beneath or outside the skin. We suggest this to be the case in biology, physiology, comparative psychology, anthropology, and behaviour analysis (Catania, 1998; Culotta & Hanson, 2004; Deguchi, Fujita, & Sato, 1988; Dugatkin, 1996; Dugatkin & Godin, 1992; Premack & Premack, 2004).

Two decades ago, Deguchi (1984) pointed out the problems in social learning interpretations (Bandura, 1977) and confusion between what constituted observational *learning* and emission of behaviours that were already in the observer's repertoire. The prior evidence base, the analysis by Deguchi, and recent research suggest empirical distinctions between observation that leads to (a) emission of a *previously acquired* repertoire, (b) acquisition of a *new repertoire*, (c) acquisition of *conditioned reinforcers by observation*, and (d) acquisition of *an observational learning repertoire*.

None of the distinctions that we propose call for mental surrogates, and analyses of the *behaviour* beneath the skin associated with these environmental controls of behaviour change, or the induction of new repertoires, can inform the work of neuroscience. We suggest new categories and definitions for observational effects on behaviour that we believe to be consistent with both prior and new evidence in order to open an empirical dialogue that will lead to greater scientific precision.

First, when learning is defined as the induction of operants and higher-order operants, we argue that there is little research in observational *learning* per se. How can this be when a casual search of the literature for the terms observational learning, vicarious behaviour change, copying, and imitation yields thousands of references! Nevertheless, it is only recently that investigations have begun to isolate variables leading to the *acquisition* of observational learning capabilities or repertoires by individuals who did not have them. Indeed, the possibility that *one, or some, may need to learn how to acquire new repertoires by observation* seems to be an ignored subject. Our interest in clarifying the terms grew out of evidence from recent research programmes— evidence that simply did not fit definitions from behaviour analysis, cognitive research, or biological research on the effects of environmental contingencies on genetically predisposed behaviour. Observation influences both performance and learning and inconsistencies in findings and interpretations reside in the lack of distinctions between these.

WHY THE DISTINCTIONS BETWEEN LEARNING AND PERFORMANCE ARE IMPORTANT

Over the last 25 years we, along with our colleagues, have been engaged in the difficult and daunting task of building schools that educate the "whole child" using a learner-driven science of schooling. First, we designed our schools to provide individualized instruction for each child based on what each child brings to the table in terms of phylogeny and ontogeny and what each child needs to receive in the way of instruction to substantially change the prognosis for the child's learning. Second, we sought to provide education that drew *solely on the use of scientific procedures* for pedagogy, supervision, administration, and curricula design. All of the components that we used involved scientific procedures for educating the children, staff, and parents, instead of approaches that treated education as an art or craft (Greer, 2002; Greer & Keohane, 2004; Greer, Keohane, & Healy, 2003; www.cabas.com)). In that effort we began to identify the difference between components of behaviour analysis that are useful in dealing with operants that exist in children's repertoires (i.e., performance), and components of our science that lead to the formation of new operants and higher-order operants (i.e., learning).

Our work has been devoted to two broad populations of children. One of the populations consisted of children with native disabilities such as autism spectrum disorders, pervasive developmental disabilities, or major learning disabilities. The other consisted of children without native disabilities who suffered from environmental deficits resulting from impoverishment (see Hart & Risley, 1996). The differences found in the Hart and Risley research are not limited to children in the USA, as our experience in developing schools in Ireland, England, and other parts of the word clearly shows. Children in these two populations all over the world are in similar straits. What they lack most are certain operants, particularly verbal operants, and higher-order operants. Without repertoires consisting of certain operants and higher-order verbal operants they simply could not progress (Greer & Keohane, 2005; Hayes, Barnes-Holmes, & Roche, 2000; Horne & Lowe, 1996; Ross & Greer, 2003). As behaviour analysis began to identify higher-order operants, and ways to develop new operants and higher-order operants when they are missing, the distinction between the branches of our science (i.e., developing new repertoires or working with existing operants) became evident.

DISTINCTIONS BETWEEN LEARNING AND PERFORMANCE

Many, if not all, of the responses emitted or elicited are present in incipient forms almost from birth. In behaviour analysis we distinguish between operant behaviour, which is emitted, and respondent behaviour, which is elicited (Skinner, 1938), and the interrelation between these (Donahoe & Palmer, 1994). In analyses of operant behaviour, it is not the behaviour per se but the relations between: (a) histories of instruction or reinforcement, (b) setting events/establishing operations, (c) discriminative stimuli, (d) responses, and (e) the consequence that are of interest. When a particular relation exists for an individual as a result of experience or instruction the operant has been learned; that is, when the relevant conditions that have been learned are present the behaviour is emitted. However, when the relation is not present the process of teaching seeks to establish that relation. The process of teaching new operants via direct contact with the contingencies involves a necessary, if not sufficient, set of interlocking contingencies between the teacher or teaching device and the student who is being taught the operant, which constitute a set of procedures identified as the *learn unit* (see Greer, 2002, for a description of the research and processes involved in the learn unit).

Investigations of the effects of variables on existing operants, or performance, constitute a large and important component of the research in behaviour analysis. Such research involves the effects of schedules of reinforcement (Catania, 1971) molar and molecular variables (Baum, 2003), immediate antecedent and postcedent variables (Skinner, 1938), drugs, and histories of reinforcement. According to Catania (1998, p. 401), "Performance [consists of] behaviour [that occurs] over extended periods of time. A subject matter in and of itself, performance has often been treated as an index of something else (e.g., learning, motivational states)." In the efforts in our schools, behaviour analysis findings on performance allowed us to have well-behaving students, maintain high levels of professional performance, motivate parents, use organizational behaviour analysis for administrative purposes, and provide noncoercive learning environments. Work in applied behaviour analysis on the "functional analysis" of "bad" behaviour is also concerned with performance rather than learning (Iwata, Dorsey, Slifer, Bauman, & Richman, 1982).

Problems in distinguishing between performance and learning also derive from the multiplicity of definitions of learning. Catania (1998, p. 395) defined learning as "roughly, acquisition, or the process by which behaviour is added to an organism's repertory, a relatively permanent change in behaviour." He then goes on to say, "The term has been used in so many different ways in both technical and colloquial vocabularies that it's of limited usefulness." However, a functional definition of learning is necessary in building a science of teaching (Greer & Keohane, 2005). Thus, our definition of learning is *the acquisition of operants or higher-order operants* as a function of direct contact with contingencies of reinforcement of punishment, *or as a function of the observation* of others receiving contact with the contingencies of reinforcement, punishment, and corrections of incorrect responses. Analyses of the acquisition of operants and higher-order operants provide the basis for teaching children, staff, or parents in our schools.

Fortunately for our effort in building scientifically based education, much recent work in behaviour analysis has been concerned with the *identification of higher-order operants* (Catania, 1998), including relational frames (Hayes, Barnes-Holmes, & Roche, 2000), naming (Horne & Lowe, 1996; Lowe, Horne, Harris, & Randle, 2002), the identification of verbal operants (Greer & Ross, 2004), and stimulus equivalence (Sidman, 1994). For us, this work began to identify specific capabilities that we could use in our efforts to teach complex missing repertoires that were key to the mastery of educational standards.

The complexity of a science of teaching and our responsibility for educating children calls for any evidence that is effective in inducing new repertoires, and we look for that evidence from any source. In the neurosciences, much of the current work involves the identification of behaviour beneath the skin as blood flow in portions of the brain, and is not related to operants or higher-order operants (for an exception, see Parkinson, Crofts, McGuigan, Davorka, Everitt, & Roberts, 2001). At present, this work has little immediate utility for our efforts. Findings from cognitive psychology on instructional interventions that have proved useful to date are essentially the same as those from applied behaviour analysis (e.g., "self-management" as contingency management under verbal stimulus control, or verbally mediated behaviour). This fortuitous agreement acts to affirm the validity of both sets of findings for our applications. Cognitive theories such as "theory of mind" have some potential as

objectives of instruction when conceptualized in relational frame theory (Barnes-Holmes, Barnes-Holmes, & Cullinan, 2001). Evidence from developmental psychology relate the emergence of repertoires to age and this work is useful in identifying missing repertoires when it can be made operational, but provides little help if students do not have the repertoire. Still other efforts that are useful for our enterprise are the identification of verbal operants and higher-order operants (Greer & Keohane, 2005; Greer & Ross, 2004). The identification of these repertoires is useful because they provide potential sources for learning difficulties that our students and teachers encounter. However, once these are identified, we require research that provides the *environmental origins* of operants, higher-order operants, repertoires, capabilities, or stages, if we are to provide pedagogical operations that lead to changes in capabilities that underlie many instructional goals associated with complex human behaviour (Greer & Keohane, 2005; Greer et al., 2004a).

BEHAVIOUR ANALYSIS AND THE ACQUISITION OF REPERTOIRES

Skinner pioneered both the performance and acquisition branches of the science of behaviour. His role in the development of the analysis of existing operants grew from *The Behaviour of Organisms* (Skinner, 1938), and this work is probably his most well known. On the other hand, his role in the development of new operants grew from his work in programmed instruction (Skinner, 1968), extrapolations of behaviour analysis to applied concerns (Skinner, 1953, 1968), and his verbal behaviour theory (Skinner, 1957) and is probably less well known. Teaching the operants that constitute the component operations for performing math (Singer-Dudek & Greer, 2005), acquiring new verbal operants (Ross & Greer, 2003; Sundberg, Loeb, Hale, & Eigenheer, 2001/2002), mastering a new language, or acquiring verbal behaviour about the science (Holland & Skinner, 1961) are very different from analyses of existing operants (Ferster & Skinner, 1957). Work that involves identifying the variables contributing to acquisition of operants or higher-order operants was made possible first by research that identified verbal operants (Lamarre & Holland, 1985; Sundberg, Michael, Partington, & Sundberg, 1996; Williams & Greer, 1989) and higher-order operants (Healy, Barnes-Holmes, & Smeets, 1998; Horne & Lowe, 1996; Lowe et al., 2002).

Teaching new operants and higher-order operants

While the focus of our paper is on observation, we are more specifically concerned with observation that results in the acquisition of new operants, higher-order operants, and new conditioned reinforcers—observational learning. For a treatment of the components of our science devoted to the acquisition of new verbal operants and higher-order operants, the reader is directed to a recent paper on the development of verbal capabilities (Greer & Keohane, 2005). In that paper we described research that led to the identification of procedures that induced new verbal capabilities in children such as naming (Greer, Stolfi, Chavez-Brown, & Rivera-Valdez, 2004c; Horne & Lowe, 1996), transformation of establishing operations across formerly independent mand and tact operant functions (Lamarre & Holland, 1985; Nuzzolo-Gomez & Greer, 2004), development of joint stimulus control across formerly independent vocal and written spelling responses (Greer, Yuan, & Gautreaux, 2004d; Skinner, 1957, p. 92), acquisition of basic listening literacy (Greer et al., 2004c), acquisition of functional vocal verbal speech in children with no prior speech (Ross & Greer, 2003; Sundberg et al., 1996; Tsiouri & Greer, 2003), and acquisition of effective writing (Greer & Keohane, 2005; Greer & Ross, 2004).

The latter work, for the most part, involved *direct application* of contingencies of reinforcement, arrangement of establishing operations, and the provision of instructional experiences that compensated for missing capabilities, which, in turn, led to the emission or production of new verbal operants, untaught responses to novel stimuli, or the emission of a single verbal form in different functions (i.e., learning a form in a mand function that results in the use of the form in a tact function without direct instruction).

However, since much of what we learn or much of how we behave results from indirect contact with contingencies, how did our students fare in this regard? The need for good observational repertoires is critical because classrooms that approach teaching as an art or craft provide inadequate exposures to direct contingencies in the form of learn units and provide even fewer exposures for children who enter school with deficit repertoires (Greenwood, Hart, Walker, & Risley, 1994; Greer, 1994; Skinner, 1968). When we began to examine the presence or absence of our children's skills in learning from observation, we realized that we needed to make more precise distinctions. We believe that these distinctions are equally important to all behavioural sciences and some areas of biology and anthropology.

DISTINCTIONS IN VICARIOUS BEHAVIOUR CHANGE, IMITATION, AND OBSERVATIONAL LEARNING

Modelling, imitation, and "learning" or other types of vicarious behaviour change received considerable attention in the literature a few decades ago. In the early 1970s, Kazdin (1973) found that children who observed other children receiving praise for certain behaviours emitted those behaviours without direct reinforcement. Ollendick, Dailey, and Shapiro (1983) found, however, that the behaviours ceased over time unless they were directly reinforced. While these findings were discussed in terms of arguments over the need or lack of need for direct reinforcement, it became clear to us that the fact that the behaviour decreased in these studies without direct reinforcement suggested that the behaviours were already in repertoire and that *learning*, as we defined earlier, was not what was occurring. The children were emitting operants that were in their repertoire when they observed the contingencies surrounding their peers' behaviour and emitting those previously learned behaviours as a function of that observation. When reinforcement was not forthcoming, they simply stopped performing.

Much of the relevant applied research over recent decades involved using modelling or the provision of an adult or peer model as a means of evoking new operants. That is, the use of models can be a means of inducing new operants—a common instructional tactic. Many times this tactic worked very well, as in the cases of the few studies that did provide evidence that the observers were missing the repertoires induced by observation. Brody, Lahey, and Combs (1979) demonstrated the effects of intermittent adult modelling on the acquisition of target behaviours by observers and Egel, Richman, and Koegel (1981) found that typically developing models evoked colour discriminations by autistic students. Goldstein and Mousetis (1989) found that all of their participants acquired matrix strategies on recombinative generalization of language responses that were modelled by their peers. Griffen, Wolery, and Schuster (1992) taught a student to prepare food in a chained fashion using a time delay tactic. At the same time two other peers observed this instruction. Werts, Caldwell, and Wolery (1996) used typically developing peers to demonstrate chains, and their developmentally disabled participants modelled these chains. MacDonald, Dixon, and LeBlanc (1986) and Latimore (2001) reported the formation of stimulus classes via observation.

However, some reports showed that sometimes some participants did not change their behaviour as a function of observing the model. For example, Christy (1975), Birnbrauer, Hopkins, and Kauffman (1981), and Drabman and Lahey (1974) failed to show consistent results when studying the effectiveness of observation on changes in the behaviour of observers. Why is this the case for some children?

When we systematically investigated the observational repertoires of the children in our schools *as a capability for other learning*, we identified children who did not learn new operants by observing other children learn new operants. One of the major goals of working with children either with or without disabilities is to provide them with the wherewithal to be successful in mainstream settings or settings that do not provide sufficient incidences of direct instruction. Since our evidence showed that learning from direct reinforcement in mainstream settings was hampered by the lack of reinforcement and sufficient numbers of learn units to acquire new operants from direct instruction, it became apparent that our students needed to have the capability of learning new operants from observation. This also appears important to those studying environmental influences on genetically evolved behaviour, those doing basic research on behaviour selection, and those concerned with cultural selection as in the evolution of language. If these distinctions are important to our efforts they are also important to all sciences concerned with natural selection, behavioural selection, and cultural selection.

We found our way to a potential solution in a serendipitous fashion. In several studies growing out of tutoring research (particularly the robust findings that tutors learn from the experience of tutoring), we began to identify procedures that led to students acquiring repertoires for learning new operants, when they could not do so prior to the experimental interventions (Greer et al., 2004a). We isolated the components of tutoring, specifically the strong effects of serving as a tutor, that appeared to produce observational learning. First, in a series of experiments in Greer et al., we found that the presence or absence of a learn unit was more important than whether teachers or children did the teaching. Moreover, correction operations by tutors or others who observed tutoring were key to learning. The components of tutoring found in the learn unit were possible sources for the

acquisition of observational *learning*. For us, these findings suggested that the process of monitoring the behaviour of others and the joint reinforcement that accrued from the tutoring role were the potential sources for learning by observation. This, in turn, led to experiments isolating these components.

Pereira-Delgado (2005) and Greer, Pereira, and Yuan (2004b) found that young children with disability diagnoses *who could not learn new operants from observation*, learned to do so following an intervention that taught them to monitor the accuracy of their peers when the peers were taught new operants. That is, we taught them to monitor (i.e., count the occurrences of correct and incorrect responses) their peers' correct and incorrect responses until they were able to do so involving a three-stage process. Stolfi (2004) found that an intervention we termed a "yoked peer contingency" also resulted in preschoolers acquiring repertoires of learning new operants from observation, as did Davies-Lackey (2004) for elementary age children with developmental disabilities. In this procedure, pairs of children played a game in which joint reinforcement for the dyad accrued when the target child emitted correct responses learned from observing corrections and reinforcement of responses emitted by her peer. Children who could not learn from observation before in pre-intervention probes learned the correct response from observing their peer in post-intervention probes. Gautreaux (2004) found that teaching middle school students, who had poor or nonexistent repertoires for acquiring new operants by observation, resulted in significantly improved observational repertoires as well as collateral behaviour changes in listening skills.

As we began to identify procedures to induce observational learning in children who were missing the repertoire, we revisited the observational learning literature. We found that that were few, if any, studies that were devoted to *inducing* observational learning repertoires. That is, changes in behaviour from vicarious sources were identified as a phenomenon leading some to call for surrogate cognitive processes (Bandura, 1986; Bandura, Adams, & Beyer, 1977) and others to test the necessity for subsequent reinforcement to maintain performance (Ollendick et al., 1983). However, *no studies were identified that induced observational learning* in children who could not learn from observation.

When we reviewed the research on vicarious reinforcemen, we found there were few studies that did pre-experimental tests of whether or not the behaviours or operants were in the participant's repertoire prior to the observational experience; most of those are cited above. In the majority of the experiments on vicarious reinforcement effects, the dependent variables were most likely existing repertoires that simply increased or were emitted because of the observed contingencies. The fact that the behaviours ceased or decreased, if direct reinforcement did not ensue, seemed to affirm that the putative responses were already in the observers' repertoires. These studies did not investigate observational *learning* as we have defined it. Rather they constituted analyses of the effects of indirect contingencies on the *emission of behaviour that was already in the observers' repertoires.* Children under the influence of the contingencies emitted by some teachers do not raise their hand for attention but do so under the influence of the teacher contingencies present in other classes. These kinds of behaviour change did not meet Catania's definition (1998, p. 399) of observational learning as "*learning* [italics added] based on observing the responding of another organism (and/or its consequences). Observational learning does not imply imitation (organisms may come to avoid aversive stimuli on seeing what happens when other organisms produce them)." Thus, while this definition works well for learning as we have defined it, it did not distinguish the performance repertoire from learning new operants and higher-order operants by observation and emitting previously acquired repertoires by observation—a distinction that Catania did make in his definition of learning. However, for our students, and we believe for other sciences, the distinction is critical.

Some definitions of observational learning incorporate the expression "one trial" learning (see Deguchi, 1984, for a review of this definition). In our experience the probability of the learning of new operants in one trial seems unlikely. We think that this definition refers to the emission of already-learned operants by observation. There is a big difference between changing the queues or lines you are waiting in for service, and emitting verbal behaviour in a new language learned by observing natives use that language. When children learn new vocabulary, it is not one trial learning; rather, first they learn to echo the speech sounds, then they learn the listener and speaker functions, usually with corrections and incidental reinforcement requiring more than one trial. We argue that one may emit a previously learned repertoire in one trial by observation, but learning by observation requires more: It requires evaluation of the response (Premack &. Premack, 2003). Moreover, learning by observation in most of the

cases we have studied requires the observer to evaluate the effects of the observed response—corrections as well as reinforcement (Greer et al., 2004a).

Based on our work and a reading of the literature, there seem to be several types of behaviour change selected out by observing the contingencies. One very basic and critical component of behaviour associated with observation is *imitation*. Baer and colleagues (Baer, Peterson, & Sherman, 1967) developed a clear empirically based definition of imitation, specifically generalized imitation. Imitation seems to be behaviour resulting from the observer being reinforced for a class of behaviours that can be characterized as learning "do as I do." Many of our children with native disabilities require special instruction to acquire this repertoire. Imitation differs from observational learning in that the latter involves the observation of the contingencies received by others that controls the behaviour of the observer (Catania, 1998). Generalized imitation is a result of direct reinforcement of a class of responding and, while it is a higher-order operant, it is not behaviour controlled by observation of the contingencies received by another. Thus, imitation is controlled by directly contacting the contingencies, while observational learning or behaviour change is controlled by indirect contact with the contingencies received by others.

To summarize, the two major classes of observation effects include: (a) emitting previously learned behaviours as a result of observing the consequences received by another (i.e., changing queues, raising your hand for teacher attention, following classroom rules, punching a bag, colouring), and (b) learning a new operant or higher-order operant as a function of observing another being taught a repertoire. The distinction between performance and acquiring behaviour extends to observation. Learning new operants or higher-order operants as a result of the observation of contingencies of reinforcement, and of correction, constitutes true observational *learning*. Since learning involves the emission of new operants, punishment is not part of the picture, although punishment can suppress the performance behaviours of an observer. That is, since the operant is not present for a learner, the operant cannot be suppressed.

Recently, we found what we believe is still another distinct type of observational learning—the acquisition of conditioned reinforcers as a function of observation. Because this is a newly identified means of conditioning reinforcers, we provide a detailed explanation.

A NEW TYPE OF OBSERVATIONAL LEARNING

Greer and Singer (2004) recently reported that translucent plastic discs, which did not act to reinforce children's performance or learning, acquired reinforcement effects after children observed peers receive the discs and the target children were denied access to the discs. The report showed that neutral stimuli, plastic discs about the size of quarters, were conditioned as generalized reinforcers for performance tasks and reinforcers for acquiring new operants *as a result of an observation process*. This appears to be a new type of observational learning.

A similar effect has been identified in research on observation that acted to reverse genetically evolved behaviour, although the effect was not identified as acquisition of reinforcement by observation. Dugatkin and Godin (1992) reported that female guppies (*Poecilla reticulata*), which were genetically predisposed to seek out brightly coloured males for mating purposes, sought out dull-coloured males after observing other female guppies mating with dull-coloured males (see also Dugatkin, 1996). Actually, the observed female guppies were not mating with the dull-coloured males; rather, the investigators, using an arrangement of mirrors, designed an ingenious experiment that provided the appearance of females selecting dull-coloured males. The observing guppies "copied" (a term used in biology that seems synonymous with modelling) the sexual selection of the observed females, thereby demonstrating a reversal of genetically predisposed behaviour as a function of observation. Changes in predisposed behaviours have also been reported as a result of observation for: conditioned snake fear in unrelated rhesus monkeys (Cook, Mineka, Wolkstein, & Laitsch, 1998), mate choice by fallow deer leks (Clutton-Brock, Hiraiwa-Hasegawa, & Robertson, 1989; Grant & Green, 1995; Prett-Jones, 1992), and transmission of enemy recognition (Curio, Ernest, & Vieth, 1978).

Conditioned reinforcers for individuals are acquired by direct experience with unconditioned or other conditioned reinforcers. No prior evidence has shown that observing another receive a consequence acts to convert the consequence itself from a neutral stimulus into one that functions to reinforce behaviour. This latter effect would constitute a new type of observational learning— the conversion of neutral stimuli to stimuli that act as generalized reinforcers as a function of observation. We argue that the reversal of sexual selection by guppies following observation is a case or

reinforcement conditioning; however, Dugatkin and Godin (1992) did not interpret the effect of the establishment of dull colouring as the conditioning of reinforcement through observation. This is understandable given that their focus as biologists was on the role of the environment in changing genetically determined behaviour. Researchers in psychology reported changes of food choice and consumption by young children or changes in reinforcement effects of tokens as a function of modelling or peer establishing operations (Birch, 1980; Greer, Dorow, Williams, McCorkle, & Asnes, 1991; Greer, McCorkle, & Sales, 1998; Sales, 1998). These studies suggested conditions that needed to be in place if reinforcement conditioning was to result from observation. However, none of the prior research identified the effect as an observational learning effect; although, given the Greer and Singer findings, we think this was probably the case.

In the Greer and Singer study, four-preschool and kindergarten age students participated in the study. Translucent circular-plastic discs (2.54 centimetres in diameter) did not act to reinforce behaviours (i.e., the discs were not conditioned generalized reinforcers) at the onset of the study. Four other students who were the same age served as the students who were observed by the target students in the observational intervention and they are referred to as the peers. The discs were already conditioned generalized reinforcers for the peers as a result of an instructional history of exchanging the discs for preferred items.

There were three stages to the experiment: (a) pre-observational experimental tests (ABAB reversals with performance tasks comparing performance with a known reinforcer and performance with the discs as consequences, and baselines with three untaught repertoires for each of the students in which they received discs for correct responses and corrections for incorrect responses), (b) the observational intervention (conditioning of tokens by observation), and (c) post-intervention tests (ABAB with the performance tasks, post-observation treatment for the three untaught repertoires). In the pre-observational test stage, the target children performed a task in which they were proficient—one that was in their repertoire and, hence, a performance task. With an experimenter and no other peers present, the target students were presented 20-trial sessions, approximately 1 minute in duration, in which they received either preferred items (e.g., edibles) as the A phases, or the discs for accurate performance, and no discs for inaccurate performance as the B phases. A second dependent variable involved learning new discriminations. These data were collected in separate sessions of the pre-observational intervention test stage, where the target students received instruction in acquiring three new operants that they did not have in their repertoire. During these 20 instructional baseline trial sessions (lasting 2 to 5 minutes), again with an experimenter and no peer present, the participants received the plastic discs for correct responses and corrective feedback for incorrect responses.

The second stage was the observational intervention in which each target child observed a peer receiving discs for responding to another performance task, while the target child, who was responding simultaneously, *did not receive the discs and could not see the peer's response*. Several sessions were conducted until the participants attempted to take the peers' plastic discs or repeatedly requested the discs. In the post-observational intervention tests, we repeated the pre-observational tests of the reinforcing effects of the discs for performance tasks and for teaching the new repertoires.

The data showed that the observational intervention acted to condition the discs as generalized reinforcers for both performance and learning. The plastic discs did not function to reinforce performance or learning prior to observing others receiving the consequence, but did so after our observational intervention; moreover, the discs continued to reinforce behaviour *without recourse to other direct forms of reinforcement* for weeks after the intervention. Initially we thought that the effect was an establishing operation (Michael, 1993), but establishing operations have only a momentary effect on consequences as reinforcers, while our effects were relatively permanent. Although we have replicated these findings in our schools with more than 20 children, they need to be replicated by others. The identification of observation as a source for young children to acquire generalized reinforcers appears to be a new and previously unidentified form of social learning and a new source for the conditioning of reinforcers. Whether the phenomenon is limited to young children is unknown at present, although related findings have been found with other species, as described earlier.

IMPORTANCE OF DISTINCTIONS FOR DIFFERENT SCIENCES

Not only are these distinctions clearly important in our efforts to provide education based solely on scientific evidence, but they may be critical to several disciplines. In prior research, in either construct psychology or behaviour analysis, on the effects of vicarious reinforcement on the responses of observers (Bandura, 1977; Kazdin, 1973; Ollendick et al., 1983), the experiments did not provide tests of the reinforcing effects of the consequence for the behaviours of observers prior to the delivery of consequences to the observed individuals. Thus, it is not known whether the prior results were due to vicarious reinforcement or whether they were a function of a change in the reinforcement effect of the consequences, as we found in the study we described. Thus, not only is it important to test whether a *repertoire is, or is not, present* in the study of what accrues from observation, but it is also important to determine *whether the contingency in effect was a reinforcer* or acquired reinforcing consequences as a function of the intervention. As a result of the evidence we cite, various theories related to behaviour change from indirect contact with contingencies, such as social learning theory, may need to be revised and new evidence gathered. For example, it is unlikely that the guppies required a mental surrogate, although some may interpret the finding as evidence that guppies have mental surrogates.

An example of the importance of the distinction for biology is found in the case of the research on mate selection by female guppies, described above, where the selection of bright-coloured males is a genetically predisposed stimulus control for behaviour. Because the dull colouring of the males selected out as mate choice of the female guppies as a result of the females' observation of other females selecting dull-coloured males, it appears also to be a case of observational conditioning of the dull colouring as a newly conditioned reinforcer for mating. If the behaviour were simply copying, the colours of the mates would be irrelevant. Indeed, the possibility that only some species may acquire generalized conditioned reinforcers may prove important to theories of evolution.

Scholars interested in the sources of language function need to take into account recent findings on observational learning of higher-order operants, specifically those involving generative language. In studies cited in Greer and Keohane (2005), several types of language function (e.g., novel tense formation, novel suffix formation, use of a form learned in a single function in a novel and untaught function, emission of untaught spelling responses after learning only one type of response) that have been attributed to nonenvironmental sources by linguists and cognitive psychologists were induced by providing multiple exemplar histories involving direct contact with the contingencies. In addition, other studies reviewed in this paper showed acquisition of novel and untaught uses that were *induced by observation or indirect contact with the contingencies*. Some, or most, incidences of novel and generative language that were previously attributed to innate capacities alone may, in fact, be a result of both direct and indirect contact with contingencies. It would appear that linguistic anthropologists might need to consider this evidence in their study of the cultural evolution of language also, since the capacity to learn generative language by indirect contact with contingencies may be key in the cultural evolution of language function.

When the technology is adequate, neuroscientists who are interested in the behaviour of the brain and its relation to overt verbal behaviour need to investigate changes in the effects of both direct and observational contact with contingencies on the presence and absence of higher-order operants. That is, in cases of individuals for whom generative verbal repertoires were not present and were induced in experiments, like those cited in Greer and Keohane (2005), neuroscientists need to determine if there were corollary changes in the brain that coincided with acquisition of the new repertoire. If changes are not present yet the repertoire is now present, what does that mean? Alternatively, if changes in blood flow were occasioned by the induction of the higher-order operants, such evidence would contribute significantly to neuroscience.

In our efforts to build a more robust science of teaching, we needed to make distinctions between types of behaviour change from indirect contact with contingencies. The distinctions are likely to be important to inquiries in other areas of psychology, environmental influences on genetically predisposed behaviour, anthropological linguistics, and neuroscience.

SUMMARY OF DISTINCTIONS AND DEFINITIONS

The studies that we have cited showed that individuals without observational learning repertoires learned them after interventions. In some cases the individuals learned new operants, and in at least two other experiments they acquired higher-order operants (Greer et al, 2004a; Yuan, 2004). This suggests that, at least for some individuals with learning delays, observational learning needs to be taught and, most importantly, it can be taught to some children. It is very

possible that certain early experiences lead to both changes in performance and true observational learning for typically developing children as well. However, there needs to be more research with typically developing children before we can declare that observational learning is itself a learned repertoire for all, or only for some children. However, this was clearly the case for the children we studied. In addition, Greer and Singer (2004) found that generalized conditioned reinforcers could be acquired by observation. How children acquire this repertoire and whether experiences contribute to its acquisition is unknown at present.

We suggest new distinctions for changes in behaviour that involve observation of others in direct contact with contingencies. Since imitation involves direct rather than observed contact, we cannot improve on Catania's (1998) definition, although imitation as he defined it is likely to be a key component or even a necessary prerequisite to some or all behaviour change emanating from observation.

However, there are some distinctions in imitation-like responding that are important. For example, there is a difference between imitating observable behaviours and *parroting or echoing* vocal responses emitted by another. Since duplicating words vocally involves unobservable behaviour, Skinner distinguished between imitation and echoing, to which we add parroting. Numerous papers in psychology refer to vocal imitation when it is clear that observation of the apparatus associated with vocal speech is not possible; hence, the term vocal imitation seems inaccurate. However, recent evidence suggests that echoing or parroting can come under a common class of responding along with other types of duplicative or copying behaviour. Reports by Ross and Greer (2003) and Tsiouri and Greer (2003) showed that rapid imitation of observable motor response under conditions in which nonvocal children were under deprivation of specific and generalized reinforcers led to the *emission of first instances of vocal verbal behaviour*. Prior research suggests that imitation of observable motor responses did not lead to vocal echoic responding. We think that the conditions of this intervention, in the studies cited, created an overarching frame or higher-order operant, bringing parroting and echoic responding into the same response class as observable motor imitation. Thus, parroting and echoic responding can become a member of a class of *generalized copying* as a result of certain instructional histories, at least for children like those we studied. It is also possible that an *overarching frame of copying* can be acquired incidentally by typically developing children in a similar fashion, but that remains to be tested.

Learning or changes in the emission of behaviours in repertoire as a function of observation of contingencies received by others is different from imitation or the formation of echoing and parroting as a member of the class of generalized copying. These distinctions need to be studied as well. We suggest the following clarifications on changes in behaviour resulting from observation of the contingencies received by others.

1. *Changes in performance.* Behaviour that is already in an individual's repertoire may be emitted as a function of observing contingencies received by a person or persons. Such behaviour probably evolves from the individual's history of contact with direct contingencies. A history of being successful with imitation of behaviour that is directly reinforced sets the stage for responding to the contingencies received by others (Curio et al., 1978). This effect is not unlike the effect engendered when an individual acquires generalized imitation. That is, "do as I do" is generalized to "do as the observed one does." Raising one's hand when others receive reinforcement for doing so is an example. In this case, extinction is likely to occur when reinforcement is not forthcoming for the behaviour emitted by the observer. However, *it is also possible* that observing others receive praise may in fact condition the praise as reinforcement in a process not unlike that which Greer and Singer (2004) found. Research needs to distinguish between these effects by providing the relevant controls.

2. *Acquisition of new operants.* New operants are acquired by observation, in cases in which pre-intervention assessments show the operant is not present, and observation of others receiving instruction with reinforcement and correction components lead to the acquisition of new operants. These include the acquisition of mands, tacts, echoics, math repertoires, and textual responding to name a few examples.

3. *Acquisition of higher-order operants.* Higher-order operants are acquired by observation when pre-observation assessments show the higher-order operants are not present in the repertoire of an individual, and following observation by the individual of others receiving contact with instruction, the higher-order operants are emitted by the observer. An example of this is the acquisition of untaught relations between selection and performance or abstraction from learning phonemes to responding to novel phoneme combinations

(Greer et al., 2004a; Pereira-Delgado, 2005; Stolfi, 2004).

4. *Acquisition of conditioned reinforcement by observation.* Conditioned reinforcers are acquired by observation when stimuli, such as tokens or non-preferred foods, acquire reinforcement functions as a result of observing others receive the stimuli *under conditions in which the observer is denied access for periods of time* (Greer et al., 1991; Greer & Sales, 1997; Greer & Singer, 2004). In the Greer and Singer study, the newly conditioned reinforcers controlled both performance and acquisition of new operants. Another example of the conditioning of reinforcement by observation occurred in guppy research on the reversal of sexual selection of mates and demonstrated the conditioning of new attributes of physiology as reinforcers for mate selection (Dugatkin, 1996). However, it should be noted that the behaviours were in the guppies' repertoire and while the reinforcer for the emission of the behaviour changed, no new operants were evoked as a function of the newly conditioned reinforcing properties. In the biological work the change was attributed to "copying" or "imitation" but clearly those terms do not characterize the phenomenon with adequate precision. New reinforcing attributes were conditioned for behaviours that were in the guppy's repertoire.

5. *Acquisition of observational learning repertoires.* An observational repertoire may be said to have been acquired when pre-intervention assessments demonstrate that an individual cannot acquire new operants or higher-order operants and following interventions the individual can acquire new operants or higher-order operants as a function of observation. We cited three experiments that used two different procedures that led to the induction of observational learning in children who did not have an observational learning capability prior to the interventions. In these studies we provided certain instructional histories that led to observational learning in children who did not have the repertoire. Are similar, but incidental, experiences necessary for typically developing children to learn by observation, or are these experiences necessary only for children with certain disabilities?

While future research will identify more precise definitions and other distinctions, we suggest that, at present, our distinctions provide or set the stage for research and discussion leading to greater precision. Because a science consists of a verbal community and newer sciences rely on pre-mathematical verbal definitions, it is essential to develop precise terminology. Clear distinctions are needed between phenomena associated the emission of behaviour already in one's repertoire and in the acquisition of repertoires that result from observation of others coming in direct contact with the contingencies of reinforcement, correction, and punishment. Precise distinctions are also key to progress in all disciplines concerned with processes of natural, behavioural, and cultural selection as they apply to adaptation, changes in performance beneath and outside the skin, learning, and the spread of cultural practices.

REFERENCES

Baer, D. M., Peterson, R. F., & Sherman, J. A. (1967). The development of imitation by reinforcing behavioural similarity to a model. *Journal of the Experimental Analysis of Behaviour, 21,* 405–416.

Bandura, A. (1977). *Social learning theory.* Englewood Cliffs, NJ: Prentice-Hall.

Bandura, A. (1986). *Social foundations of thought and action.* Englewood Cliffs, NJ: Prentice-Hall.

Bandura, A., Adams, N. E., & Beyer, J. (1977). Cognitive processes mediating behavioral change. *Journal of Personality and Social Psychology, 35,* 125–139.

Barnes-Holmes, D., Barnes-Holmes, Y., & Cullinan, V. (2001). Relational frame theory and Skinner's Verbal Behaviour. *The Behaviour Analyst, 23,* 69–84.

Baum, W. M. (2003). The molar view of behaviour and its usefulness to behaviour analysis. *The Behaviour Analyst Today, 4,* 78–81. Retrieved 15 November, 2003, from http://www.behavior-analyst-today.org

Birch, L. (1980). Effects of peer models' food choice and eating behavior in preschoolers' food preferences. *Child Development, 51,* 14–18.

Birnbrauer, J. S., Hopkins, N. R., & Kauffman, J. M. (1981). The effects of vicarious prompting on attentive behavior of children with behavior disorders. *Child Behavior Therapy, 3,* 27–41.

CABAS®. (2005). Retrieved 7 March, 2005, from http://www.cabas.com

Catania, A. C. (1971). Reinforcement schedules: The role of responses preceding the one that produces the reinforcement. *Journal of the Experimental Analysis of Behavior, 15,* 271–278.

Catania, A. C. (1998). *Learning* (4th ed.). Englewood Cliffs, NJ: Prentice-Hall.

Christy, P. R. (1975). Does use of tangible rewards with individual children affect peer observers? *Journal of Applied Behavior Analysis, 8,* 187–196.

Clutton-Brock, T. H., Hiraiwa-Hasegawa, M., & Robertson, A. (1989). Mate choice on fallow deer leks. *Nature, 340,* 463–465.

Cook, M., Mineka, S., Wolkstein, B., & Laitsch, K. (1998). Conditioning of snake fear in unrelated rhesus monkeys. *Journal of Abnormal Psychology, 94,* 591–610.

Culotta, E., & Hanson, B. (2004). First words. *Science, 303,* 1315.

Curio, E., Ernest, U., & Vieth, W. (1978). Cultural transmission of enemy recognition: One function of mobbing. *Science, 202,* 899–901.

Davies-Lackey, A. J. (2004). *Yoked contingencies and the acquisition of observational learning repertoires.* Unpublished dissertation, Columbia University.

Deguchi, H. (1984). Observational learning from a radical-behavioristic viewpoint. *The Behavior Analyst, 7,* 83–95.

Deguchi, H., Fujita, T., & Sato, M. (1988). Reinforcement and the control of observational learning in young children: A behavioral analysis of modeling. *Journal of Experimental Child Psychology, 46,* 326–371.

Donahoe, J. W., & Palmer, D. C. (1994). *Learning and complex behavior.* Boston: Allyn & Bacon.

Drabman, R. S., & Lahey, B. B. (1974). Feedback in classroom behaviour modification: Effects on the target and her classmates. *Journal of Applied Behavior Analysis, 7,* 591–598.

Dugatkin, L. A. (1996). The interface between culturally based preference and genetic preference: Female mate choices in *Poecilla reticulata. Proceedings of the National Academy of Science, USA, 93,* 2770–2773.

Dugatkin, L. A., & Godin, J. G. (1992). Reversal of female mate choice by copying in the guppy (*Poecilla reticulata*). *Proceedings of the Royal Society of London B, 249,* 179–184.

Duncker, K. (1938). Experimental modification of children's preference through social suggestion. *Journal of Abnormal Psychology, 33,* 489–507.

Egel, A. L., Richman, G. S., & Koegel, R. L. (1981). Normal peer models and autistic children's learning. *Journal of Applied Behavior Analysis, 14,* 3–12.

Ferster, C. B., & Skinner, B. F. (1957). *Schedules of reinforcement.* New York: Appleton-Century-Crofts.

Gautreaux, G. (2004). *The effects of monitoring on the acquisition of observational learning by middle school students.* Dissertation in progress.

Goldstein, H., & Mousetis, L. (1989). Generalized language learning by children with severe mental retardation: Effects of peers' expressive modelling. *Journal of Applied Behavior Analysis, 22,* 245–259.

Grant, J. W. A., & Green, L. D. (1995). Mate copying versus performance for actively courting females by female Japanese medaka (*Oryzias latipes*). *Behavioral Ecology, 9,* 534–539.

Greenwood, C. R., Hart, B., Walker, D., & Risley, R. (1994). The opportunity to respond and academic performance revisited: A behavioural theory of retardation and its prevention. In R. Gardner III, D. M. Sainato, J. O. Cooper, T. E. Heron, W. L. Heward, J. Eshleman, & T. A. Grossi (Eds.), *Behaviour analysis in education: Focus on measurably superior instruction.* Pacific Grove, CA: Brooks/Cole.

Greer, R. D. (1994). The measure of a teacher. In R. Gardner III, D. M. Sainato, J. O. Cooper, T. E. Heron, W. L. Heward, J. Eshleman, & T. A. Grossi (Eds.), *Behaviour analysis in education: Focus on measurably superior instruction.* Pacific Grove, CA: Brooks/Cole.

Greer, R. F. (2002). *Designing teaching strategies: An applied behavior analysis systems approach.* New York: Academic Press.

Greer, R. D., Dorow, L., Williams, G., McCorkle, N., & Asnes, R. (1991). Peer-mediated procedures to induce swallowing and food acceptance in young children. *Journal of Applied Behavior Analysis, 24,* 783–790.

Greer, R. D., & Keohane, D. (2004). A real science and technology of teaching. In J. Moran & R. Malott (Eds.), *Evidence-based educational practices* (pp. 23–46). New York: Elsevier/Academic Press.

Greer, R. D., & Keohane, D. (2005). The evolution of verbal behaviour in children. *Behavioral Development, 1,* 31–48.

Greer, R. D., Keohane, D., & Healey, O. (2002). Quality and applied behaviour analysis. *The Behaviour Analyst Today, 3*(2), 2002. Retrieved 20 December, 2003, from http://www.behavior-analyst-online.org

Greer, R. D., Keohane, D., Meincke, K., Gautreaux, G., Pereira, J., Chavez-Brown, M., & Yuan, L. (2004a). Key components of effective tutoring. In J. Moran & R. Malott (Eds.), *Evidence-based educational practices.* New York: Elsevier/Academic Press.

Greer, R. D., McCorkle, N. P., & Sales, R. D. (1998, June). *Conditioned reinforcement as a function of peer contingencies with pre-school children.* Paper presented at the annual meeting of the International Association for Behavior Analysis, Washington, DC.

Greer, R. D., Nirgudkar, A., & Park, H. (2003, June). *The effect of multiple exemplar instruction on the transformation of mand and tact functions.* Paper presented at the International Conference of the Association for Behavior Analysis, San Francisco, CA.

Greer, R. D., Pereira, J., & Yuan, L. (2004b, August). *The effects of teaching children to monitor learn unit responses on the acquisition of observational learning.* Paper presented at the Second International Conference of the Association of Behavior Analysis, Campinas, Brazil.

Greer, R. D., & Ross, D. E. (2004). Research in the induction and expansion of complex verbal behaviour. *Journal of Early Intensive Behavioural Intervention, 1.2.* Retrieved 20 May, 2005, from http://www.behavior-analyst-today.org

Greer, R. D., & Sales, C. D. (1997). *Peer effects on the conditioning of a generalized reinforcer and food choices.* Paper presented at the Annual International Conference of the Association for Behavior Analysis, Chicago, IL.

Greer, R. D., & Singer, J. (2004). *A new type of observational learning.* Manuscript submitted for publication.

Greer, R. D., Stolfi, L., Chavez-Brown, M., & Rivera-Valdez, C. (2004c). *The emergence of the listener to speaker component of naming in children as a function of multiple exemplar instruction.* Manuscript submitted for publication.

Greer, R. D., & Yuan, L. (2003). *Kids say the darnedest things.* Paper presented at the International Conference of the Association for Behavior Analysis and the Brazil Association for Behavior Medicine and Therapy.

Greer, R. D., Yuan, L., & Gautreaux, G. (2004d). *Novel dictation and intraverbal responses as a function of a multiple exemplar instructional history.* Manuscript submitted for publication.

Griffen, A. K., Wolery, M., & Schuster, J. W. (1992). Triadic instruction of chained food preparation responses: Acquisition and observational learning. *Journal of Applied Behavior Analysis, 25,* 193–204.

Hart, B., & Risley, T. (1996). *Meaningful differences in the everyday life of America's children.* New York: Paul Brookes.

Hayes, S. C., Barnes-Holmes, D., & Roche, B. (2000). *Relational frame theory: A post-Skinnerian account of human language and cognition.* New York: Kluwer/Plenum.

Healy, O., Barnes-Homes, D., & Smeets, P. M. (1998). Stimulus equivalence as an operant: The effects of between session feedback, *The Psychological Record, 48,* 522–536.

Holland, J. G., & Skinner, B. F. (1961). *The analysis of behavior.* New York: McGraw Hill.

Horne, P. J., & Lowe, C. F. (1996). On the origins of naming and other symbolic behavior. *Journal of the Experimental Analysis of Behavior, 65,* 185–241.

Iwata, B. A., Dorsey, M. F., Slifer, K. J., Bauman, K. E., & Richmond, G. S. (1982). Towards a functional analysis of self-injury. *Analysis and Intervention in Developmental Disabilities, 2,* 3–20.

Kazdin, A. E. (1973). The effect of vicarious reinforcement on attentive behavior in the classroom. *Journal of Applied Behavior Analysis, 6,* 71–78.

Lamarre, J., & Holland, J. (1985). The functional independence of mands and tacts. *Journal of Experimental Analysis of Behaviour, 43,* 5–19.

Latimore, D. L. (2001). Observational learning and stimulus equivalence in children with autism. *Digital Dissertations.*

Lowe, C. F., Horne, P. J., Harris, D. S., & Randle, V. R. L. (2002). Naming and categorization in young children: Vocal tact training. *Journal of the Experimental Analysis of Behavior, 78,* 527–549.

MacDonald, R. P. F., Dixon, L. S., & LeBlanc, J. M. (1986). Stimulus class formation following observational learning. *Analysis and Intervention in Developmental Disabilities, 6,* 73–87.

Michael, J. (1993). Establishing operations. *The Behaviour Analyst, 16,* 191–206.

Nuzzolo-Gomez, R., & Greer, R. D. (2004). Emergence of untaught mands or tacts with novel adjective-object pairs as a function of instructional history. *The Analysis of Verbal Behavior, 24,* 30–47.

Ollendick, T. H., Dailey, D., & Shapiro, E. S. (1983). Vicarious reinforcement: Expected and unexpected results. *Journal of Applied Behavior Analysis, 16,* 485–491.

Parkinson, J. A., Crofts, H. S., McGuigan, M., Davoraka, T. L., Everitt, B. J., & Roberts, A. C. (2001). The role of the primate amygdala in conditioned reinforcement. *The Journal of Neuroscience, 21,* 7770–7780.

Pereira-Delgado, J. A. (2005). *Effects of teaching peer monitoring on the acquisition of observational learning.* Unpublished doctoral dissertation, Columbia University, New York, USA.

Premack, D., & Premack, A. (2003). *Original intelligence: Unlocking the mysteries of who we are.* New York: McGraw-Hill.

Prett-Jones, S. G. (1992). Independent versus non-independent mate choice: Do females copy each other. *American Naturalist, 140,* 1000–1009.

Ross, D. E., & Greer, R. D. (2003). Generalized imitation and the mand: Inducing first instances of speech in young children with autism. *Research in Developmental Disabilities, 24,* 58–74.

Sales, C. D. (1998). *Peer effects on the conditioning of a generalized reinforcer on preschool aged children.* Columbia University dissertation, Proquest AAT 9909429.

Sidman, M. (1994). *Equivalence relations and behavior: A research story.* Boston: Authors Cooperative.

Singer-Dudek, J., & Greer, R. D. (2005). A long-term analysis of the relationship between fluency and the training and maintenance of complex math skills. *The Psychological Record, 55,* 361–376.

Skinner, B. F. (1938). *The behavior of organisms.* New York: Appleton-Century-Crofts.

Skinner, B. F. (1953). *Science and human behaviour.* New York: Macmillan.

Skinner, B. F. (1957). *Verbal behaviour.* Acton, MA: Copley Publishing Group and the B. F. Skinner Foundation.

Skinner, B. F. (1968). *The technology of teaching.* New York: Appleton-Century-Crofts.

Skinner, B. F. (1992). *Verbal behaviour.* Englewood Cliffs, NJ: Prentice-Hall (Originally published 1957).

Stolfi, L. (2004). *The effects of yoked contingencies on the acquisition of observational learning by preschoolers.* Dissertation in progress.

Stolfi, L., & Greer, R. D. (2004). *The effects of yoked contingencies on the acquisition of observational learning by preschoolers.* Paper presented at the Annual International Conference of the Association for Behavior Analysis, Boston, MA.

Sundberg, M. L., Loeb, M., Hale, L., & Eigenheer, P. (2001/2002). Contriving establishing operations for teaching mands for information. *The Analysis of Verbal Behavior, 18,* 15–30.

Sundberg, M. L., Michael, J., Partington, J. W., & Sundberg, C. A. (1996). The role of automatic reinforcement in early language acquisition. *The Analysis of Verbal Behavior, 13,* 21–37.

Tsiouri, I., & Greer, R. D. (2003). Inducing vocal verbal behaviour through rapid motor imitation training in young children with language delays. *Journal of Behavioral Education, 12,* 185–206.

Werts, M. G., Caldwell, N. K., & Wolery, M. (1996). Peer modelling of response chains: Observational learning by student with disabilities. *Journal of Applied Behavior Analysis, 29,* 53–66.

Williams, G., & Greer, R. D. (1993). A comparison of verbal-behavior and linguistic-communication curricula for training developmentally delayed adolescents to acquire and maintain vocal speech. *Behaviorology, 1,* 31–46.

Yuan, L. (2004). *The effects of tutoring on the emergence of higher order operants.* Unpublished manuscript, Columbia University, New York.

INTERNATIONAL JOURNAL OF PSYCHOLOGY, 2006, 41 (6), 500–513

Challenging collective violence: A scientific strategy

Mark A. Mattaini and Joseph Strickland

University of Illinois at Chicago, IL, USA

C ollective violence (war, terrorism, violent political conflicts, genocide, repression, organized criminal activity, disappearances, torture, and a range of other abuses of human rights) killed at least 200 million persons directly or indirectly, and injured many more, during the 20th century (Krug, Dahlberg, Mercy, Zwi, & Lozano, 2002). Recent advances in the science of behaviour can help to explain why humans turn so quickly to collective violent actions in response to threat or opportunity, and why such actions are in a real sense "natural." However, in the contemporary world the potential costs of relying on these nearly automatic responses are unacceptably high. This paper explores the roots of this violence from the perspective of the natural science of behaviour. Strategies for modifying collective violence should take into consideration motivational factors such as verbal processes and cultural perceptions, shifting motivating antecedents, etc. Rules, models, and structural conditions are also relevant. The potential contribution of behaviour science in changing collective violence is very important. The analysis suggests that policy-makers often rely on responses and preventive strategies that are inherently weak or counterproductive, and often politically manipulated. Potentially more powerful strategies, meanwhile, remain largely unrecognized. Programs of research that expand strategic options could meaningfully contribute to human well-being, but pursuing this work will require courageous scholarship conducted in solidarity with those at risk.

L a violence collective (guerre, terrorisme, conflit politique violent, génocide, répression, activité criminelle organisée, disparition, torture et un éventail d'autres abus aux droits humains) a tué au moins 200 millions de personnes directement ou indirectement et a blessé encore plus de gens au cours du vingtième siècle (Krug, Dahlberg, Mercy, Zwi, & Lozano, 2002). Les progrès récents en science du comportement peuvent aider à expliquer comment les êtres humains s'adonnent aussi rapidement à des actes de violence collective en réponse à la menace ou dès que l'occasion se présente, et pourquoi de tels actes sont en réalité «naturels». Cependant, dans le monde contemporain, les coûts potentiels à recourir à ces réponses presque automatiques sont élevés à un point inacceptable. Cet article explore les racines de la violence à partir de la perspective de la science naturelle du comportement. Les stratégies de modification de la violence collective doivent prendre en considération les facteurs motivationnels tels que les processus verbaux et les perceptions culturelles, les antécédents de changements de motivation, etc. Les règles, modèles et conditions structurelles sont aussi appropriés. La contribution potentielle de la science du comportement pour le changement de la violence collective est très importante. L'analyse suggère que les décideurs politiques recourent souvent à des réponses de stratégies préventives qui sont fondamentalement faibles, contreproductives et souvent manipulées politiquement. En contrepartie, les stratégies potentiellement plus puissantes demeurent très peu reconnues. Les programmes et la recherche qui développent des options stratégiques pourraient contribuer significativement au bien-être humain, mais la poursuite de ce travail requiert des études vaillantes menées en solidarité avec les personnes qui sont à risque.

L a violencia colectiva (la guerra, el terrorismo, los conflictos políticos violentos, el genocidio, la represión, la actividad criminal organizada, las desapariciones, la tortura, y una variedad de otros abusos de los derechos humanos) mató al menos 200 millones de personas directa o indirectamente, e hirió muchas más, durante el siglo XX (Krug, Dahlberg, Mercy, Zwi, y Lozano, 2002). Avances recientes en la ciencia de la conducta pueden ayudar a explicar por qué los seres humanos utilizan tan rápidamente las acciones de violencia colectiva como respuesta a la amenaza o a la oportunidad de hacerlo, y por qué tales acciones son "naturales" en un sentido real. Sin embargo, en el mundo contemporáneo los costos potenciales de confiar en estas respuestas casi automáticas son

Correspondence should be addressed to Mark Mattaini, Jane Addams College of Social Work, University of Illinois at Chicago (MC 309), 1040 West Harrison Street, Chicago, IL 60607-7134, USA (E-mail: mattaini@uic.edu).

For further information or discussion of the content of this paper, readers may contact Dr Mattaini by e-mail. Potential collaborators in the programs of research outlined here are particularly sought.

http://www.psypress.com/ijp

DOI: 10.1080/00207590500492484

inaceptablemente altos. El presente artículo explora las raíces de esta violencia desde la perspectiva de la ciencia natural de la conducta. Las estrategias para modificar la violencia colectiva deben tomar en cuenta factores motivacionales tales como los procesos verbales y las percepciones culturales, los cambios en las motivaciones antecedentes, etc. Las reglas modelos y condiciones estructurales también son relevantes. La contribución de la ciencia del comportamiento para cambiar la violencia colectiva es muy importante. El análisis sugiere que los responsables de las políticas generalmente se fundamentan en respuestas y estrategias preventivas que son inherentemente débiles o contraproductivas, y que con frecuencia están manipuladas políticamente. Por otra parte las estrategias potencialmente más poderosas en muchos casos no se reconocen. Los programas de investigación que amplían las opciones estratégicas podrían en forma significativa contribuir al bienestar humano, pero llevar a cabo este tipo de trabajo requiere investigación valiente conducida en forma solidaria con las personas en riesgo.

INTRODUCTION

The World Health Organization defines collective violence as: "The instrumental use of violence by people who identify themselves as members of a group—whether this group is transitory or has a more permanent identity—against another group or set of individuals, in order to achieve political, economic or social objectives" (Krug et al., 2002, p. 215). Included in this definition are war, terrorism, violent political conflicts, genocide, repression, organized criminal activity, disappearances, torture, and a range of other abuses of human rights. Such violence has been an issue for millennia (Ferguson, 2003), but advances in communication, transportation, and technologies of killing and destruction have dramatically increased the associated costs.

Governments, arms manufacturers, multinational corporations, international terrorist networks, paramilitary groups, drug cartels, street gangs, and others, responding to environments of threat, coercion, and potential profit—all have contributed to the expansion of collective violence. The level of financial and scientific resources dedicated to reducing violence, in contrast to that associated with the science and technology of killing, is vanishingly small. Growing income inequities, violent media, expanded arms and drug trade, and related processes associated with globalization further support escalating patterns of violence (Buvinic & Morrison, 2000). While the actions taken by members of such disparate groups as drug cartels and modern armies may not be morally equivalent, many of the behavioural dynamics involved in multiple forms of collective violence have much in common.

Recent advances in the science of behaviour can help to explain why humans turn so quickly to collective violent actions in response to threat or opportunity, why such actions are in a real sense "natural" (Sidman, 2001). For example, the natural responses to violent threats or actions by one group toward another are those associated with countercontrol (Delprato, 2003), including striking back or taking preemptive ("preventive") action. In the contemporary world, however, the potential costs of relying on these nearly automatic responses—levels of casualties and desperate pain; loss of human potential, mutual trust and personal integrity; destruction of cultural and economic systems, and ultimately escalating violence—are unacceptably high.

The analysis elaborated here suggests that critical links in the interlocking behavioural and cultural contingencies that shape and maintain cultures of collective violence are commonly overlooked or misunderstood by policy-makers. In this paper, we examine the context and behaviour dynamics of collective violence. While there is much to learn, it is already clear that a thoughtful scientific analysis can provide some level of useful guidance, and suggest critical directions for further research that could progressively refine that guidance.

THE EXTENT AND COSTS OF COLLECTIVE VIOLENCE

According to data gathered by the World Health Organization, at least 200 million persons died during the 20th century as the direct or indirect result of collective violence, as defined earlier. The majority of those deaths were of noncombatants. Indirect deaths include those that occur due to interruptions in the availability of food, medical care, and other human necessities, as well as those that can be attributed to poor conditions in refugee camps and other factors associated with displacement. Nearly unimaginable numbers of persons also were wounded, tortured, raped, or otherwise severely injured, physically and emotionally.

There are other serious costs associated with collective violence, including the escalating costs of police, military, and security efforts, and the sometimes dramatic effects on the quality of life of those touched by the issues. The severe developmental impact on children in war zones, for example, is well known. Less obvious, but also damaging, are the multiple impacts associated with living in an uncertain and fearful cultural environment in which extreme aversive events are seen as constant threats, and as a result of these many are willing to accept limits on civil liberties and personal dignity. Violence typically leads to violence, aversive leads to aversive, in dangerously escalating spirals (Sidman, 2001), even when such escalation is clearly counterproductive in the long run. Nevin's recent analyses (2003, 2004), for example, suggest that retaliation for terrorist acts is common, generally ineffective, and may even be associated with increases in such acts. Another important conclusion from Nevin's analyses is that terrorist campaigns have often been successful in achieving at least some of the goals of the terrorist groups, which naturally may encourage those groups and others to take similar actions.

The World Health Organization analysis (Krug et al., 2002) has clarified critical risk factors for collective violence. These include unequal access to power, grossly inequitable distribution of resources, control over drug production or trading, inequality between distinct cultural groups, the fueling of group fanaticism along ethnic, national, or religious lines, the ready availability of weapons, and rapid demographic change. (Policy shifts that remove existing barriers among diverse racial, religious, or ethnic groups may also result in conflict and competition over resources; Olzak, 2003.) Most of these risk factors are not surprising; addressing them, however, will require the political will to take on difficult challenges like redistribution of scarce resources.

The costs of collective violence are not evenly distributed. The rate of war-related deaths, for example, was six times higher in low- and middle-income states than in the most prosperous nations in the year 2000. In prosperous nations like the US and the UK, major public concerns focus on terrorism and gang violence, but such nations are also directly and indirectly linked to many other violence-related issues around the world, in ways that may sometimes reduce but often increase levels of violent acts. The specific issues in such disparate and severely affected areas as Iraq, Israel/Palestine, India/Pakistan, and Colombia are dramatically different, of course, but a general scientific analysis appears to have promise for

offering initial guidance for local applications. A scientific analysis can also help us to understand why some of the conditions listed increase the risks (Mattaini, 2003b).

THE POTENTIAL CONTRIBUTIONS OF BEHAVIOUR SCIENCE

Behaviour analytic and cultural analytic sciences provide a unique perspective on the dynamics of collective violence. Dramatic advances have been made in these behaviour sciences over the past three decades, although awareness of those advances is uneven. (Many other disciplines, of course, ranging from cognitive science and social psychology to history and political science, have their own contributions to make as well.) Among central recent advances are (1) dramatic increases in understanding of the dynamics of interlocking contingencies at the collective or cultural level, (2) the discovery of quantitative models and approaches like the matching law and behavioural economics that clarify understanding of multiple behaviours embedded in complex matrices of concurrent contingencies, and (3) advances in understanding of rule-governed behaviour and equivalence relations that have enabled behaviour analysis to deal effectively with what are often viewed as exclusively cognitive factors. The key variables in the sciences of behaviour, however, remain the behaviours themselves (defined as "things done," Lee, 1988), antecedent and postcedent events and conditions associated with those behaviours over the course of learning history, and the genetic substrates upon which learning processes rest. Elementary behavioural units, however, rather like genes, can now be understood in much more complex and transactional combinations than was the case even a few years ago.

Technically, despite loose common usage, only individuals behave; the dynamics of collective action therefore depend on understanding the contingencies that shape and maintain individual acts, as well as how those contingencies interlock and interact to produce emergent collective and cultural processes. The analysis here, therefore, begins with a model for understanding an act of violence at the individual level, then moves to a model for examining the matrices of interlocking contingencies involved in collective processes.

The importance of being able to understand such complex collective processes is enormous, given the realities of collective violence in many parts of the world. As just one example, consider the situation in Colombia (Leech, 2002). This is not simply a matter of the military against left-wing insurgents. There are also right-wing paramilitary groups, which have had many incarnations and reincarnations and have often, but not always, been allied to segments of the military. These groups also, however, have in some cases been allied with or under the control of narco-traffickers. The current major insurgent group, the Revolutionary Armed Forces of Colombia (FARC), has also long raised revenues from taxing drug traffic. Until about a decade ago, major drug cartels were an additional factor supporting violence. The enduring impacts of historical factors including numerous civil wars during post-colonial history, the enormous increase in violence in the late 1940s (*La Violencia*), and unrelenting experiences of collective violence since that time contribute to the complexities that need to be addressed to move toward a peaceful solution.

Analysing participation in collective violence

Figure 1 is a simplified diagram introducing some of what is currently known about the dynamics of violent action at the level of an individual participant in an act of collective violence (e.g., a suicide bomber or a low-ranking member of a paramilitary group). Although a great deal more technical detail is important to a full analysis and each situation is unique, even this quite general image indicates where many of the issues lie. A number of antecedent events and conditions are associated with the act, as are a number of concurrent and postcedent events and conditions. Many of these factors are considered in detail in the material that follows, but a few preliminary points are important here.

Beginning with postcedents: Sometimes key determinants of behaviour, certain events that follow participation in an act of violence (for example, threatened punishment by the other side) do not act as effective or active consequences. They may be too unlikely or uncertain to have a powerful impact on the associated behaviour, or may not be viewed as genuinely aversive (e.g., the threat of martyrdom). Many of the most common current responses to acts of violence, however, rely precisely on such postcedents. By contrast, powerful recognition by peers within the group, future rewards in an afterlife viewed as certain to occur, and opportunities to exercise countercontrol (e.g., to damage the enemy) in many cases serve as effective consequences. Some other postcedents may in fact be the result of actions taken but may not be known or understood by the participants

(e.g., increases in disease among populations indirectly affected by campaigns of collective violence, or rippling economic effects).

Another common emphasis in efforts to reduce violence is a focus on structural conditions (e.g., efforts to reduce access to weapons or to harden possible targets). While sometimes necessary, the record of efforts to address terrorism suggests that there are too many accessible targets, variations of violence, and potential recruits to groups engaged in violence to make a focus on structural conditions a realistic primary strategy over the long term (Mattaini, 2003b). There also can be substantial costs, for example the losses of dignity and privacy associated with increased surveillance and security measures.

By contrast, as will be seen in the material that follows, very little real emphasis has been placed on efforts to shift antecedents, particularly potent antecedents that motivate action (technically, establishing and abolishing operations[1]), although as will become clear below, these appear to be among the most promising areas for preventive action. For example, some discussion is currently occurring in policy circles related to the importance of reducing the number of potential recruits of groups associated with violence, whether youth gangs or terrorist networks. To the extent that these efforts rely principally on threat and punishment, they are unlikely to produce the desired effects (see Sidman, 2001); sophisticated efforts to shift motivating antecedents, however, are much more promising alternatives. Verbal rules, equivalence relations, and models are among other powerful antecedents that in some cases may offer accessible intervention points, as discussed later.

Interlocking contingencies at the collective level

While the behavioural relationships sketched in Figure 1 already offer considerable information that might usefully inform policy, the realities are far more complicated. Antecedents and consequences affecting the actions of members of the leadership group are usually substantially different from those affecting the actions of less central members, like those who personally perpetrate acts

---

[1]Establishing and abolishing operations are events and conditions that increase or decrease the valence of available reinforcers and thereby the rate of behaviours associated with those reinforcers. These include deprivation, presence of certain types of aversive conditions, reinforcer sampling, as well as some verbal processes as described later in this paper. See Michael (1993) for detail.

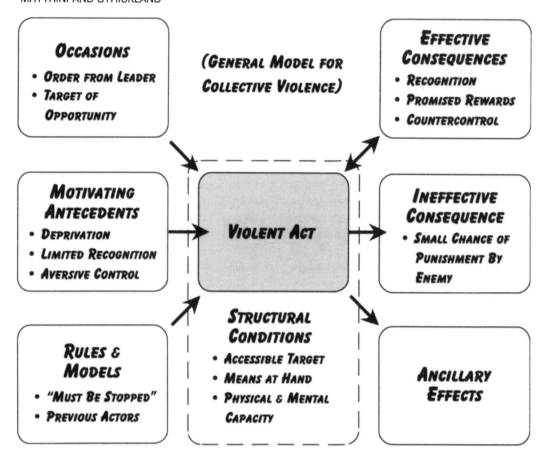

Figure 1. The contingency matrix associated with individual participation in an act of collective violence. (© 2004, Mark A. Mattaini, used with permission)

of violence in the name of the group. Malott (1988) has persuasively argued that cultural leaders often act based on perceptions of longer-term consequences, while most participants respond to much more immediate factors. Foot soldiers consistently report that in battle their moment-by-moment actions are often focused on keeping themselves and other members of their immediate combat unit as safe as possible. Collective violence often, in fact, has political or economic objectives that may be of limited benefit to those actually involved in direct action (Rauf, 2004). Decisions to send participants into harm's way, by contrast, are made by commanders who must weigh short-term human costs against possible long-term strategic gains.

In the case of collective terrorist or drug cartel actions, for example, the contingency matrices within which leaders operate may be similar in some areas to those shaping the actions of their followers, but in other areas are likely to be quite distinct. The opportunity to order a violent action now that is likely to damage the economic situation of an enemy later, and which may subsequently result in the enemy's withdrawal

from territory important to the leader, may be the primary active consequence for that leader. Understanding the connections between current actions and longer-range impacts may require a vision well beyond the moment. Those who actually perform the action, however, may be motivated by personal recognition, immediate financial gain, or other immediate effects. Seeing the World Trade Center towers fall may be satisfying for the rank and file (simple damage to the enemy), but reverberating economic and political impacts around the world are more likely to be the active consequences for the leader.

Scientifically, armies, gangs, terrorist networks, and other groups that maintain an internal culture leading to collective action (including violent action) are examples of *autopoietic* (self-organizing) systems (Hudson, 2000). The behaviour of their constituent members is to a substantial degree shaped and maintained in mutual transaction with other members of the group, rather than by outside forces. This reality obviously complicates efforts to change the behaviour of individual members of the group. While living systems always require resources from outside, these may figure

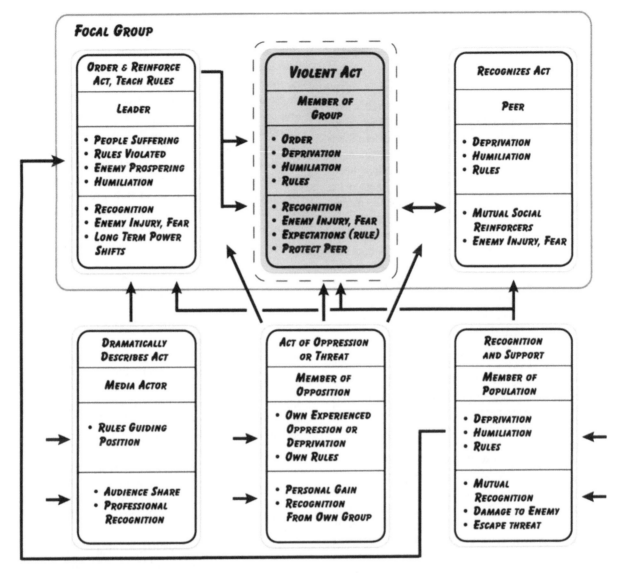

Figure 2. Interlocking contingencies associated with collective violence. In this diagram, the cultural practice is listed at the top of each class, followed by the actor, antecedents, and consequences in descending order. Short arrows directed toward actors outside the focal group represent contingencies involving actors not shown on this diagram. (© 2004, Mark A. Mattaini, used with permission)

only to a limited extent in the contingencies shaping behaviour of members of the self-organizing system. Examining the full transactional network, as outlined in simple form in Figure 2, sees both potential intervention points and their limitations begin to emerge.

As a result of the largely self-organizing nature of such networks, it can be difficult for outsiders, even those who appear to wield great power, to have a significant impact on the behaviour of persons within the network. Potential and peripheral members of the group (be that a street gang, insurgent group, or elite military unit) are also often members of other cultural networks like families and religious congregations, however, which in some cases may provide accessible points

for intervention as discussed below. (In fact, more militant groups often try to limit contacts between their members and such other networks to maintain tight control of the social and verbal environment.) Adequate scientific analysis needs, as far as possible, to take all of these concurrent processes into account.

ACTION TO CHALLENGE COLLECTIVE VIOLENCE

A number of tentative directions for limiting collective violence that might be immediately pursued, as well as critical questions that need to be explored in detail in future research, are sketched below. These should be viewed as strategic directions, rather than well-established prescriptions.

Occasions

Most acts of collective violence are initiated when ordered or encouraged by a person in a leadership position. In tightly organized and disciplined groups like modern armies, positive consequences for the actor only follow the act if it has been directly ordered. In less structured networks (including some terrorist and special forces groups), however, explicit orders may not be required. The availability of a target of opportunity may, for members of such groups, function as an occasion for action that will be recognized or reinforced. One common strategy for preventing action by an opponent is reduction of opportunities for enemy leadership to give coordinated instructions to act. In military situations, this is often discussed in terms of damaging command and control systems. The justice system attempts to do something similar when it targets gang leaders or organized crime leadership structures. Attempts to assassinate leaders represent a related strategy. Under some circumstances, the approach appears to be somewhat successful. There are clearly limitations as well, particularly when dealing with groups that are organized as loosely knit networks like al-Qa'ida rather than in rigid hierarchies such as those in West often expect. Such groups function as networks of variably autonomous groups in which relative power shifts depending on resources needed and changing events (Ackerman & Kruegler, 1994). For example, new leadership has continuously emerged in the Palestinian group Hamas when leadership figures have been assassinated, increasing anger among the Palestinian people each time. A danger associated with targeting such figures is that such action may increase their stature (as appears to have happened with bin Laden in the 1990s), or may create a powerful symbolic presence should the person targeted be killed. The imprisonment of Nelson Mandela is another example, and a reminder that one side's "terrorist" is commonly the other side's "liberator."

Motivating antecedents

Deprivation or the threat of loss of something highly valued can be powerful motivating forces for action among human beings (Michael, 1993). Relative economic deprivation is one important example, but so is the possible loss of more abstract values (freedom, or a morally upright social environment). Such experiences of deprivation are deeply rooted in culture. Recent actions by Western nations in the Arab world are commonly viewed as representative of the "moral degeneracy and consequent weakness of Western civilization" (Lewis, 2003, p. 22), a degeneracy that many in the Muslim world believe is intentionally being inflicted on them by the "Crusaders" of the West. A powerful aversive event for most human beings is the experience of being coerced by someone else to act in ways that are aversive or that violate one's values. There is considerable scientific evidence that such coercive control often leads to "countercontrol"—actions that are oriented toward "controlling the controller" (Sidman, 2001). Nonviolent campaigns like the US Civil Rights movement are examples of countercontrol, as are military responses to attacks, or terrorist strikes responding to experiences of occupation. Unfortunately, the US has recently explicitly endorsed a strategic stance that relies on establishing supposedly invincible coercive power. This stance is precisely the one most likely to lead to countercontrolling actions, including terrorist strikes (Nevin, 2003, 2004). (Recent terrorist actions demonstrate that effective countercontrol need be neither technologically complex nor prohibitively expensive, even against a self-proclaimed "superpower.") So long as members of some groups are motivated by shared experiences of aversive control, such acts are likely to continue.

Although often neglected, strategies grounded in shifts in motivating antecedents, and verbal phenomena including rules and equivalence relations (e.g., the US="the Great Satan") are among the most important and promising currently available. Perhaps the major reason why attention to motivating antecedents has not been greater is that, to be effective, action in these areas should be taken preventively rather than reactively. Focusing preventively, however, requires a significant shift in the way inter-group relations are usually dealt with in areas of the world that are most heavily immersed in collective violence. If levels of deprivation were universally low (as the Universal Declaration of Human Rights would suggest they should be), there would be many fewer young people (and others) motivated to take violent action. The science suggests that fewer young people lacking alternative opportunities for gaining status and demonstrating their worth, fewer young people lacking real hope for a satisfying life in their own terms, would result in fewer terrorist recruits. Experiencing reductions in aversive control (being forced to act against one's will) and reductions in other aversive conditions (e.g., the presence of non-Muslims on sacred ground) should also, the science suggests, reliably reduce acts of countercontrolling violence (Sidman, 2001).

Verbal processes and cultural perceptions. Verbal processes are the key to understanding cultural perceptions. As an example, the 1998 "Declaration of the World Islamic Front for Jihad against the Jews and the Crusaders," signed by bin Laden and leaders of other radical Islamic groups, lists three main complaints: the occupation of the holiest lands of Islam (in Saudi Arabia), the destruction of the Iraqi people at the hands the "Crusader Jewish alliance," and the occupation of Jerusalem (Lewis, 2003). It is noteworthy that radical leaders have utilized complaints that are based on injustice and oppression; it would be impossible to gain broad Muslim support for a platform of violent action based on hate, or for that matter on expanding Islam. In particular, a call for "terrorist" action would be entirely inconsistent with Islam. Any effort to rally Muslims must be grounded in an Islamic objective of ending injustice or protecting the faith (Nasr, 2002). The verbal underpinnings of the issues noted in the Declaration reflect long-standing Islamic tradition; for some Muslims, non-Muslims desecrate the most sacred Islamic places (which theologically are viewed as including much of Saudi Arabia) by their very presence. For others, many common actions of non-Muslims in Saudi Arabia violate core cultural and religious values in ways not at all apparent to those involved. Iraq and Jerusalem also include sacred sites. The increased presence of Westerners, particularly Americans, in certain parts of the Islamic world is therefore deeply troubling or offensive to many.

Many contemporary Muslims regard Islam's normative call for *jihad* as a call for moral striving. According to Nasr (2002), "In Arabic the term jihad is derived from the root *jhd*, meaning 'to strive' or 'to exert effort,' and in the context of Islam this striving and exertion are understood to be in the path of God" (p. 256). Many others—including but not limited to those associated with radical Islamist terrorist groups—interpret that binding moral directive as a call to continuing action, military if necessary, to achieve the final ascendancy of Islam worldwide (Lewis, 2003). The Holy Qur'an instructs believers to "fight in the cause of Allah those who fight you..." (Ali & Ali, 1990), so events such as an unwelcome occupation could inspire Muslims to violently oppose foreign forces. In addition, some of those who see *jihad* as moral striving can be moved towards more radical approaches if they experience their way of life as under threat. The West also often tends to take most seriously those with worldviews similar to their own and those who carry threat power, rather than religious leaders who see the world in more moderate terms, limiting the potential influence of the latter.

The problem of cultural humiliation is particularly challenging to address, since that experience can be so deeply rooted in cultural specifics. Aversive conditions and events (experiences one would avoid if possible) serve as powerful motivating antecedents. What is perceived as aversive, however, and the ways that experiences are described verbally, are deeply rooted in cultural values and networks of social reinforcement. Relevant aversive conditions and events may also range from the immediate to the historical. For example, frequent complaints about the way US troops "stare" at Iraqi women have been reported during the occupation. Such behaviour, normative for one group, is experienced as highly aversive by Iraqis. On the other hand, for radical Islamists, but for many other Muslims worldwide as well, the dissolution of the caliphate at the hands of occupying Western powers and secularized Muslims early in the 20th century—about which most in the West know nothing—remains a deeply humiliating and ever-present experience (Lewis, 2003). The Holy Qur'an instructs Muslims that persecution is worse than death, a message similar to historical cries for freedom and justice such as "give me liberty or give me death" or "live free or die" in the US and related messages in other cultures. Religious, cultural, and national duties can be deeply interwoven when core values are perceived to be at risk. (Similar analyses of motivating antecedents and verbal processes can be developed for many other instances of collective violence and conflict.)

Shifting motivating antecedents. Changes in the processes that establish and maintain some conditions as aversive can be quite challenging. Behaviour that has been richly reinforced is more difficult to shift when conditions change than is behaviour that has been less richly reinforced (Dube & McIlvane, 2002; Nevin, Milo, Odum, & Shahan, 2003), and the kinds of experiences and verbal descriptions under discussion here have often been culturally reinforced innumerable times over the lives of members of groups at risk of engaging in violence. Equivalence relations (which include values and views of other groups, e.g.,

"Arabs=terrorists"), once firmly established, are difficult to disrupt (Spradlin, Saunders, & Saunders, 1992). Disputing established equivalences, according to the research, is not likely to change them (e.g., repeating "Arabs are not evildoers!" over and over is unlikely to be effective). In fact, such disputation may *strengthen* the equivalence (Dixon, Dymond, Rehfeldt, Roche, & Zlomke, 2003). Rather, the more powerful approach is to strengthen competing relations (e.g., "We are partners," initially in particular projects) through experience (Spradlin et al., 1992).

Interestingly, a suggestion by President Khatami of Iran may be roughly accurate in terms of how to begin to construct such competing equivalences. He recently called for "a continuous dialogue between cultures and to work toward an alliance for spreading peace" while clarifying that this could not be done through surrender under force (CNN.com, May 13, 2003). Increased exposure can expand sensitivity to multiple equivalences of which participants are members (e.g., diplomat, thoughtful problem solver, parent, soccer fan). Importantly, the Committee on the Present Danger (CPD), a somewhat diverse but relatively conservative US group including the Democratic Senator Joseph Lieberman and the conservative commentator Newt Gingrich, suggests a number of steps to "reconnect with the Iranian people" that are highly consistent with Khatami's suggestion. Those steps include dramatically expanding cultural, academic, and professional exchanges; increasing information outreach; and ongoing diplomatic, military, and law enforcement contacts—a plan highly consistent with the strategy suggested here (some of the CPD's other recommendations are not consistent with the present analysis; Committee on the Present Danger, 2004).

Another direction that emerges from this analysis involves the construction of legitimate avenues of contact among individuals and groups who do not possess the economic and political means for ongoing experience with members of other cultures, races, and religions. Historical divisions and feuds can sometimes be manipulated by the powerful and by the media to construct barriers to peace. Throughout the world, people at grassroots levels who desire peace lack avenues for meaningful dialogue with their counterparts in other groups. Persistent contact is necessary to produce shifts in verbal processes associated with collective violence (Dixon et al., 2003), and the construction of alternative cognitive and cultural

structures rooted in understanding, ongoing dialogic processes, and human affiliation.

Such continuous mutual experience at multiple levels appears promising given basic behavioural theory (Mattaini, 2003b), but is difficult to establish since in international relations dialogue is often viewed as a reward for acting as the other party wishes. Breaking off dialogue and severing relations are commonly used as punishments, but such actions preclude the continuous contact necessary to build robust competing equivalences in which members of all groups come progressively to be viewed as genuinely human and valuable—a view inconsistent with propaganda practices of most groups today. As noted by Hayes, Niccolls, Masuda, and Rye (2002), "virtually all cultures openly amplify" processes of negative labelling toward opposing groups (p. 296); and such constructions, once learned, are very difficult to disrupt. Propaganda can also shift verbal categories directly and powerfully. A number of observers suggest that mutual hatred among groups in the former Yugoslavia, for example, was dramatically amplified by the mass media on each side (Jarman & Jarman, 2000; Nagler, 2001).

Scientifically, then, key questions to be asked take forms like, "How can we act to reduce deprivation for peoples who are currently struggling?" and "In what ways do other groups experience us as threatening or aversively controlling, and what could we do to reduce those perceptions?" The answers would open a range of preventive possibilities. Current science suggests that active work to reduce deprivation and aversive conditions, produce humanizing shifts in verbal processes, and build mutual experiences among peoples may be among the most predictable and powerful ways to shift levels of motivation, and thereby levels of collective violence.

Rules and models

Technically, rules and modelling involve establishing operations and, in some cases, discriminative functions, so a brief note here may be useful. Rules (Malott, Malott, & Suarez, 2003) are verbal and cognitive phenomena that state the connections between behaviour and its consequences (e.g., "martyrdom leads to glory" or "allowing the infidels to be present desecrates sacred places"). Such rules are powerful determinants of human behaviour, and are generally the results of simple social learning processes including vicarious and direct reinforcement. Such processes also lead to the formation of equivalence relations. Members of groups supporting violence often observe others verbally supporting violence or actually participating in it, and the modelling involved certainly is a major factor supporting continuation of violence within such groups.

Preventive and interventional options for dealing with these factors involve provision of different models and social networks supporting different rules and equivalences. Powerful alternative groups supporting effective nonviolent action, for example, would offer such models, as discussed in detail below. Approaches that could shift equivalence relations and those that reduce deprivation and other motivating antecedents will also collectively shift rules and modelled action over time.

Structural conditions

A common emphasis for reducing acts of collective violence is the control of structural variables, for example, enhancing airport security to reduce access to planned targets as well as targets of opportunity. Such efforts have some utility, at least in reducing the likelihood of the repetition of certain specific threats, but they also have important limitations. The first is cost; there are an almost infinite number of vulnerable points requiring protection, especially given the continuously advancing state of the knowledge and technology of killing. Surveillance, once established, typically needs to be maintained indefinitely, and with high levels of attention that are difficult to maintain. Security measures also increase the level of aversive experiences for the general population, as is currently evident at airports worldwide. When distinguished elderly persons are compelled to walk barefoot through security checkpoints, pilots are afraid to fly without firearms, and the next generation of scanners will electronically undress each passenger, such costs are evident.

While devoting resources to limiting access to targets as well as to possible instruments of attack (e.g., low-grade nuclear material that could be used for dirty bombs) is only prudent, over the long term such approaches are limited and costly strategic options. These approaches do not reduce the motivation to act, and highly motivated individuals and groups will ultimately find a way (Sidman, 2001). In the long run, therefore, attention to motivating factors and to consequences (discussed next) is likely to be far more powerful because these involve work with the basic dynamics of human behaviour.

Certain structural factors may, however, be effectively but indirectly influenced through attention to motivating antecedents and consequences. Most groups engaged in violence, including national armies and many terrorist networks, require extensive resources (financing, weapons, shelter, assurances of anonymity, and other necessities) to maintain their efforts over the long term. Populations and their leaders who do not share the values of those engaged in violence are less likely to provide such resources, and more likely to share information about the group with officials, thus limiting the availability of structural factors required for effective action. Families who see better avenues for their children to act that are consistent with core values, and who recognize that alternative sets of more positive consequences are available, are likely to support and reinforce actions consistent with those alternatives, thus reducing the availability of potential recruits (a necessary resource for continued action).

Consequences

Figures 1 and 2, and the science that underlies them, provide initial guidance for work with consequences as well. The risk of punishment is not high for any particular act associated with being a member of a street gang, terrorist network, or violent insurgent group, and is even lower for a member of a legitimated army, even if that army is producing heavy casualties among noncombatants. Any punishment that may occur is likely to be far off in an uncertain future. Behaviour scientists have known for decades that effective punishment must be quick and inescapable (Azrin & Holz, 1966; Sidman, 2001). In addition, what some regard as punishment (e.g., death) is often not viewed in the same way by those involved in the violence (an issue of conflicting equivalence relations). In addition, the threat of punishment often sparks countercontrol, so threats may paradoxically *increase* the risk of further violent acts, further shaping a reciprocal spiral of threat and violence.

Turning to positive consequences, there is often a range of these associated with acts of collective violence; some are tangible and immediate, some are distant but made immediate through verbal processes. These include, for example, recognition from other members of the group, injury to the enemy, or promised glory in afterlife. These are powerful reinforcers for a young person who finds other paths essentially absent, and in whose social world large portions of the population share the experiences of deprivation and humiliation that support violence. Young people who, by contrast, find opportunity and a social and cultural network whose values support nonviolent action, and not the violent alternative, are much less likely to be recruited to violent groups. Such supports appear to be the strongest prescription we currently have for gang-involved youth (Garbarino, 1999; Goldstein & Huff, 1993), and are likely to hold significant promise for reducing other forms of collective violence as well. The best current science suggests that supporting cultural practices that recognize alternative choices, provide alternative forms of power, and discourage involvement with groups supporting violence would have a powerful effect on young people in vulnerable regions (Mattaini, 2001).

A final strategy grounded in consequences, perhaps among the most promising, may be the development of effective alternative models for nonviolent social change. The analysis above clarifies that acts of collective violence are functional for both the individual and the group; such acts occur because they produce (or may produce) desirable effects. Decades of behavioural research clarify that the best way to reduce an undesirable behaviour is often to shape a more desirable alternative repertoire that produces similar effects (e.g., asking for what one wants rather than having a tantrum) (Goldiamond, 1974/2002). Collective nonviolent actions that produce some of the same results as violence, at less cost and potentially more effectively, could serve as functional equivalents to acts of violence. Groups having such alternatives available would be less likely to turn to collective violence, threat, and terrorism. Behavioural theory suggests, for example, that a rigorous strategy of nonviolence would better serve the Palestinians than a violent *intifada* (cf. Hahn, 2004). While groups with great power may be as likely to resist change that is being advocated nonviolently as that being supported by the violent force, and the associated costs are not small, the evidence nevertheless suggests that nonviolent action can in many cases be the most effective alternative (Mattaini, 2003a). This strategic direction is further discussed below.

IMPLICATIONS OF THE ANALYSIS

The most powerful possible interventions are also politically challenging. If science is to contribute to solutions to the problem, adventuresome and often frankly courageous scholarship will be required. Some of the steps that need to be taken

may initially be politically unpopular, and the work may not be uniformly valued in the academy. Nonetheless, more important scientific work is difficult to imagine. Consistent with the analysis presented, among the directions such work might take are the following:

1. *Analyses of motivating antecedents related to initiation and maintenance of collective violence within particular cultural settings.* These analyses would entail detailed exploration and cultural interpretations of motivating and verbal factors affecting specific groups (nations, peoples, domestic minorities, and other networks) currently or potentially involved in collective violence. Both subjective (emic) experiences of those within the culture and (etic) observations by those outside it should be included in these analyses. Early work may begin with science-based analyses of existing technical, historical, and even popular literature (which may clarify popular rules and equivalences). It would then be essential, however, to move subsequently to observational, ethnographic, and interview methods with members of the groups involved to test, clarify, and elaborate initial hypotheses further. Behaviour analysts, ethnographers, and persons professionally trained in international relations would be important contributors to this work, but the critical importance of including members of the cultures involved as active participants with strong voices should not be underestimated. Honouring those voices in a genuine way will require great humility; it is extraordinarily difficult to truly accept that the experiences and values of the other are as real or as important as one's own, or that one's own supposedly expert perspective could be wrong. This is, in fact, one of the great challenges that anthropology has struggled with, often unsuccessfully, throughout its history, and the challenges for behaviour scientists are no smaller. Hypotheses for preventive action that address accessible dynamics and shifting patterns of aversive control and countercontrol will emerge from these analyses.

2. *Identification and field testing, in partnership with the groups involved, of the action options that emerge in the previous step.* These options may include the initiation and maintenance of particular kinds of inter-group dialogues, novel policy initiatives, particularly around opportunities, new joint efforts among networks of nongovernmental organizations, principled withdrawals of forces, or any number of other possibilities. What is important here is not just to participate in ongoing campaigns, but to collaboratively experiment with options that emerge from systemic analyses. Based

on the current state of knowledge discussed above, a focus on preventive steps is likely to be among the most powerful, but the full range of possibilities, once elaborated, can and should be explored and tested. The results of this testing are likely to lead to new questions that need to be explored through observation and cultural contact, and to refined preventive and interventional procedures. In this area, the need for active, respectful partnerships with those involved in nonviolent action is immediately clear.

3. *Scholarship oriented toward the development of an effective science of nonviolent action.* Although Mahatma Gandhi repeatedly indicated that nonviolence is a science, and many contemporary nonviolent theoreticians (e.g., Nagler, 2001) agree, rigorous conceptual and empirical work elaborating such a science has until now been largely lacking. This science now appears possible, however, and dedicating relatively modest resources to these efforts (as compared to the enormous resources dedicated to violence-grounded strategies) may be a crucial step toward cultural advance and even human survival. For further discussion beyond the brief comments here, refer to Mattaini (2003a).

There is now substantial empirical evidence that nonviolent (and less coercive) actions can be powerful under a wide range of conditions (see Mattaini, 2003a, for a review; see also Ackerman & Kruegler, 1994). Violent behaviour continues because it produces valued outcomes, ranging from temporary diminution of personal rage to major shifts in intercultural power dynamics (Nevin, 2003, in press; Sidman, 2001). Violence, therefore, is functional—it provides power. Consistent with the work of Goldiamond and many other behaviour scientists, reducing or eliminating collective violence is likely to require the development and dissemination of functionally equivalent individual and collective repertoires that offer alternative, more desirable, and less destructive forms of power. Groups who experience their situation as highly aversive can be expected to forego strategies of violence only if potent nonviolent alternatives are available.

Contrary to common belief, effective nonviolent action does not rely primarily on the actions of a few spiritually exemplary individuals. Well-organized collectives of average people have generally been the principal active force in effective nonviolence (Ackerman & Kruegler, 1994). In fact, and perhaps surprisingly to many, collective nonviolent action has been characteristic of major social change through the ages, although it has seldom attracted the attention that collective violence has (Ackermann & Duvall, 2000; Schell, 2003).

Some nonviolent approaches clearly work better than others under some circumstances, but careful work to determine why this is true, and therefore which actions are most likely to be effective under which circumstances, remains to be done. The precision of behaviour science can move beyond description to provide a *functional classification*, which is likely to help answer the question, "What is most likely to be useful under these particular circumstances?" In addition, it is likely that a thoroughgoing analysis will suggest additional nonviolent strategies that have not yet been identified—empty cells in the analysis. As discussed elsewhere (Mattaini, 2003a), a science of nonviolent action is likely to begin with scientific exploration of historical and current examples of more successful and less successful nonviolent campaigns that examines individual and collective dynamics at the level of interlocking practices and the transactional contingencies that support them. The work is then likely to advance toward experimental praxis in partnership with groups willing to experiment with empirically grounded nonviolent alternatives.

A science of nonviolent action often will not change the goals of cultural groups. Rather, such a science may provide less costly and possibly more effective strategic and tactical tools for achieving those goals. Opposing groups might be expected to prefer being confronted by nonviolence, but if it is powerful, nonviolence will also be experienced as threatening to groups currently exercising economic, military, and other forms of power that can be used coercively or exploitatively. We are concerned in this paper with reducing collective violence of all kinds, certainly including terrorism and gang violence, but also violence associated with civil wars and separatist ethnic and religious movements, as well as violence legitimated by governments. A science of nonviolent action may produce radical shifts in understanding, leading to transformations in the moral acceptability of many forms of collective violent and coercive action, given a context of realistic alternatives. The refinement of nonviolent alternatives, and scholarship supporting them, is not therefore likely to be immediately or universally accepted, but appears critical to pursue.

4. *Other research directions.* In addition to the research directions mentioned here, Volume 12, Number 2 of the open access journal *Behaviour and Social Issues* discusses a number of other science-based strategies for reducing collective violence that appear worth further study. This

material is available on the web at http://www.bfsr.org/BSIOnLine.html. Of particular note are the quantitative analyses of Nevin (2003, 2004), which provide a model for evaluating the associations among the incidence of acts of violence and responses to those acts, and the relational frame analyses discussed by Dixon and colleagues (Dixon et al., 2003), which may provide substantial guidance for public information and public education efforts grounded in verbal processes.

CONCLUSION

Changes that could shift cultural practices in ways likely to reduce collective violence will be difficult, since some steps (such as engaging those labelled as enemies or responding affirmatively to active nonviolence) may be inconsistent with common public values. Ongoing public education efforts that provide opportunities for members of the public to actively weigh the multiple effects of possible policy options based on accurate information, perhaps utilizing a behavioural procedure called *consequence analysis* (Sanford & Fawcett, 1980; Moore & Mattaini, 2001), are therefore critical. Consequence analysis works to shift public opinion in respectful and nonmanipulative ways. By contrast, efforts to manipulatively manage public opinion are unlikely to be consistent with the long-range reduction of collective violence, since they tend to rely on behavioural processes associated with such violence.

An essential consideration is that all of this work, if it is to be of maximum utility, needs to be conducted with the active participation of and in true solidarity with those who are most at risk. Such solidarity requires a willingness to acknowledge and include in the analyses the ways in which oneself and one's own group may participate in oppressive processes, and a commitment to acting to address that participation. Exploring collective violence inevitably embeds one in deep pain, devastation, and death, and therefore requires an active commitment to stay with the work, honestly report one's findings, and remain involved over the long term in a process of reflective praxis.

While nearly everyone might naively agree that they want to live in peaceful, nonviolent societies in a peaceful, nonviolent world, contemporary societies rely extensively on the manipulation of verbal processes and on coercive processes of threat and punishment. Moving toward the alternatives sketched here will be difficult, and the challenges of the underlying science are enormous.

Nonetheless, behaviour science appears to be reaching a stage of development such that it can contribute to addressing crucial social issues like collective violence and other violations of human rights and social justice. Supporting and conducting that science may be the most critical challenge of the present age, but it will not be universally embraced. In fact, this work is likely to require some of the most courageous, and at the same time humble, scholarship that can be imagined.

REFERENCES

Ackerman, P., & Duvall, J. (2000). *A force more powerful: A century of nonviolent conflict.* New York: Palgrave.

Ackerman, P., & Kruegler, C. (1994). *Strategic nonviolent conflict: The dynamics of people power in the Twentieth Century.* Westport, CT: Praeger.

Ali, Y., & Ali, A. Y. (1990). *The Holy Qur'an: Text, translation, and commentary.* Beltsville, MD: Amana Publications.

Azrin, N. H., & Holz, W. C. (1966). Punishment. In W. K. Honig (Ed.), *Operant behaviour: Areas of research and application* (pp. 380–447). New York: Appleton-Century-Crofts.

Buvinic, M., & Morrison, A. R. (2000). Living in a more violent world. *Foreign Policy, 118,* 58–72.

Committee on the Present Danger. (2004). *Iran: A new approach.* Available at http://www.fightingterror.org/newsroom/CPD_Iran_policy_paper.pdf).

Delprato, D. J. (2002). Countercontrol in behavior analysis. *The Behavior Analyst, 25,* 191–200.

Dixon, M. R., Dymond, S., Rehfeldt, R. A., Roche, B., & Zlomke, K. R. (2003). Terrorism and relational frame theory. *Behavior and Social Issues, 12,* 129–147.

Dube, W. V., & McIlvane, W. J. (2002). Reinforcer rate and stimulus control in discrimination reversal learning. *The Psychological Record, 52,* 405–416.

Ferguson, R. B. (2003). The birth of war. *Natural History, 112,* 28–35.

Garbarino, J. (1999). *Lost boys: Why our sons turn violent and how we can save them.* New York: Free Press.

Goldiamond, I. (2002). Toward a constructional approach to social problems: Ethical and constitutional issues raised by applied behavior analysis. *Behavior and Social Issues, 11,* 108–197 (Originally published 1974).

Goldstein, A. P., & Huff, C. R. (1993). *The gang intervention handbook.* Champaign, IL: Research Press.

Hahn, T. N. (2004). *Peace begins here: Palestinians and Israelis listening to each other.* Berkeley, CA: Parallax Press.

Hayes, S. C., Niccolls, R., Masuda, A., & Rye, A. K. (2002). Prejudice, terrorism, and behavior therapy. *Cognitive and Behavioral Practice, 9,* 296–301.

Hudson, C. G. (2000). From Social Darwinism to self-organization: Implications for social change theory. *Social Service Review, 74,* 533–559.

Jarman, R., & Jarman, P. (2000). The hidden costs of war. In J. Lampen (Ed.), *No alternative? Nonviolent responses to repressive regimes* (pp. 1–11). York, UK: William Sessions.

Krug, E. G., Dahlberg, L. L., Mercy, J. A., Zwi, A. B., & Lozano, R. (2002). *World report on violence and health*. Geneva, Switzerland: World Health Organization.

Lee, V. L. (1988). *Beyond behaviorism*. Hillsdale, NJ: Lawrence Erlbaum Associates Inc.

Leech, G. M. (2002). *Killing peace: Colombia's conflict and the failure of US intervention*. New York: Information Network of the Americas.

Lewis, B. (2003). *The crisis of Islam*. New York: Modern Library.

Malott, R. W. (1988). Rule-governed behavior and behavioral anthropology. *The Behavior Analyst, 11*, 181–203.

Malott, R. W., Malott, M. E., & Suarez, E. A. T. (2003). *Principles of behavior* (5th ed.). Upper Saddle River, NJ: Pearson Education.

Mattaini, M. A. (2001). *Peace power for adolescents: Toward a culture of nonviolence*. Washington, DC: NASW Press.

Mattaini, M. A. (2003a). Constructing nonviolent alternatives to collective violence: A scientific strategy. *Behavior and Social Issues, 12*, 148–163.

Mattaini, M. A. (2003b). Understanding and preventing collective violence. *Behavior and Social Issues, 12*, 90–108.

Michael, J. L. (1993). *Concepts and principles of behavior analysis*. Kalamazoo, MI: Society for the Advancement of Behavior Analysis.

Moore, S. K., & Mattaini, M. A. (2001). Consequence analysis: An on-line replication. *Behavior and Social Issues, 11*, 71–79.

Nagler, M. N. (2001). *Is there no other way? The search for a nonviolent future*. Berkeley, CA: Berkeley Hills Books.

Nasr, S. H. (2002). *The heart of Islam: Enduring values for humanity*. San Francisco: Harper SanFrancisco.

Nevin, J. A. (2003). Retaliating against terrorists. *Behavior and Social Issues, 12*, 109–128.

Nevin, J. A. (2004). Retaliating against terrorists: Erratum, reanalysis, and update. *Behavior and Social Issues, 13*, 154–158.

Nevin, J. A., Milo, J., Odum, A. L., & Shahan, T. A. (2003). Accuracy of discrimination, rate of responding, and resistance to change. *Journal of the Experimental Analysis of Behavior, 79*, 307–321.

Olzak, S. (2003). Racial policy and racial conflict in the urban United States, 1869–1924. *Social Forces, 83*, 481–517.

Rauf, A. F. (2004). *What's right with Islam: A new vision for Muslims and the West*. New York: Harper Collins.

Sanford, F. L., & Fawcett, S. B. (1980). Consequence analysis: Its effects on verbal statements about an environmental project. *Journal of Applied Behavior Analysis, 13*, 57–64.

Schell, J. (2003). *The unconquerable world: Power, nonviolence, and the will of the people*. New York: Metropolitan Books.

Sidman, M. (2001). *Coercion and its fallout*. Boston: Authors Cooperative.

Spradlin, J. E., Saunders, K. J., & Saunders, R. R. (1992). The stability of equivalence classes. In S. C. Hayes & L. J. Hayes (Eds.), *Understanding verbal relations* (pp. 29–42). Reno, NV: Context Press.

INTERNATIONAL JOURNAL OF PSYCHOLOGY, 2006, 41 (6), 514–522

Recombinative generalization: Some theoretical and practical remarks

Monika Suchowierska

Warsaw School of Social Psychology, Warsaw, Poland

A primary goal of behavioural interventions aimed at teaching skills is to establish generative responding. Recombinative generalization, which has been defined as the demonstration of novel arrangements of previously established linguistic units, is a process involved in generative responding. Successful recombinations contribute to the development of a functional, not rote, language repertoire that often generalizes across stimuli, responses, and time. Although research on recombinative generalization began some 80 years ago, understanding of this process is still not complete. Furthermore, programming for successful recombinations when teaching language and reading to typically and not-typically developing children is still minimal. The early recombinative generalization studies worked on a "miniature linguistic system"; the referential stimuli (words) were arranged in a pattern that included all possible combinations of the dimensions of interest. Matrix training approaches to recombinative generalization showed how to produce functional language. In the present paper, I will (1) review research on recombinative generalization, (2) discuss conditions necessary for successful recombinations, and (3) make suggestions for practice relating to recombinative generalization. The discrimination required for successful recombinations fits well in the definition of "abstraction": a discrimination based on a single property of a stimulus, independent of other properties; thus, generalization to other stimuli with that property. Abstraction is demonstrated when an individual correctly identifies untrained stimuli based on property of interest. Recombinative generalization contributes to achieving functional language. Further research on recombinative generalization will broaden the understanding of basic processes and their application to teaching language and early literacy skills.

L 'objectif primaire des interventions comportementales qui visent à enseigner des compétences est d'établir une génération de réponse. La généralisation recombinante, définie comme étant une démonstration de nouveaux arrangements des unités linguistiques établies préalablement, est un processus qui implique la génération de réponse. Les recombinaisons réussies contribuent au développement d'un répertoire de langage fonctionnel, pas mécanique, qui se généralise souvent à travers les stimuli et le temps. Même si la recherche sur la généralisation recombinante a débuté quelque 80 ans plus tôt, la compréhension de ce processus est toujours incomplète. De plus, la programmation pour des recombinaisons réussies est encore minimale pendant l'enseignement d'une langue ainsi que de la lecture à des enfants qui se développent typiquement et des enfants atypiques. Les premières études portant sur la généralisation recombinante ont porté sur le «système linguistique miniature»; les stimuli référentiels (les mots) étaient arrangés selon un patron qui a inclus toutes les combinaisons possibles des dimensions d'intérêt. Les approches fondées sur une matrice d'entraînement pour la généralisation recombinante ont montré une production de langage fonctionnel. Dans le présent article, l'auteur: (1) révisera la recherche sur la généralisation recombinante, (2) discutera les conditions nécessaires pour la réussite des recombinaisons, et (3) proposera des suggestions pour la pratique reliées à la généralisation recombinante. La discrimination requise pour la réussite des recombinaisons entre bien dans la définition de «l'abstraction»: une discrimination basée sur la propriété unique d'un stimulus, indépendamment des autres propriétés; d'où la généralisation à d'autres stimuli avec la même propriété. L'abstraction est démontrée lorsqu'un individu identifie correctement les stimuli sans entraînement en se basant sur la propriété d'intérêt. La généralisation recombinante contribue à parvenir au langage fonctionnel. La recherche future sur la généralisation recombinante élargira la compréhension des processus de base et de leur application à l'enseignement d'une langue et aux capacités précoces d'alphabétisation.

Correspondence should be addressed to Monika Suchowierska, PhD, Warsaw School of Social Psychology, Ul. Nowoursynowska 143 K. m. 2, 02-776 Warsaw, Poland (E-mail: msuch@aster.pl).

© 2006 International Union of Psychological Science

DOI: 10.1080/00207590500492534

*U*na meta fundamental de las intervenciones conductuales que buscan enseñar habilidades es establecer respuestas generativas. La generalización recombinatoria que se define como la demostración de arreglos novedosos de unidades lingüísticas previamente establecidas, es un proceso que toma parte en las respuestas generativas. Las recombinaciones exitosas contribuyen al desarrollo de un repertorio funcional del lenguaje, no mecánico, que con frecuencia se generaliza a través de los estímulos, las respuestas y del tiempo. Aunque la investigación acerca de la generalización recombinatoria comenzó hace aproximadamente 80 años, el proceso no se entiende completamente. Más aún, la programación de recombinaciones exitosas para enseñar lenguaje y lectura a niños con desarrollo típico y con desarrollo atípico, es todavía mínimo. Los estudios iniciales sobre generalización recombinatoria se referían a "sistemas lingüísticos en miniatura"; los estímulos de referencia (palabras) se organizaban en una pauta que incluía todas las posibles combinaciones de las dimensiones de interés. Los enfoques de matriz de entrenamiento para investigar la generalización recombinatoria mostraron que produce lenguaje funcional. En el presente artículo, la autora: (1) revisa la investigación sobre generalización recombinatoria, (2) discute las condiciones necesarias para las recombinaciones exitosas, y (3) presenta sugerencias para la práctica relacionada con la generalización recombinatoria. La discriminación que se requiere para combinaciones exitosas encaja bien en la definición de "abstracción": una discriminación basada en una sola propiedad de un estímulo independiente de las otras propiedades; en esta forma ocurre la generalización a otros estímulos que posean esa propiedad. La abstracción se demuestra cuando un individuo identifica correctamente sin entrenamiento estímulos basados en esta propiedad que nos interesa. La generalización recombinatoria contribuye al logro del lenguaje funcional. Investigaciones adicionales sobre la generalización recombinatoria aumentará nuestra comprensión de los procesos básicos y de su aplicación a la enseñanza del lenguaje y a las habilidades tempranas de lecto-escritura.

INTRODUCTION

Learning has been defined as a process during which behaviour is added to an organism's repertoire (Catania, 1998). Sometimes the result—a relatively permanent change in behaviour—is a function of direct teaching of skills of interest, but more often, it is a function of discovering, based on what has been taught, relations between stimuli or generalizing the newly acquired skills to different stimuli and behaviours. Indeed, a primary goal of behavioural interventions aimed at teaching skills is to establish generative responding (Bergman & Gerdtz, 1997; Lord & McGee, 2001). Generative responding refers to emitting behaviours that have not been previously demonstrated by an individual and have not been directly trained, but may be related to other, trained responses (Schumaker & Sherman, 1970). In the context of language, generative responding means comprehending questions, requests, and comments (receptive language) that an individual has not heard before and producing utterances (expressive language) that have not been produced before. Both skills are crucial in the development of flexible and functional, not stereotypical and rote, language. Some typically developing children and many persons with developmental disabilities have great difficulties with achieving generative responding. It is, thus, a formidable task for researchers and practitioners to understand basic processes responsible for generative responding. Previous research indicates that recombinative generalization is involved in generative responding (Peterson, Larsson, & Riedesel, 2003).

Recombinative generalization has been defined as "differential responding to novel combinations of stimulus components that have been included previously in other stimulus contexts" (Goldstein, 1983, p. 281). When familiar stimuli are recombined in novel ways and stimulus elements continue to exert precise and appropriate control over corresponding portions of the response, recombinative generalization has occurred (Wetherby & Striefel, 1978). In the context of language, recombinative generalization refers to the demonstration of novel arrangements of previously established linguistic units (Goldstein, 1993). Although research on recombinative generalization began some 80 years ago, understanding of this process is still not complete. Furthermore, programming for successful recombinations when teaching language and early literacy skills to typically and not-typically developing children is minimal. In the present paper, I will: (1) review research on recombinative generalization, (2) discuss conditions necessary for successful recombinations, and (3) make several suggestions for programming recombinative generalization.

RESEARCH ON RECOMBINATIVE GENERALIZATION

The recombinative generalization literature includes two types of studies: those in which the recombined units are whole words and those in which the units are smaller than words (e.g., syllables). Both groups of studies will be discussed in this section.

The early recombinative generalization studies originated from Esper's (1925) work on a "miniature linguistic system" (as reported by Wetherby, 1978, p. 401). In this system, the referential stimuli (i.e., words) are arranged in a pattern that includes all possible combinations of the dimensions of interest. For example, if the dimensions of interest are colour and shape, the words representing different colours are placed in rows and the words representing different shapes are placed in columns. Thus, a matrix is formed in which separate cells, the intersections of each row and column, contain a two-word utterance referring to a colour–shape combination (e.g., green square). Within the whole matrix, there is an overlap between the two-word utterances because each colour is paired with each shape (e.g., green square, green circle, green triangle). In Esper's study, four colour and four shape stimuli were used, thus the whole system consisted of 16 colour–shape labels. Esper showed that participants, who were trained to expressively name 14 stimuli using appropriate labels, identified correctly the 2 untrained colour–shape combinations. However, when the labels in cells did not correlate with the colour and shape names (i.e., each stimulus combination received a different, unsystematically chosen name), such generalization did not occur (Esper, 1925, 1933). Thus, the orderliness of the miniature linguistic system, as shown by the overlap in the labels, facilitated recombinative generalization. What Esper did not examine was how many labels had to be taught minimally and in what order to produce novel responding.

The results of studies by Foss (1968a, 1968b), Striefel, Bryan, and Aikins (1974), Striefel and Wetherby (1973), and Striefel, Wetherby, and Karlan (1976) delineated the training conditions necessary for recombinative generalization to occur. Those researchers distinguished between diagonal and stepwise training, which differed in the selection of training items. In diagonal training, the participants were trained on labels that did not have an element in common (e.g., red circle, yellow triangle, blue square). Stepwise training, in contrast, provided an overlap among the stimulus components (e.g., red circle, red triangle, yellow triangle, yellow square, blue square, blue heart). The combined results of the studies showed that only the stepwise training resulted in correct labelling of the untrained stimuli, presumably by establishing stimulus control of both elements in

each two-word utterance (Striefel et al., 1976). Thus, overlap among stimulus components is vital because it facilitates subjects making the discriminations necessary to demonstrate recombinative generalization. The stepwise training is also called matrix training.

Recombinative generalization of whole words was also investigated by Goldstein and colleagues (Goldstein, 1983; Goldstein, Angelo, & Mousetis, 1987; Goldstein & Mousetis, 1989). The researchers applied matrix training to a more complex language system, one that included three dimensions. Goldstein and Mousetis, for example, constructed an object–preposition–location matrix. Three object labels were combined with five prepositions and six locations, yielding 90 three-word utterances (e.g., "button under cabinet"). The participants identified expressively and receptively all three objects, two prepositions, and three locations before training. Within the matrix, there was a submatrix consisting of the known words (18 three-term utterances) and three other submatrices of unknown propositions and locations. Training, which consisted of modelling and differential reinforcement of correct responses, began with a single item from the submatrix of known words. The participants were to answer the experimenter's question "What did I do?" using a three-word utterance (e.g., "penny on rug"). Upon reaching mastery of this utterance, three participants with mental retardation responded correctly to the remaining 17 items. Training of one item from the other three submatrices resulted sequentially in generalization to the remaining items from those matrices. In sum, recombinative generalization accounted for 95–98% of responses learned. The authors point out that the positive results might have been heightened by teaching recombinations of known items before introducing unknown items (Goldstein et al., 1987; Goldstein & Mousetis, 1989).

Lutzker and Sherman (1974) investigated generalized use of two sentence forms corresponding to subject–verb agreement (e.g., "Boy is running" versus "Boys are running") in response to appropriate pictures. The authors pretrained expressive labelling of the pictures, which depicted either a single object or two objects, as well as different activities. The main training consisted of teaching use of the appropriate auxiliary verb when answering the question "What's happening?" in a complete sentence. Four of five children began to produce correct sentences in response to untrained pictures following training. Although the researchers did not use matrix training, Wetherby (1978) pointed out that their work could be analysed within the miniature linguistic system framework because of the repetition and overlap among trained units (e.g., "boy is fishing," "boys are fishing," "cow is running," "cows are running"). In summary, when two- and three-word phrases and simple sentences are trained in the context of several and varied stimuli that contain overlapping components, the emergence of novel labels in response to new arrangements of the trained stimulus components demonstrates recombinative generalization.

The role of recombinative generalization in teaching early literacy skills (e.g., naming printed words or spelling) has been shown in studies examining recombination of within-word units. Within-word units are syllables, onsets (the consonant or consonant cluster, which precedes the vowel in a syllable) or rimes (the vowel and succeeding consonants), morphemes, and individual phonemes (Bernstein & Treiman, 2003).

A series of studies by Guess and colleagues demonstrated that parts of words could be recombined (e.g., Guess, 1969). Guess, Sailor, Rutherford, and Baer (1968), for example, taught a girl with mental retardation to correctly label objects when they were presented singly or in pairs. The trained expressive responses to objects in pairs contained /s/ at the end (e.g., "cups"). The generalized use of the plural morpheme /s/ emerged following training of a several singular and plural labels. The generalization results can be conceptualized as abstraction of the plural morpheme /s/ in the presence of more than one object. Thus, a novel stimulus configuration—several of the same object (the participant had learned to name a single object)—resulted in a recombination of the name of the object with the /s/.

Mueller, Olmi, and Saunders (2000) investigated recombinative generalization of within-syllable units (i.e., onsets and rimes) using matrix training. Three kindergartners were taught, using a match-to-sample procedure, to select several printed words containing overlapping onsets and rimes (e.g., mat/sat/sop/sug) upon hearing those words. The researchers were interested in whether the children would correctly select untrained printed words formed by rearranging letters of the trained words (e.g., mop/mug). The three participants demonstrated generalization after little training (on one or two word sets out of six). This performance indicates the recombination of onset and rime units. The researchers also asked the participants to name the 21 words used in the study before and after the match-to-sample training. None of the children read any of the words at the beginning of the study. At the end, the participants read 65%, 0%, and 20% of the words. The word naming results for the first participant suggest, similar to the de Rose, de Souza, and Hanna (1996) study, the development of control by smaller units (individual phonemes in this case). Because there was a considerable overlap in letters among the study words (e.g., "mop" and "map"), the first participant's word naming was most likely under the control of all of the letters. Such performance is not common in beginning readers as they often name words based on the first letter only (Ehri, 1992).

Finally, Goswami (1993) showed that when young prereaders were taught to read a "clue" word (e.g., "bug"), they were more likely to read correctly untrained words with a rime that overlapped with the "clue" word (e.g., "rug"). However, the generalization results were modest, potentially due to a lack of prerequisite skills for complete generalization (i.e., cue words containing the initial consonants were taught). Goswami (1986) referred to the children's performance as reading by analogy, but the participants' performance was clearly an example of recombination.

To conclude this section, recombinative generalization is a process involved in generative responding in language acquisition and in early literacy skills (de Rose et al., 1996; Wetherby & Striefel, 1978). Matrix training approaches to recombinative generalization have been shown to produce functional language and this approach appears to hold promise for learning more about basic processes involved in language acquisition.

CONDITIONS NECESSARY FOR SUCCESSFUL RECOMBINATION

One condition that has been shown to result in generalized responding is conditional discrimination (Saunders & Spradlin, 1990, 1993). Conditional discrimination is a discrimination in which responding to a certain stimulus is reinforced depending on an additional—conditional—stimulus (Catania, 1998; Saunders & Williams, 1998). For example, a child may say "cat" when presented with the printed word "cat" and asked "What does it say?" or he might say "c" when asked "What letter does this word start with?" Which response to a printed word "cat" is reinforced depends on the teacher's question.

In order to successfully recombine multiple-term phrases (e.g., blue cup, yellow plate), a child must learn multiple-term conditional discrimination. In the example given, the conditional discrimination would be two-term (adjective-noun). The conditional discrimination is possible when, during teaching of "blue cup" and "yellow plate," distracters for both terms (adjective and noun) are present (i.e., blue cup, yellow cup, blue plate, yellow plate). If the discriminative stimulus is "blue cup" and on the table there are a blue cup, a yellow cup, and a blue plate, the response becomes conditional when the adjective determines which cup is correct (i.e., the blue cup). In other words, the adjective "blue" is a conditional stimulus. A correct conditional discrimination is only made when both terms are simultaneously discriminated to produce one correct response. Thus, acquisition of multiple-term conditional discriminations results in attending to all terms comprising the discriminative stimulus. If, then, those terms are recombined in novel ways (e.g., blue plate, yellow cup) and stimulus elements continue to exert precise and appropriate control over corresponding portions of the response, successful recombination has occurred. Peterson et al. (2003) show examples of teaching two-term (e.g., subject-action), three-term (e.g., action-adjective-object), four-term (e.g., subject-preposition-adjective-object), and five-term (subject-action-preposition-adjective-object) discriminations. In practice, effective conditional discrimination may be trained to the eight-term level (e.g., adjective-adjective-subject-action-adverb-preposition-adjective-object).

The discriminations required for successful recombinations seem to fit well the definition of "abstraction," as proposed by Catania (1998): Namely, abstraction is a discrimination based on a single property of a stimulus, independent of other properties; thus, generalization to other stimuli with that property (p. 250). Abstraction is demonstrated when an individual correctly identifies untrained stimuli based on the property of interest (e.g., if the property is "redness," abstraction is shown when a child identifies a red, and not a blue, ball the first time the child sees the red ball). Saunders (2002) distinguishes between visual abstraction (discrimination based on a visual property of a stimulus) and auditory abstraction (discrimination based on an auditory property). Visual and auditory abstractions seem to play a role in the development of early literacy skills. That is, in order to establish a basic reading repertoire, beginning readers must name printed words they have been taught and words they have not previously encountered (Ehri, 1991). Prereaders are more likely to demonstrate these performances if they master the alphabetic principle (Foorman et al., 2003; Thompson, 1999). The alphabetic principle refers to "useable knowledge

of the fact that phonemes can be represented by letters, such that whenever a particular phoneme occurs in a word, and in whatever position, it can be represented by the same letter" (Byrne, 1998, p. 313). Thus, in the next section, I discuss the role of visual and auditory abstraction in the development of the alphabetic principle.

Visual abstraction involves recognizing individual printed letters or letter combinations within the complex, whole-word stimuli (Saunders, Johnston, & Brady, 2000). For example, a student is shown the printed word "six" and taught to select printed words that begin with the same letter (e.g., "sat, sick, set" and not "pat, pick, pet"). If, later, on a test, when presented with the written word "six," the student independently selects the untrained words "simple, sage, sill" and not "pimple, page, pill," the student would demonstrate visual abstraction of the printed letter "s." When investigating the acquisition of the alphabetic principle, the visual part, as compared to the auditory part, of the letter–sound relation has received little attention from practitioners and scientists (Saunders et al., 2000). One reason for this might be that teachers and researchers assume that students who discriminate printed letters presented in isolation can also focus on individual letters or letter combinations within whole words. However, that is sometimes not the case, especially with young prereaders or individuals with mental retardation (NICHD, PO1 HD18955-18S1A1; Snow, Burns, & Griffin, 1998).

Saunders and colleagues (2000) reported that typically developing prereaders showed at least 90% accuracy at matching individual letters. In contrast, their accuracy on matching consonant-vowel-consonant (CVC) words that differed only in the initial letter was sometimes at chance levels. The children's responding did not indicate that they visually abstracted the initial consonant, that is, made a discrimination based on this property of the written stimuli. The authors concluded that failing to isolate individual letters embedded in words could compromise linking appropriate phonemes to those letters, thus demonstrating the alphabetic principle.

Similarly, McCandliss, Beck, Sandak, and Perfetti (2003) asserted that focusing attention on each individual letter within a word may play an important role in learning to name and identify novel words. The authors supported their assertion by investigating the effectiveness of an instructional programme that taught children to form and read words by manipulating a single letter in a previously constructed word. A child was, for example, taught to change "sat" to "sap" to "tap" to "top," etc and to name those words. The authors attributed positive effects of the intervention, in part, to the fact that the programme trained the children to attend to each letter and link it to the appropriate phoneme. However, this study did not provide empirical evidence for this claim because the authors did not specifically evaluate the role of visual abstraction.

Finally, Byrne (1992) investigated the differences in learning to name printed words that were visually more similar (e.g., rat, ran, rag) or less similar (e.g., two, boo, you). The results showed that the participants learned the less similar words more readily and with fewer mistakes. The authors concluded that the difficulties in naming similar words might have been related to the visual, not auditory, resemblance and, potentially, to the children's lack of skill in focusing on individual letters. This study provides indirect evidence that if children do not abstract individual letters within a word, they might not read similar words correctly. In summary, visual abstraction is a component of learning the alphabetic principle. Although there are few studies on the role of visual abstraction, this skill seems to be logically necessary for learning to name novel words (Snow et al., 1998). However, it is not sufficient. Visual abstraction must be accompanied by auditory abstraction if children are to master early reading skills (Byrne, 1992).

Auditory abstraction involves recognizing individual sounds or sound combinations within a spoken word (Saunders, 2002). For example, a student is taught that the spoken words "mat, milk, mouth" start with the same /m/ sound and that "sat, silly, sandwich" all start with the same /s/ sound. If, on the test, the student responds correctly to the question: "Which word starts with the same sound as 'mat,' is it 'mum' or 'sum'?", the student would demonstrate auditory abstraction of the sound /m/. Thus, following Catania's (1998) definition of abstraction, auditory abstraction is a discrimination based on a single phoneme in a word, independent of other phonemes, so there can be generalization to other words with that phoneme. In terms of reading, if children learn to break spoken words into smaller units and to relate those units to printed letters within words, they will be demonstrating the alphabetic principle (Murray, 1998).

Traditionally, individual phonemes have been the starting point in teaching children to read (e.g., Buchanan, 1973). More recently, however, researchers have shown that larger sound segments (e.g., onset and rime) might be abstracted by children earlier than individual phonemes (Treiman, 1992; Treiman & Zukowski, 1996). In a syllable, the term "onset" refers to the initial consonant and "rime" to the vowel and subsequent consonants (e.g., in "run," "r" is the onset and "un" is the rime) (Bernstein & Treiman, 2003). Consequently, studies examining the role of auditory abstraction in the development of the alphabetic principle focused on onsets and rimes.

Byrne and Fielding-Barnsley (1989, 1990, 1991, 1993, 1995) have conducted a series of experiments investigating the conditions necessary for mastery of the alphabetic principle. They mainly investigated onset sounds. In the 1989 study, for example, the researchers first taught 12 typically developing preschoolers to name two written words ("mat" and "sat"). Then, the researchers administered segment identity training, which consisted of teaching each child that a testing word (e.g., "mum") has the same onset as the training word (e.g., "mat"). Five children mastered the segment identity task, but none performed correctly on the transfer task (answering the question: "Does this say 'sum' or 'mum'?" when presented with the written word "mum"). Finally, the children were trained on letter–sound relations. That is, they were taught that the letter "m" corresponds to the sound /m/ and the letter "s" to the sound /s/. All 12 children learned this relation. During the next transfer test, six children showed generalization. Five of those children mastered both segment identity and letter–sound correspondence training. From this and other studies in the series (e.g., Byrne & Fielding-Barnsley, 1990, 1991), the authors concluded that the two skills necessary for the development of the alphabetic principle were segment identity and letter–sound relation.

Segment identity is auditory abstraction. That is, segment identity training taught the children to isolate the onset from the rest of the word and to discriminate among words based on their onsets. The reported studies also showed that once children master auditory abstraction for a particular phoneme in a particular position, they are likely to generalize this skill to other phonemes in other positions (Byrne & Fielding-Barnsley, 1990, 1991). However, it appears that auditory abstraction is not sufficient for mastery of the alphabetic principle. It needs to be supplemented by direct letter–sound training (Fielding-Barnsley, 1997). Both skills in combination seem to promote acquisition of the alphabetic principle and early reading skills.

Saunders (NICHD, PO1 HD18955-18S1A1) also examined conditions necessary to establish the alphabetic principle. Regarding onset abstraction, the researchers taught five typically developing kindergartners and three adults with mental retardation (MR) to select the printed letters "m" or "s" corresponding to the onset sound of several spoken CVC words beginning with those letters. Essentially, the researchers trained segment identity and letter–sound correspondence at the same time. All of the children and two adults with MR readily selected the letter corresponding to the onset sound of words they had not been trained on (NICHD, PO1 HD18955-18S1A1), while one adult with MR required some additional training before generalization was shown (Vaidya & Saunders, 2000). Those results clearly indicate abstracted stimulus control by the onset sound, which is a component of the alphabetic principle.

In the Mueller et al. (2000) study, auditory abstraction of both onsets and rime units was investigated in the context of selecting novel printed words upon hearing them read. Two children demonstrated generalization after training on one set only and the third child after training on two sets. All three children continued to select untrained words throughout six word sets. This performance indicates that the children abstracted onset and rime units and demonstrated the alphabetic principle. The skills that the children had to master to select untrained words were: (1) discriminating letters within written words, (2) discriminating phonemes within spoken words, and (3) relating those phonemes to printed letters. The results of Mueller et al. were reproduced using adults with mental retardation by Saunders, O'Donnell, Vaidya, and Williams (2003).

Goswami (1986, 1993) and de Rose et al. (1996) also demonstrated, although they did not directly assess, the role of auditory abstraction in early reading. De Rose et al. showed that three of seven children who were taught to read 51 words, read correctly at least 65% of the 45 untrained words. The untrained words were constructed by rearranging the syllables of the training words. Thus, correct performance on the generalization task indicated that the children learned that spoken words consist of syllables (i.e., auditory abstraction) and that those syllables correspond to specific letter combinations no matter in which word they occur or in what position. The three children's performance demonstrated the alphabetic principle.

To conclude this section, two conditions that seem to be necessary for successful recombination of whole words and within-word units are mastery of multiple-term conditional discrimination and ability to visually and auditory abstract.

SUGGESTIONS FOR PROGRAMMING RECOMBINATIVE GENERALIZATION

Teaching in a way that promotes recombinative generalization is very important because of its role in generative responding. The most important suggestion is to *programme* for recombination. One way to achieve this is to teach with the use of matrix training, which ensures that the trained words incorporate all of the test-word components. Matrix training can be used for whole-word or within-word unit recombinations and correct recombinations may be facilitated if the matrix consists in part of known items. The second suggestion is to not overlook the role of visual and auditory abstraction in basic literacy skills. Reading/writing of novel words will be possible if the child learns that a spoken/written word consists of smaller units (e.g., syllables), and that those units correspond to specific letter combinations, no matter what their position. Furthermore, successful recombinations may be hastened by establishing multiple-term conditional discrimination performance. Before each multiple-term discrimination is taught, each component term should be taught until generative. Lastly, successful recombinations may be promoted if, during teaching, equivalence classes are formed, especially in the context of reading and writing. Thus, procedures that facilitate development of relations between printed words, dictated words, and environmental events or their corresponding pictures should be used in teaching.

To summarize, recombinative generalization contributes to achieving functional language. Learning more about this process is important for both researchers and teachers. For a researcher, a child's correct identification of untrained words/phrases (in an expressive or receptive task) indicates that this child's responding is under the control of small units that were not presented independently, but rather developed from larger units (Skinner, 1957). For a teacher, the same performance indicates that this child does not always have to be taught to respond to every single novel stimulus, but rather that generative responding might emerge. Further research on recombinative generalization will broaden the understanding of basic processes and their application to teaching language and early literacy skills.

REFERENCES

Bergman, J. D., & Gerdtz, J. (1997). Behavioral interventions. In D. J. Cohen & F. R. Volkmar

(Eds.), *Handbook of autism and pervasive developmental disorders*. New York: Wiley.

Bernstein, S. E., & Treiman, R. (2003). Learning a novel grapheme: Effects of positional and phonemic context on children's spelling. *Journal of Experimental Child Psychology, 79*, 56–77.

Buchanan, C. D. (1973). *Teacher's guide to programmed reading* (rev. ed., Book 1, Series 1). St Louis, MO: McGraw-Hill.

Byrne, B. (1992). Studies in the acquisition procedure for reading: Rationale, hypotheses, and data. In P. B. Gough, L. C. Ehri, & R. Treiman (Eds.), *Reading acquisition* (pp. 1–34). Hillsdale, NJ: Lawrence Erlbaum Associates Inc.

Byrne, B. (1998). *The foundation of literacy: The child's acquisition of the alphabetic principle*. Hove, UK: Psychology Press.

Byrne, B., & Fielding-Barnsley, R. (1989). Phonemic awareness and letter knowledge in the child's acquisition of the alphabetic principle. *Journal of Educational Psychology, 81*, 313–321.

Byrne, B., & Fielding-Barnsley, R. (1990). Acquiring the alphabetic principle: A case for teaching recognition of phoneme identity. *Journal of Educational Psychology, 82*, 805–812.

Byrne, B., & Fielding-Barnsley, R. (1991). Evaluation of a program to teach phonemic awareness to young children. *Journal of Educational Psychology, 83*, 451–455.

Byrne, B., & Fielding-Barnsley, R. (1993). Evaluation of a program to teach phonemic awareness to young children: A 1-year follow-up. *Journal of Educational Psychology, 85*, 104–111.

Byrne, B., & Fielding-Barnsley, R. (1995). Evaluation of a program to teach phonemic awareness to young children: A 2- and 3-year follow-up and a new preschool trial. *Journal of Educational Psychology, 87*, 488–503.

Catania, A. C. (1998). *Learning*. Upper Saddle River, NJ: Prentice-Hall.

de Rose, J. C., de Souza, D. G., & Hanna, E. S. (1996). Teaching reading and spelling: Exclusion and stimulus equivalence. *Journal of Applied Behavior Analysis, 29*, 451–469.

Ehri, L. C. (1991). Development of the ability to read words. In R. Barr, M. Kamil, P. B. Mosenthal, & P. D. Pearson (Eds.), *Handbook of reading research, Vol. 2* (pp. 383–417). New York: Longman.

Ehri, L. C. (1992). Reconceptualizing the development of sight word reading and its relationship to recoding. In P. B. Gough, L. C. Ehri, & R. Treiman (Eds.), *Reading acquisition* (pp. 107–143). Hillsdale, NJ: Lawrence Erlbaum Associates Inc.

Esper, E. A. (1925). A technique for the experimental investigation of associative interference in artificial linguistic material. *Language Monographs, No. 1.*

Esper, E. A. (1933). Studies in linguistic behavior organization: I. Characteristics of unstable verbal reactions. *The Journal of General Psychology, 8*, 346–379.

Fielding-Barnsley, R. (1997). Explicit instruction in decoding benefits children high in phonemic awareness and alphabet knowledge. *Scientific Studies of Reading, 1*, 85–98.

Foorman, B. R., Chen, D. T., Carlson, C., Moats, L., Francis, D. J., & Fletcher, J. M. (2003). The necessity of the alphabetic principle to phonemic awareness instruction. *Reading and Writing: An Interdisciplinary Journal, 16*, 289–324.

Foss, D. J. (1968a). An analysis of learning in a miniature linguistic system. *Journal of Experimental Psychology, 76*, 450–459.

Foss, D. J. (1968b). Learning and discovery in the acquisition of structured material: Effects of number of items and their sequence. *Journal of Experimental Psychology, 77*, 341–344.

Goldstein, H. (1983). Recombinative generalization: Relationship between environmental conditions and the linguistic repertoires of language learners. *Analysis and Intervention in Developmental Disabilities, 3*, 279–293.

Goldstein, H. (1993). Structuring environmental input to facilitate generalized language learning by children with mental retardation. In A. P. Kaiser & D. B. Gray (Eds.), *Enhancing children's communication: Research foundations for intervention, Vol. 2* (pp. 317–334). Baltimore: Brookes.

Goldstein, H., Angelo, D., & Mousetis, L. (1987). Acquisition and extension of syntactic repertoires by severely mentally retarded youth. *Research in Developmental Disabilities, 8*, 549–574.

Goldstein, H., & Mousetis, L. (1989). Generalized language learning with severe mental retardation: Effects of peers' expressive modeling. *Journal of Applied Behavior Analysis, 22*, 245–259.

Goswami, U. (1986). Children's use of analogy in learning to read: A developmental study. *Journal of Experimental Child Psychology, 42*, 73–83.

Goswami, U. (1993). Toward an interactive analogy model of reading development: Decoding vowel graphemes in beginning reading. *Journal of Experimental Child Psychology, 56*, 443–475.

Guess, D. (1969). A functional analysis of receptive language and productive speech: Acquisition of the plural morpheme. *Journal of Applied Behavior Analysis, 2*, 55–64.

Guess, G., Sailor, W., Rutherford, G., & Baer, D. M. (1968). An experimental analysis of linguistic development: The productive use of the plural morpheme. *Journal of Applied Behavior Analysis, 1*, 297–306.

Lord, C., & McGee, J. P. (2001). *Educating children with autism*. Washington, DC: National Academy Press.

Lutzker, J. R., & Sherman, J. A. (1974). Producing generative sentence usage by imitation and reinforcement procedures. *Journal of Applied Behavior Analysis, 7*, 447–460.

McCandliss, B., Beck, I. L., Sandak, R., & Perfetti, C. (2003). Focusing attention of decoding for children with poor reading skills: Design and preliminary tests of the word building intervention. *Scientific Studies of Reading, 7*, 75–104.

Mueller, M. M., Olmi, D. J., & Saunders, K. J. (2000). Recombinative generalization of within-syllable units in prereading children. *Journal of Applied Behavior Analysis, 33*, 515–531.

Murray, B. A. (1998). Gaining alphabetic insight: Is phoneme manipulation skill or identity knowledge causal? *Journal of Educational Psychology, 90*, 461–475.

NICHD, PO1 HD18955-18S1A1, 2001-2005, *Generative recombination at the single word level*. Saunders, K. J.

Peterson, G. B., Larsson, E. V., & Riedesel, K. L. (2003). A conceptual toolkit for intensive behavioral intervention teachers. *Journal of Behavioral Education, 12*, 131–146.

Saunders, K. J. (2002, October). *Abstraction and recombinative generalization of within-syllable units.* Invited presentation at the Southeastern Association for Behavior Analysis, Charleston, SC.

Saunders, K. J., Johnston, M. D., & Brady, N. C. (2000). Identity matching of consonant-vowel-consonant words by prereaders. *Journal of Applied Behavior Analysis, 33*, 309–312.

Saunders, K. J., O'Donnell, J., Vaidya, M., & Williams, D. C. (2003). Recombinative generalization of within-syllable units in nonreading adults with mental retardation. *Journal of Applied Behavior Analysis, 36*, 95–99.

Saunders, K. J., & Spradlin, J. E. (1990). Conditional discrimination in mentally retarded adults: The development of generalized skill. *Journal of the Experimental Analysis of Behavior, 54*, 239–250.

Saunders, K. J., & Spradlin, J. E. (1993). Conditional discrimination in mentally retarded subjects: Programming acquisition and learning set. *Journal of the Experimental Analysis of Behavior, 60*, 571–585.

Saunders, K. J., & Williams, D. C. (1998). Stimulus-control procedures. In K. A. Lattal & M. Perone (Eds.), *Handbook of research methods in human operant behavior* (pp. 193–228). New York: Plenum.

Schumaker, J., & Sherman, J. (1970). Training generative verb usage by imitation and reinforcement procedures. *Journal of Applied Behavior Analysis, 3*, 273–287.

Skinner, B. F. (1957). *Verbal behavior.* New York: Appleton-Century-Crofts.

Snow, C.E., Burns, M.S., & Griffin, P. (Eds.). (1998). *Preventing reading difficulties in young children.* Washington, DC: National Academy Press.

Striefel, S., Bryan, K. S., & Aikins, D. A. (1974). Transfer of stimulus control from motor to verbal stimuli. *Journal of Applied Behavior Analysis, 7*, 123–135.

Striefel, S., & Wetherby, B. (1973). Instruction-following behavior of a retarded child and its controlling stimuli. *Journal of Applied Behavior Analysis, 6*, 663–670.

Striefel, S., Wetherby, B., & Karlan, G. R. (1976). Establishing generalized verb-noun instruction-following skills in retarded children. *Journal of Experimental Child Psychology, 22*, 247–260.

Striefel, S., Wetherby, B., & Karlan, G. R. (1978). Developing generalized instruction-following behavior in severely retarded people. In C. E. Meyers (Ed.), *Quality of life in severely and profoundly mentally retarded people: Research foundations and improvement.* Washington, DC: American Association on Mental Deficiency.

Thompson, G. B. (1999). The processes of learning to identify words. In G. B. Thompson & T. Nicholson (Eds.), *Learning to read: Beyond phonics and whole language* (pp. 25–54). New York: Teachers College Press.

Treiman, R. (1992). The role of intrasyllabic units in learning to read and spell. In P. B. Gough, L. C. Ehri, & R. Treiman (Eds.), *Reading acquisition* (pp. 65–106). Hillsdale, NJ: Lawrence Erlbaum Associates Inc.

Treiman, R., & Zukowski, A. (1996). Children's sensitivity to syllables, onsets, rimes, and phonemes. *Journal of Experimental Child Psychology, 61*, 193–215.

Vaidya, M., & Saunders, K. J. (2000). Establishing abstracted stimulus control by the beginning sounds of spoken words in an adult with mental retardation. *Experimental Analysis of Human Behavior Bulletin, 18*, 30–32.

Wetherby, B. (1978). Miniature languages and the functional analysis of verbal behavior. In R. L. Schiefelbusch (Ed.), *Language intervention series: Bases of language interventions, Vol. 1* (pp. 397–448). Baltimore: University Park Press.

Wetherby, B., & Striefel, S. (1978). Application of miniature linguistic system or matrix training procedures. In R. L. Schiefelbusch (Ed.), *Language intervention series: Language intervention strategies, Vol. 2* (pp. 317–356). Baltimore: University Park Press.

INTERNATIONAL JOURNAL OF PSYCHOLOGY, 2006, 41 (6), 523–526

Psychology Press
Taylor & Francis Group

Training parents and professionals to help children with autism in China: The contribution of behaviour analysis

Guo Yanqing

Peking University, Beijing, China

A training programme is presented with two parts. (1) Professional training is received by graduate students at the Institute for Mental Health of Beijing University, based on the principles of behaviour assessment and modification, radical behaviourism, and applied research methods. (2) Parent training focused on parents with autistic children, using the behaviour analysis and modification methods. China has between 400,000 and 800,000 children with autism. In comparison to its fast economic growth the development of social welfare and social insurance systems are far behind. Once the child is diagnosed with autism, the parents or the primary caregivers of the child, not the government or the community, take the responsibility for the child's rehabilitation. The diagnosis of autism was first introduced in China in 1982, and for years the work was based on clinical appearances and diagnosis. The main mission of child psychiatrists was early diagnosis, but there was little change obtained with autistic children. From the year 2000 more people were interested in rehabilitation rather than in diagnosis and medical treatments. Behaviour analysis methods are now extensively used in interventions in children with autism in this country. There is a great need in China for this kind of work, but there are few professionals with the appropriate scientific knowledge and skills to work with autistic children. These professionals will help to further develop the area of behaviour analysis in China.

*U*n programme d'entraînement est présenté en deux parties: (1) l'entraînement professionnel est reçu par les étudiants gradués à l'Institut pour la Santé Mentale de l'Université de Beijing, basé sur les principes de l'évaluation et de la modification du comportement, le comportementalisme (ou le behaviorisme) radical et les méthodes de recherche appliquées. (2) Un entraînement aux parents centré sur les enfants autistes, en utilisant l'analyse comportementale et les méthodes de modification. La Chine possède entre 400,000 et 800,000 enfants avec autisme. En comparaison avec sa rapide croissance économique, le développement du bien-être social et des systèmes d'assurance sociale sont loin derrière. Une fois l'enfant diagnostiqué avec l'autisme, ce sont les parents ou les premiers soignants, et non pas le gouvernement ou la communauté, qui prennent la responsabilité de la réadaptation de l'enfant. Le diagnostic de l'autisme a été introduit en Chine pour la première fois en 1982, et pendant des années le travail était basé sur les apparences cliniques et sur le diagnostic. La mission principale des pédopsychiatres était le diagnostic précoce mais il y avait peu de changement obtenu avec les enfants autistes. Depuis l'année 2000, plus de personnes se sont intéressées à la réadaptation plutôt qu'au diagnostic et aux traitements médicaux. Les méthodes d'analyse comportementale sont maintenant utilisées extensivement dans l'intervention auprès des enfants avec autisme dans ce pays. Il y a une forte demande en Chine pour ce genre de travail mais il existe peu de professionnels avec les connaissances scientifiques et les compétences appropriées pour travailler avec les enfants autistes. Ces professionnels aideront à développer davantage le domaine de l'analyse comportementale en Chine.

*S*e presenta un programa de entrenamiento con dos partes: (1) Entrenamiento profesional que reciben estudiantes graduados en el Instituto de Salud Mental de la Universidad de Beijing (China), basado en los principios de la evaluación y la modificación conductuales, el conductismo radical, y los métodos de investigación aplicada. (2) Entrenamiento a padres centrado en aquéllos que tienen niños autistas, utilizando el análisis conductual y los métodos de modificación. China posee entre 400,000 y 800,000 niños con autismo. En comparación con su rápido desarrollo económico, el desarrollo del bienestar social y de los sistemas de seguridad social están muy atrás. Cuando a un niño se le diagnostica con autismo, la responsabilidad de su rehabilitación recae en los padres o en los cuidadores, y no en el gobierno o en la comunidad. El diagnóstico de autismo se

---

Correspondence should be addressed to Guo Yanqing, Institute of Mental Health, Peking University, Beijing, China, 100083 (E-mail: gyq1201@sohu.com).

DOI: 10.1080/00207590500492575

introdujo por primera vez en China en 1982 y durante años el trabajo con esta población se limitó al aspecto clínico y al diagnóstico. La principal misión de los psiquiatras infantiles fue el diagnóstico temprano, pero se lograron pocos cambios con los niños autistas. A partir del año 2000 más y más personas se interesaron en la rehabilitación que en el diagnóstico y en los tratamientos médicos. Los métodos del análisis conductual se utilizan ahora extensamente en las intervenciones con niños en autismo en este país. Existe en China una gran necesidad para esta clase de trabajo, pero hay muy pocos profesionales con los conocimientos científicos apropiados y con las habilidades para trabajar con niños autistas. Tales profesionales ayudarán eficazmente a desarrollar el área del análisis conductual en China.

BACKGROUND OF TRAINING CHILDREN WITH AUTISM IN CHINA

China is the most populous country in the world. According to the State Statistics Bureau, up to the end of 2004, China had a population of 1,299,880,000, with 279,470,000 children between 0 and 14 years of age. It is estimated that there are at least 400,000 to 800,000 children with autism. In comparison to its fast economic growth, the development of social welfare and social insurance systems in China lag far behind. Once a child is diagnosed with autism, usually it is not the government or community but rather the parents or the primary caregivers of the child who take responsibility for the child's rehabilitation.

The diagnosis of autism was first introduced and described in China in 1982, more than 40 years later than Leo Kanner's first descriptions of such cases in the West. In nearly 10 years, the main interests in autism were based on clinical appearances and diagnosis; many kinds of hypothesis were suggested without any effective treatments being provided. During the next 10 years (1990 to 2000), early diagnosis was still the main mission of child psychiatrists in dealing with autistic children. However, there was a little change during this period; many self-help organizations, such as the *Beijing Association of Rehabilitation for Autistic Children* (BARAC, founded in 1993) were established. Although many of these organizations could not provide any specific directions or instructions on rehabilitation, they at least provided an opportunity for parents to share their feelings and experiences, and helped parents face their difficulties with a more realistic attitude and in a more rational way. From the year 2000, more and more people are now interested in rehabilitation rather than diagnosis and medical treatments. Behaviour analysis has been mentioned more often, and is popular in all kinds of newly established centres. However, the work carried out by professionals is not as good as it should be. At the same time, parents still lack knowledge and skills about rehabilitation; they just blindly invest their energy and money in such newly established centres. Each parent starts with hope, followed afterwards by a deep feeling of failure and despair. Both parents and professionals are in great need of any true effective intervention information, knowledge, and skills.

Behaviour analysis methods and techniques have been developed very well in Western countries and are now extensively used in interventions in children with autism in China. In considering them, a programme focused on training parents to train their children at home was developed. Concurrently, professionals would also be trained gradually to meet professional guidelines for parents and professional services for children with autism. The professional training sessions would not only educate professionals to provide support for parents with autistic children, but also foster interest in several areas of applied behaviour analysis.

PARENTAL TRAINING PROGRAMMES

Training materials

Guidelines for parental training at home. This is a training manual made up of the PowerPoint presentations of the lectures. It includes the behavioural characteristics of children with autism, the experiences of parents facing children with autism, applied behaviour analysis and autism, the principles of behaviour analysis, strategies for enhancing children's social-communicative interactions, and operating skills and procedures. This manual is the main reference during the short-term on-site training period.

Typical behaviour analysis programmes for children with autism. This is a manual that parents can refer to and adapt to their own children's conditions. It is edited from the translation of part of the book *Behavioural Interventions for Young Children with Autism*, edited by Catherine Maurice.

Activity schedules for children with autism. This is a translation of a book with the same title, which tells parents or professionals how to teach independent behaviour to children with autism. Once the children with autism make the connections between schedules and behaviours (or activity), they would behave more like a normal child in a familiar background, or even in some unfamiliar environments once they get their schedules.

Training process

For each of the training sessions, the process will be divided into three parts. The first part focuses on theoretical training; the training manual of *Guidelines for Parental Training at Home* is a framework for this. The second part focuses on hand-in-hand instructions on training skills and processes of teaching models, such as discrete trial, incidental teaching, most-to-least prompting, least-to-most prompting, the observation and assessment of behaviour, etc. We also provide videotaped records to illustrate the models of correct and incorrect behaviour in the training process at this period. The third part focuses on post-training activities, for those who will do training tasks by themselves at home. A videotaped follow-up service is provided on appointment. The initial training protocol is done with the cooperation of parents and professionals, and the following changes of the protocol are done by the parent under the guidance of professionals. The videotaped follow-up is usually intensive at the beginning, for example, twice a week for the first month. However, it will fade out as parents progress in their training procedure. After 2 or 3 months of follow-up, parents are competent to perform training protocols independently, and then they can get help on appointment if required. For those who do not want to do the training themselves, we provide professional training on site at the rehabilitation centre.

TRAINING TASKS AND RESULTS

Three training sessions have been finished and altogether 129 parents from 67 families (17 for the first session, 24 for the second session, and 26 for the third session) have benefited from them. For each session, both parents would be encouraged to participate. Each training session provides 32 hours of training and flexible hours of videotaped follow-ups on appointment. For the first training session, there were three families, for the second training session three families, and in the third session five families who performed training

tasks and made videotaped follow-ups on appointments. All have been very successful in training children and are satisfied with the processes and outcomes of their children. All the families who participated in the training sessions think such training is very helpful for them, both in understanding and in controlling their children's behaviour. For those (56) who did not make videotaped follow-ups on appointments, most (37) of the families also tried to perform training tasks using behaviour analysis methods for at least for a week; however, only a few of them persisted. The main reasons they stopped were the problematic behaviours the children exhibited during the training processes and their own lack of confidence in doing such tasks. For those (35) who also sent their children to institutional training centres, the feedback from the institution professionals showed that these parents were more cooperative and more understanding about the training processes and training contents. The training sessions are described in Table 1.

The results of the parental training sessions indicated that short-term intensive training sessions on theoretical issues and practical issues alone are not enough to allow the family to give long-term training tasks to their children. They need to follow up instructions on both their behavioural performance and their problem-solving skills. However, such training tasks do help parents on the following points: (1) they have a better understanding of their children's problematic behaviours as well as behaviour deficits; (2) they have a better understanding of the difficulties as well as the ways of rehabilitating their children; (3) they become more cooperative with professionals if their children are institutionalized.

PROFESSIONAL TRAINING PROGRAMMES

Professional training takes the form of self-learning combined with room (Salon) discussions. The learning materials are the textbooks or study materials presented by the University of Nevada,

TABLE 1
Description of parental training

Training sessions	No. of families			
	Enrolment	Follow-up	Home training	Centre training
First session	17	3	10 (+3)	11
Second session	24	3	14 (+3)	9
Third session	26	5	13 (+5)	15
Total	67	11	37 (48)	35

Reno (USA), including topics such the ones found in the books *About Behaviorism, Beyond Freedom and Dignity;* radical behaviourism, assessments and intervention strategies, behaviour modification, the science of learning, tactics of scientific research and single case research designs. Most of the Salon members are postgraduate students of the Institute of Mental Health, Peking University. The only requirement to be a Salon member for the postgraduate students is interest; another Salon member is the young psychiatrist from the same Institute. Salon activity, which is now being held on a monthly basis, will be intensified to a weekly basis in the near future. Most Salon members will also participate at least in one or two parental training sessions.

CHALLENGES

The training tasks have just started; there are only a few families who have had the opportunity to be followed up on appointment. Many others are not yet proficient in training children with autism, and have been unable to get sufficient instructions from trained professionals. Some of them might give up training and depend again upon the institutions or training centres.

A few of the followed-up families also have problems. First, we did not have a very good assessment or evaluation system that could give us a comprehensive description of the profile of any individualized child with autism—his/her unique behavioural characteristics on social, language and communication, and play activity. Although each of the followed-up cases reported great progress in attention, communication, and self-management skills, we lack integrated evaluations of such progresses, which could tell us in detail how far and in what degree they are behind normal children. Second, we are not good at providing instructions on incidental teaching strategies. Incidental teaching strategies are very important because they provide opportunities for children with autism to learn social or communicating skills in a normal background or context. Third, we are not very good at instructing parents to use all kinds of communicating systems, such as gestures, pictures, and communication books. Fourth, we also need to continue working on how to teach children with autism to use token systems and activity schedules.

INTERNATIONAL JOURNAL OF PSYCHOLOGY, 2006, 41 (6), 527–540

Operant conditioning and errorless learning procedures in the treatment of chronic aphasia

Zuilma Gabriela Sigurðardóttir and Magnús Blöndahl Sighvatsson

University of Iceland, Reykjavik, Iceland

*I*n the field of aphasia, the processes that enable improvements in fluent speech, e.g., in naming, reading, sentence structure, etc., are not well understood. At the present time the fields of cognitive psychology, clinical neuropsychology, and cognitive neuropsychology are limited with regard to explaining the causes of different symptoms of aphasia. Treatment based on operant conditioning or stimulus control procedures seems to be very promising. In the present study, four participants with chronic aphasia, aged between 52 and 62 years, received treatment based on errorless learning procedures and operant conditioning for 7 months. Treatment effects were evaluated with a multiple-baseline design across behaviours. The performances that were treated varied across participants but were two or three of the following in each case: naming people or objects, making sentences, sequencing stimuli, discriminating written words, and unassisted recall. Treatment variables were clearly defined and systematically used in standard ways across participants with flexibility for adaptation to individual outcomes using clearly defined criteria. Prompts that were used in training faded out as performances improved. The performances of all participants improved significantly in all tasks; they all reached 100% correct performance without any prompts from the experimenter in at least one task. Generalization measures across stimuli and settings demonstrated that their improved performances generalized to novel stimuli and novel settings.

*D*ans le domaine de l'aphasie, les processus qui facilitent les améliorations du langage fluent, e.g., la nomination, la lecture, la structure de la phrase, etc., ne sont pas bien compris. En ce moment, les domaines de la psychologie cognitive, de la neuropsychologie clinique, et de la neuropsychologie cognitive sont limités en ce qui concerne l'explication des causes des différents symptômes de l'aphasie. Le traitement basé sur le conditionnement opérant ou sur les techniques de contrôle du stimulus semble très prometteur. Dans la présente étude, quatre participants avec une aphasie chronique, âgés entre 52 et 62 ans, ont reçu un traitement basé sur les techniques d'apprentissage sans erreur et le conditionnement opérant pendant sept mois. Les effets du traitement ont été évalués avec un protocole à niveaux de base multiples à travers les comportements. Les performances qui ont été traitées ont varié à travers les participants mais elles étaient deux ou trois des suivantes dans chacun des cas: nommer les gens ou les objets, faire des phrases, faire la séquence des stimuli, discriminer les mots écrits et le rappel non assisté. Les variables du traitement étaient clairement définies et systématiquement utilisées de manière standardisée à travers les participants avec une flexibilité pour pouvoir s'adapter aux résultats individuels en utilisant des critères définis. Les indices qui ont été utilisés pendant l'entraînement ont disparu tout au long de l'amélioration des performances. Les performances de tous les participants se sont améliorées significativement dans toutes les tâches, toutes ont atteint 100% de performance correcte sans aucun indice de la part de l'expérimentateur dans au moins une tâche. Des mesures de généralisation à travers les stimuli et les contextes ont démontré que leurs performances améliorées se sont généralisées aux nouveaux stimuli et aux nouveaux contextes.

*E*n el campo de la afasia, los procesos que permiten lograr mejorías en el lenguaje fluido, por ejemplo nombrar, leer, dar estructura a las frases, etc., no se entienden suficientemente bien. En este momento los campos de la psicología cognitiva, la neuropsicología clínica, y la neuropsicología cognitiva, poseen limitaciones para explicar las causas de los diferentes síntomas de la afasia. El tratamiento basado en el condicionamiento operante o en los procedimientos de control de estímulo parece ser muy promisorio. En el presente estudio cuatro

Correspondence should be addressed to Zuilma Gabriela Sigurðardóttir PhD, Associate Professor, University of Iceland, Psychology Division, Oddi v/ Sturlugötu, 101, Reykjavik, Iceland (E-mail: zuilma@hi.is).

This study was made possible by grants from Iceland's Research Institute, The University of Iceland's Research Fund, and The Students' New Creations Fund in the year 2002. Further information can be acquired from the first author.

DOI: 10.1080/00207590500492625

participantes con afasia crónica, con edades entre los 52 y los 62 años, recibieron tratamiento basado en procedimientos de aprendizaje sin error y en condicionamiento operante durante siete meses. Los efectos del tratamiento se evaluaron con un diseño de base múltiple entre conductas. Las ejecuciones tratadas variaron entre los participantes pero en cada caso eran dos o tres de las siguientes: nombrar personas u objetos, construir frases, hacer secuencias de estímulos, discriminar palabras escritas y recordar sin ayuda. Se definieron clara y sistemáticamente las variables de tratamiento utilizadas en forma estándar a través de los participantes, y con flexibilidad para adaptarlas a los resultados individuales usando criterios claramente definidos. Se usaron instigadores en el entrenamiento que se desvanecieron al mejorar las ejecuciones. Las ejecuciones de todos los participantes mejoraron significativamente en todas las tareas, y siempre alcanzaron el 100% de ejecución correcta sin ninguna instigación del experimentador en al menos una tarea. Las medidas de generalización a través de los estímulos y de los ambientes demostraron que las ejecuciones mejoradas se generalizaban a estímulos nuevos y a ambientes nuevos.

INTRODUCTION

Very few researchers in the field of aphasia have studied the effects of treatment based on operant conditioning or stimulus control procedures. The processes that enable improvement in fluent speech, e.g., in naming, reading, sentence structure, etc., among persons with aphasia are not well understood. Cognitive psychologists have proposed theories about the processes that take place (e.g., perception, discrimination, retrieval) when specific behaviours are displayed (e.g., naming objects or people, reading). Some aphasiologists are looking at available models of normal cognitive processing to understand how those processes may be affected in aphasia (Mitchum, 1994). They compare the performances of people with aphasia to performances of nonaphasics in a certain task (Albert & Helm-Estabrooks, 1988; Thompson, 1996). Unfortunately, neither normal nor abnormal processing is well understood as yet. Presently, the fields of cognitive psychology, clinical neuropsychology, and cognitive neuropsychology remain limited with regard to explaining the causes of different symptoms of aphasia. Direct correspondence between specific parts of the brain and specific components of language is nonexistent (Albert & Helm-Estabrooks, 1988). Plasticity of the brain is not well understood, although recent studies on plasticity as a result of training are enlightening (Raymer, 2001; Thulborn, Carpenter, & Just, 1999). Finally, a clear relation between specific symptoms and underlying deficits has not been established (Hillis, 1989; Thompson, 1996). The process of spontaneous recovery, the reasons why specific interventions affect the performances of aphasics, and the way different types of interventions shown to be effective affect hypothesized cognitive processes remain unknown. As a result, development of treatments based on specific cognitive neuropsychological theories about the

causes of aphasia symptoms is still very slow (Byng & Black, 1995; Mitchum, 1994). Treatment variables that can be linked directly to elements that are believed to be causes of specific symptoms remain undeveloped. However, it has been established that therapy for symptoms of aphasia is effective (Fridriksson & Holland, 2001; Holland, Fromm, DeRuyter, & Stein, 1996; Orange & Kertesz, 1998; Poeck, Huber, & Willmes, 1989; Robey, 1998). Unfortunately, most available language therapy is still poorly specified (Byng & Black, 1995; Robey, 1998). A process of relearning through known learning principles could be the main explanation of patients' improvements both while spontaneous recovery lasts and after that. Treatment seems to speed up recovery at any stage (Robey, 1998). A learning paradigm is an attractive, parsimonious alternative to the cognitive and cognitive neuropsychological approaches in the study of aphasia. A learning paradigm looks at symptoms leading to a diagnosis of aphasia as behavioural deficits that may be rectified with training that is based on known learning principles. Training that is based on learning principles has been used with efficacy, effectiveness, and efficiency with persons with various learning disorders, e.g., developmental disabilities (including autism), learning disabilities, traumatic brain injuries, attention deficit disorder with and without hyperactivity, and psychiatric disorders, to name just a few (Bellack, Hersen, & Kazdin, 1993; Jacobs, 2000). These disorders have sometimes known and sometimes unknown neurological causes that lead to either behavioural excesses and/or deficits. Those excesses and/or deficits interfere with a person's functioning in activities of daily living. The ability to learn from ordinary interactions with the environment is diminished, thus making special and extraordinary ways of teaching and training necessary. A review of the literature on the successes of the behavioural approach to teaching and training persons who have a myriad of learning or adaptation problems due to either an unknown or well-known aetiology is beyond the scope of this article. However, on the basis of what is known about the effects, efficiency, and efficacy of operant conditioning and stimulus control techniques in the field of applied behaviour analysis, a study was undertaken to measure the effects of an intervention for symptoms of aphasia purely based on those techniques.

Effects of treatment based on operant conditioning are most often measured in well-controlled single-subject experimental designs. This methodology is quite common in the literature on effects of treatment for aphasia; however, direct and systematic replications of original studies (Barlow & Hersen, 1984; Sidman, 1960) are uncommon or nonexistent. Direct and systematic replications of single-subject experimental studies of treatment effects are necessary to establish the generality and limitations of those effects. Only with direct and systematic replications of single-subject experimental studies is it possible to ultimately determine which type of therapy is effective for what type of patient with what type of aetiology and symptoms in which particular situation. The systematic search for the generality and limitations of effects on a few individuals of available language therapies for aphasics has not yet begun. Perhaps one of the reasons for this present state is that language treatments have not been well defined (Byng & Black, 1995; Orange & Kertesz, 1998; Robey, 1998).

Definitions and operationalization of treatment variables and treatment procedures is a necessary prerequisite for experimental replication. Treatments that are based on operant procedures and stimulus control are usually well defined, which should make this approach an attractive model for designers of language therapy for aphasia who are trying to find effective, efficient, and efficacious treatments. Unfortunately, only two studies of the effects of operant conditioning on symptoms of aphasia were found in the literature. Bardin Ayers, Potter, and McDermon (1975) monitored the error rate of four aphasic persons who had suffered from aphasia from between 1 month and 10 years. They were asked to work on different tasks depending on their main deficit according to test results (on the Minnesota Test for Differential Diagnosis of Aphasia). Their performances were monitored and a check was made for each correct response. With this type of simple feedback on their performances the error rate decreased considerably. When participants

took the test again after 17 sessions over a period of 11 weeks their scores had increased significantly. The results were homogeneous for all four participants so their aphasic stage did not seem to affect the results. Doyle, Goldstein, Bourgeois, and Nakles (1989) worked with four aphasic participants who had suffered aphasia for 29 to 195 months. In their study, participants had to ask questions of their trainers on specific topics. They were given 20 seconds to ask a question after they got information about the topic. If no response occurred within 20 seconds the trainers provided a prompt. If the prompt was not sufficient to result in an adequate response from the participant within the next 20 seconds then a request was modelled for the participant to repeat. Adequate responses were praised and resulted in the provision of the requested information. The number of questions and their content was monitored. All the participants' performances improved considerably. Generalization of requests was measured by exposing participants to strangers of whom they were supposed to ask questions. Participants' performances towards trainers were better than towards strangers; however, their performances towards the latter group were comparable to the performances of a nondisabled comparison group. Training effects had not deteriorated after 12 weeks. Unfortunately, there was no evidence of generalization to themes not used during training. Sveinsdóttir and Sigurðardóttir (1999) worked with one elderly man with Broca's aphasia, 3 years post-onset. A multiple baseline across behaviours was used to evaluate the effects of treatment on four conversational behaviours, i.e., rate of correct responding to questions leading to a simple "Yes" or "No" answer, clarity of speech, rate of eye contact, and initiation of conversation. The intervention, which was only 20 sessions over 4 weeks, consisted of instructions for each task, praise and other social reinforcements for correct performance in 100% of all training trials, verbal performance feedback at the end of each session, and visual performance feedback in the form of graphs once per week. Clinically significant changes were made in all dependent variables; especially striking was the change in performance in the initiation of conversation task, which went from almost nothing to 35 times during a 20-minute session as a result of training. At 16 weeks follow-up, measures showed that training effects maintained and his performances had improved, perhaps because family members, for whom the intervention was explained and modelled, kept using the main treatment variables after formal training had ceased.

In the study presented here, care has been taken to operationalize and describe treatment variables, treatment procedures, and criteria used for evaluation of progress/deterioration. Instructions and ways of intervening when deterioration occurred were kept constant. Replication of this study should not be difficult and so the authors hope for systematic replications. A direct replication shows encouraging results.

METHOD

Participants

There were four participants, aged between 52 and 62 years. All had suffered a single cerebrovascular accident. Twenty-three to 55 months had passed since the incident took place that led to their aphasia; thus, the spontaneous recovery stage had ended in all cases when this study began. All participants had access to occupational and physical therapy but not all of them took advantage of it. Participants 2–4 had lived very fulfilling career, social, and family lives before their stroke. Participant 1 had lived a difficult life with various emotional crises resulting in a pattern of substance and self-abuse but had not abused drugs or alcohol after having the stroke.

Participant 1. Aged 55 (23 months post-stroke), Participant 1, the only female, lived alone in an apartment. She began receiving speech therapy 1 month after being admitted to the hospital. She was initially diagnosed with global aphasia. Three to five 30-minute sessions were provided per week for 3 months, after which she was diagnosed with Broca's aphasia. She then took a 3-month vacation. After that she received three 30-minutes sessions per week of speech therapy for 5 months. Three months later, she began to attend speech therapy sessions with a different speech therapist, once per week for 40 minutes.

Participant 2. Aged 52 (55 months post-stroke), Participant 2 lived in a nursing facility. He had hemiplegia of the right side and used a wheelchair. His speech was very clear. Attempts were made 1 and 3 months post-stroke to begin speech therapy, but he was totally unresponsive. He began receiving speech therapy 7 months post-stroke for 9 months, three times per week, for 30 minutes each time. He was diagnosed with severe aphasia when therapy ended. He had not received any speech therapy for almost 4 years when the study began.

Participant 3. Aged 62 (25 months post-stroke), Participant 3 lived with his adult son at their own home. He began receiving speech therapy 1 month post-stroke. He was diagnosed initially as having severe aphasia and mixed nonfluent aphasia; his scores were on the border of a global aphasia diagnosis. He attended four to five 30-minute sessions per week for 2 months. After a 1-month break he received 2 months more of speech therapy in three 30-minutes sessions per week. At the end of this period, his performance in reading comprehension was the best compared to his performance in other tasks. He suffered from severe apraxia.

Participant 4. Aged 59 (30 months post-stroke), Participant 4 lived with his wife in their own home. He was diagnosed with global aphasia 2 weeks post-stroke. He began receiving speech therapy after diagnosis, three to four times per week, for 30 minutes each time, for 5 months. One month after speech therapy began he scored 100% correct in the simple comprehension task of the Communication Independence Profile for Adults and scored 70% in the simple expression task of the same test. Three months after speech therapy began his performances in all tasks of the Boston Diagnostic Aphasia Examination were mostly average, or within one standard deviation above or below average. He received speech therapy occasionally, for a few weeks at a time, at least twice per year for 2 years prior to this study.

Setting

Baseline and training sessions were conducted in the participant's kitchen (Participants 1, 3, and 4) on the kitchen table or, for Participant 2, in the private rooms in the nursing home where he resides, on a small table with wheels. No distracting stimuli like radio, television, or phones were allowed. Almost all sessions ran smoothly with no disturbances. During sessions only the experimenter and the participant were present, except when reliability measures were taken; in those sessions two experimenters were present. Also, once in a while, a family member, friend, or staff observed the training session.

Generalization measures were taken in participants' homes and in an office in the rehabilitation/day-care facility that Participants 1, 3, and 4 attended. In the office there was a desk, a computer, a closet, three chairs, and a side table. The atmosphere was peaceful with no disturbances.

Experimental stimuli

Baseline and training. Visual stimuli were glued onto the centre of 21 × 15 cm index cards that were laminated. Almost the entire set of visual stimuli consisted of colour photographs acquired from magazines and catalogues; a few were black-and-white drawings. The same pictures were used during baseline and training trials. For the naming objects task a total of 77 stimuli were used. The stimuli were very simple, with no distracting stimuli surrounding the target stimulus. For the naming people task a total of 14 to 20 stimuli were used with Participants 1, 2, and 3; the set of pictures used with each participant was made of personal photographs of the participant, his/her family, and friends. For Participant 4, a total of 55 stimuli were used for this task, both personal photographs and pictures of people who are regularly in the news (politicians, musicians, entertainers, and royal families). For the sentence construction task a total of 64 stimuli were used. Stimuli used for sentence structure were complicated, showing scenarios, events, and people or animals engaging in different activities. Stimuli for the reading task were on 10.5 × 6 cm white cards. One to five letter words were centred on the cards in black print. During baseline measures, three words of each length were used, i.e., three 5-letter words, three 4-letter words, etc. During training only three 1-letter words were used.

Verbal stimuli were used in the sequencing and unassisted recall naming task. A total of 15 different sequences were used and a total of 99 different questions were used in the latter task.

Generalization. For the naming objects and sentence structure tasks, 15 × 10 cm colour photographs (photo cue cards) (Kerr, 1979, 1985) were used. A total of 15 pictures that were similar to those used in training were used first. Participants whose performances allowed were then exposed to a total of 15 new pictures. For the naming people task, real persons (co-workers, co-inhabitants, and staff of the day-care and rehabilitation or nursing facilities) were selected and participants were asked for their names. Participant 4, however, was exposed to new pictures of people in the news and historically important sites or buildings, a total of 76 new pictures. Some of the new pictures were small, others large; some were in black-and-white, others in colour; some were of persons whose pictures had been used during training but taken from different angles—some were even unclear; many were of politicians, musicians,

entertainers, sites, and buildings not seen in training. For the sequencing task, eleven new verbal stimuli were used. For the nonassisted naming task, seven new verbal stimuli were used.

Tasks, scoring, and dependent variables

Tasks. Tasks for baseline measures were selected on the basis of recommendations made by a speech therapist who had provided speech therapy to participants, on information participants and their families had given about their most salient dysfunction, and on a review of the literature on speech therapy. Three to four tasks were selected in each case out of the following. (1) Answering "Yes" or "No" to factual questions, e.g., "Is it Sunday today?" "Is there snow outside?" etc. Fifteen questions were used in this task. (2) Naming objects. Fifteen stimuli were always used in this task. (3) Naming people. Ten stimuli were used in this task. (4) Making sentences. Fifteen stimuli were used in this task. (5) Sequencing (e.g., counting weekdays, months, the alphabet, numbers, etc. in the correct order with different starting points). Three to five stimuli were used in this task. (6) Unassisted recall (i.e., name three stimuli on a particular theme, e.g., three types of cakes you like, three soccer teams, three countries in Europe, three roads to drive out of town). Three questions were asked each time. (7) Reading. Three stimuli were used in this task. Only the performances of Participants 3 and 4 on sequencing were assessed, Participant 4 was the only one who took the unassisted naming task, and Participant 2 was the only one who got the reading task. After this initial assessment, tasks were selected for use during intervention with each participant.

Scoring. Participants' responses were scored as correct, incorrect, or no answer. Clarity of speech was also scored as intelligible or unintelligible according to the primary experimenter's perception. After giving the participant an opportunity to respond, the experimenter waited for at least 10 s for an answer and gave a second opportunity to respond by repeating the question. If the participant did not respond then the experimenter scored "no answer" and initiated the next trial. The experimenter could also initiate the next trial if the participant refused to try to respond and requested to see the next picture or said "I don't know the name for it" or "I can't."

Dependent variables. The main dependent variable in all tasks was number of correct responses out of opportunities given. In some tasks, e.g., in the naming people task with Participant 4, the number of opportunities changed after measurements began and so the performances are shown as percentages. The answering time of Participant 4 was measured in the naming people task.

Independent/Therapeutic variables

The intervention consisted of the following. (1) Giving standardized instructions about the tasks and the target behaviours in each task. (2) Setting the occasion for the target behaviour, e.g., asking a question (and in some tasks simultaneously showing a picture) and waiting at least 10 seconds. (3) Providing prompts and the instruction to imitate. (4) Providing encouragement like "relax and try again," or "you got it almost right, try again." (5) Correcting errors after scoring by imitation and rehearsal. (6) Praising the appropriate response in a cheerful and respectful manner in 100% of trials. Prompts were faded out as performance improved. In addition, (7) once per week, participants received visual performance feedback when they were shown a graph of their performance in each task during the previous week. All progress was noted and praised. Participants were encouraged to do even better and to continue making progress.

Procedure and experimental design

A multiple-baseline across behaviours design was used to assess the effects of the treatment on aphasia symptoms of three different participants. Assessment began in all assessed variables simultaneously; however, with Participant 4, whose baseline performance was generally high, tasks were dropped and new tasks were selected. Thus, the experimental design used to assess the effects of training on this participant's performances changed from a multiple-baseline design to an AB design with three separate variables. Generalization was assessed with new stimuli and by conducting sessions in a new setting.

Baseline. Baseline measures of all dependent variables commenced simultaneously. Measures were taken daily. Sessions lasted for 25–45 minutes each time. Instructions used for each task were standardized across participants. No prompts or performance feedback were provided during baseline measures; the experimenter was careful to maintain a flat, inexpressive face throughout the baseline. Only comments like "you have worked so hard that we are almost done for the day" or "thank you for seeing us today" were used during baseline sessions as praise for the participant's cooperation. At least five baseline measures were taken before the intervention began on the first behaviour. Whichever behaviour was most stable or had a decreasing baseline was chosen for intervention first.

Intervention. The intervention lasted for 7 months. Sessions were held daily (except for weekends and sick or vacation days) and lasted for 30–60 minutes each time, depending on the type of tasks each participant worked on and on their performances. Sessions were held at approximately the same time throughout the study. A 25-year-old graduate student of psychology (second author), under daily supervision and guidance of a behaviour analyst (first author), carried out the intervention. This was a response guided experimentation study (Barlow & Hersen, 1984; Johnston & Pennypacker, 1993; Sidman, 1960), thus decisions on changes in the intervention depended on what the data showed each day about the effects of the current intervention on the performance of each participant in each task. Variations in the intervention were principally made in the kind of prompts (amount of help) provided to the participant in each task. Three kinds of prompts (or levels of help) were manipulated. In the beginning stages, for all participants in all variables, the target response was modelled. If the participant had not responded within 10 seconds after the experimenter asked a question, the experimenter either provided a name or a sentence and the participant was asked to imitate. Prompts used with each stimulus were held constant to avoid variability in the experimenter's behaviour between sessions and to facilitate reliability measures. When a participant had shown 100% correct performance in a task (prompted or unprompted) on six consecutive sessions, the amount of help was reduced to the next level, level 2. On level 2, the experimenter waited for 10 seconds and then gave only the first two sounds of a name or the first two words of a sentence and the participant had to finish the word or sentence. In the reading task, the mouth was moved and positioned as if the experimenter was ready to say the one-letter word but no sound was made. In the sequencing task and the unassisted recall task, only the first two sounds of each element of the required sequence/names were provided after 10 seconds of waiting from the last response made. When participants had shown

100% correct performance on three consecutive sessions, the amount of help was again decreased to the next level of help, level 1. On level 1 participants got an indirect prompt, e.g., "his name starts with the same letter as your name does," or "tell me, what is the first thing you think about when you see this scene?" In level 1 and level 2 participants were given three opportunities to respond correctly, if they did not, their response was scored as incorrect or as "no response" and then they were told the correct answer, were asked to repeat or rehearse, and were praised for correct responses.

Recycling. If a participant's performance in a task deteriorated two or three times in a row, the level of help was increased in the following session. Also, if the level of help was decreased and that led to an unstable performance that seldom reached 100% correct, the level of help was increased again. In addition, the criteria for decreasing the level of help increased to six consecutive performances that were 100% correct.

Generalization. Generalization measures were taken in the last 4 weeks of the study. If training sessions lasted 1 hour then training was skipped and only generalization was measured. If training lasted about half an hour, then both training and generalization measures were conducted. No prompts were provided during generalization measures but subtle, intermittent feedback, e.g., "Yes, let's continue" or "OK" was provided without eye contact. During the naming people task, the experimenter walked with the participant and pointed at the person that the participant had to name.

Reliability

Reliability was scored both with regard to the dependent variables and one independent variable, i.e., prompt level. The main experimenter was the main observer. One specially trained reliability observer scored agreements with regard to the participants' responses in each task, intelligibility of each response, prompt provided by experimenter, and in the case of Participant 4 in the naming people task, the length of the response in seconds. Reliability scores were calculated by comparing observers' scores trial by trial in each task used with each participant. The number of agreements in each task was counted and divided by the sum of observers' agreements and disagreements (i.e., the total number of opportunities given in the task), then multiplied by 100.

RESULTS

Reliability

Reliability measures were taken in 5–35% of baseline sessions across participants and tasks. During intervention, reliability was measured in 32–48% of sessions across participants and tasks. During generalization, reliability was measured in 28–80% of sessions across participants and tasks. Mean reliability for measures taken during training across participants and tasks ranged between 81–100% and was above 90% in 21/22 cases, over 95% in 19/22 cases, and was 100% in 4/22 cases. Mean reliability during generalization measures ranged between 81–100%, but were 100% in 5/10 cases and 95% or better in 2/10 cases. Table 1 shows mean reliability for each participant in each task during training and generalization. Table 2 shows mean reliability for measures of usage of correct prompt with each participant in each task.

TABLE 1
Mean reliability scores during training and generalization in each task with each participant

	Participant			
	1	2	3	4
	%	%	%	%
Training task				
Naming objects		97.85	99.28	
Naming people	98.8	100	95.21	98.13
Sentences	90			
Sequencing			100	99.43
Unassisted recall				95.83
Reading		96.78		
Generalization task				
Naming objects		86.6	95.72	
Naming people	100	86	100	100
Sentences	81.55			
Sequencing			95	100
Unassisted recall				100

TABLE 2
Mean reliability measures for use of correct prompt

	Participant			
	1	2	3	4
Correct prompt use	%	%	%	%
Naming objects		97.68	97.68	
Naming people	100	97.75	99.11	91.26
Sentences	97.10			
Sequencing			96.93	100
Unassisted recall				95
Reading		99.08		

Effects of training

Baseline measures of all participants' performances in the answer to "Yes" and "No" factual questions demonstrated very high performances. This led to the decision to drop this task entirely. Performances of participants during baseline and training in the tasks that remained can be seen in Figures 1 through 4. In general, the intervention had clinically significant effects on the performances of all participants across tasks. Correct responding that was independent of available prompts increased throughout the training phase and all participants reached the point in at least

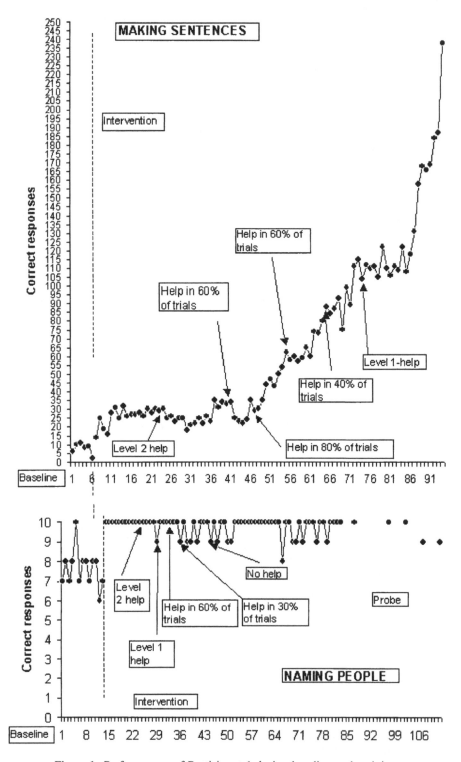

Figure 1. Performances of Participant 1 during baseline and training.

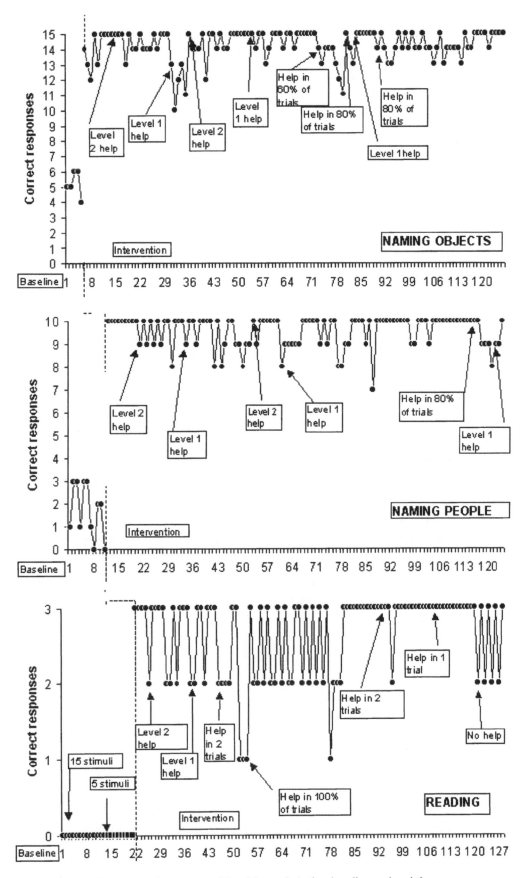

Figure 2. Performances of Participant 2 during baseline and training.

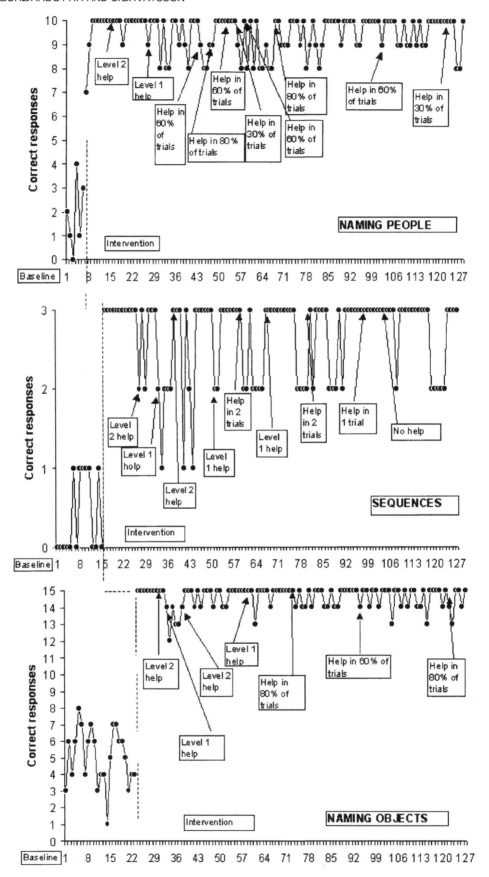

Figure 3. Performances of Participant 3 during baseline and training.

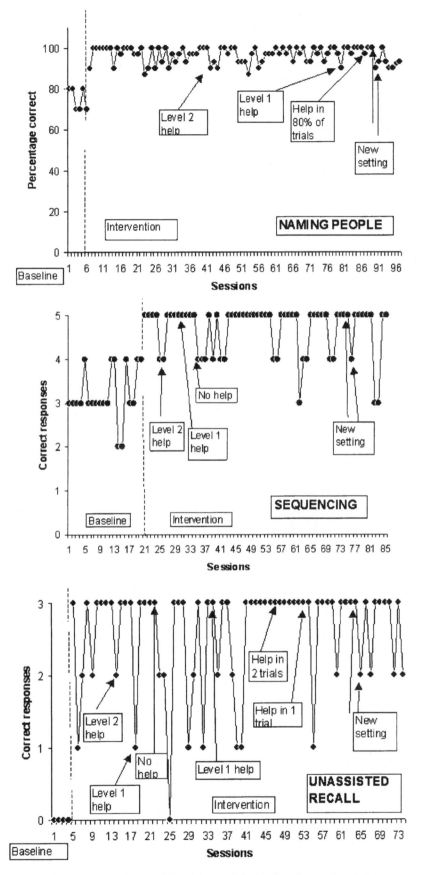

Figure 4. Performances of Participant 4 during baseline and training.

one task where their performance was so good that all prompts were withheld without detrimental effects to the point of needing recycling. Several measures were taken of the performances of three participants after this point was reached, however, this does not apply to Participant 2; far fewer measures were taken of his performance after reaching the point when no prompts were available to him because the experiment ended, which was too bad. Moreover, generalization measures showed that in general all participants generalized their performances to new stimuli, even when sessions were conducted in a different setting. The performances of Participants 1 and 4 show a more immediate and stable generalization pattern than those of Participants 2 and 3, which show a less stable (Participant 2) and less immediate (Participant 3) generalization pattern. However, all participants in all tasks showed generalization.

Participant 1. The intervention had a very clear effect on the performances of this participant on two tasks, i.e., making sentences and naming people. Moreover, her improvements generalized to a different task, i.e., to the naming objects task, in which no intervention took place. The participant's performances in the sentence construction task and the naming objects task seem to correlate, which makes them both members of the same response class. This participant's performance in the sentence construction task went from occasionally saying very simple subject-verb sentences during baseline when shown the 15 stimuli used to saying 245 sentences of different types, lengths, and complexity. Moreover, she consistently took less and less advantage of the help that was made available to her. Her performance in the naming people-task also improved considerably with training (Figure 1) and reached the point when no help was available to her without this affecting her performance to any significant degree. After she had repeatedly shown very good performance in this task without any help, it was considered unnecessary to provide further training. Measures of her performance were taken once per week to check maintenance of treatment effects. Those weekly probes show good maintenance of treatment effects. Generalization measures show that improvements in the naming people task generalized to naming other persons than those who were on the photographs used in training. Generalization measures were taken in a different setting without affecting her performance.

Participant 2. Training had clinically significant effects on the performances of this participant in three tasks: naming objects, naming people, and reading (Figure 2). This participant had the longest history of aphasia, is physically disabled, and received the least amount of speech therapy after he had a stroke compared to the other participants. He showed remarkable although variable progress. In the reading task, baseline measures showed 0% performance when 15 stimuli were used, i.e., 3 stimuli each of 5 different lengths (1- to 5-letter words). Baseline measures were then taken with only 5 stimuli, 1 each of 5 different lengths (1- to 5-letter words). His performance remained at 0%. During the intervention, he was taught to discriminate between three 1-letter words "á," "í," and "ó." He was able to learn to discriminate between these. He reached the point where he did not get any help because of his repeated 100% performance when minimum help was available to him. His performance became variable when he did not have access to help; it remained perfect only half of the time. He discriminated "á" and "ó" very well but did not reliably respond correctly to "í" after all prompts were withdrawn. Unfortunately, the experiment ended. In the future, if he receives more training, it would be necessary to assess and train discrimination between shapes like lines of various lengths and in different directions, circles, half circles, etc. that are elements of written letters. Breaking the task down into smaller steps may lead to successful results. However, the training provided in this experiment clearly resulted in learning that could have continued had the experiment not ended. Variability in his performance decreased in all tasks with training. He did not show a very clear tendency to decrease the use of help available to him at different levels although there was decrement. During generalization, at first, measures showed immediate, perfect generalization that became variable but later returned to high levels. As novel generalization stimuli were added, generalization measures showed an increasing pattern.

Participant 3. Clinically significant changes in performances were achieved with this participant in three tasks: naming people, sequencing, and naming objects. He consistently decreased the use of prompts available to him in all tasks. Variability in his performances in all tasks decreased with training (Figure 3). In the sequencing task, his performance reached the point when he was provided no prompts because he repeatedly scored 100%. After no prompts were available to him he performed 100% correctly in 80% of cases (17/23 times) before the experiment ended. His baseline performance in this task had repeatedly been 0%

correct in 9/15 measures; thus the changes in his performance from baseline to the end of the experiment were considerable. Generalization was assessed both in the regular training setting and in a new setting. Measures showed immediately that some generalization occurred but that progress was slow. This participant suffers from severe apraxia. Training does not seem to have affected this symptom; however, his motivation for speaking and trying to produce intelligible speech increased significantly.

Participant 4. This participant is the least disabled by aphasia. His baseline performance in the naming people task was very high, i.e., 70–80% correct; however, he consistently was unable to name his grandchildren and other family members. Thus, performance in this task was targeted for intervention. His baseline performance in the sequencing task was not far from perfect but there was room for improvement. Finally, his baseline performance in the unassisted recall task was 0%. The intervention had notable effects on this participant's performances in all tasks (Figure 4); however, due to his initial performance during baseline it is not possible to state that the intervention had radical effects on his performances, except in the unassisted recall task. His ability to name three examples to an open-ended request to name three items in a particular context went from 0% to 100% with minimal help. He made decreasing use of the prompts available to him as training proceeded. Generalization measures showed immediate generalization, except in the unassisted recall task, where generalization was not seen until the second measure both when one and later two novel stimuli were used. In addition, when training took place in a different setting, i.e., in the setting where generalization measures were taken, his performance deteriorated in all tasks.

DISCUSSION

The effects of training based on learning principles for symptoms of aphasia were demonstrated in three single-subject experiments with a multiple-baseline design across behaviours. In addition, the same effects were demonstrated in one additional experiment, on three behaviours of one participant with an AB design. Thus, the effects of training were demonstrated 11 times. Internal validity in these studies is high because no other new treatment was available to them while this study was conducted and no other changes took place in the participants' lives during the 7 months of the

study. The effects of the intervention were immediate in all cases and the amount of progress was clinically significant in 9 behaviours out of 11 studied. Generalization measures show that most performances generalized to a new setting and to new stimuli, in some cases immediately and in others more slowly. Anecdotal reports from co-workers and family claim that all participants' motivation to speak and to take part in conversation increased, and that behaviours that had not occurred in a long period of time, e.g., using the telephone to call somebody, speaking in a supermarket, calling somebody by a nickname, were becoming more common.

Treatment was composed of several variables, i.e., performance feedback, social reinforcers, instructions, prompts that were faded out, recycling, etc. It is impossible to say which variables were the most important, sufficient, or necessary to achieve the results attained. However, the treatment did have clinically significant effects on most behaviours of all participants treated and this is important in and of itself. Many studies have looked at the size and location of a cerebral lesion, the aetiology of the lesion, and individual variables like age and level of education, in an attempt to understand what affects recovery. This is, of course, very important; however, treatment and intervention in general and its parameters must also be looked at. It is crucial to develop effective intervention procedures that can speed up recovery or at least initiate it and stimulate it. It is necessary to examine exactly what type of intervention is effective and to examine its parameters. It is crucial to examine also whether and how a particular type of intervention with specific parameters interacts with specific personal variables like site and size of lesion, age, and aetiology of lesion. In the initial stages of development of an intervention and its parameters, it is important and practical to set together a number of variables that may affect outcome to try to design as effective an intervention as possible. If experimental results confirm that the intervention is effective and direct replications of the experiment confirm this outcome, then the next step is to try to find its limitations, i.e., In what cases does the intervention not work? What changes are needed to have the same effect that had been established in former tests? For a long time it was not known whether interventions would affect recovery from the symptoms of aphasia. Several studies have now established that treatment is better than no treatment. For a long time it was not known whether recovery could take place after the period when spontaneous recovery occurs. Several studies have now established that recovery can continue with treatment long after spontaneous recovery ends. What is needed now is better examination of the exact variables that make an effective intervention. This study is one step forward in that search.

REFERENCES

Albert, M., & Helm-Estabrooks, N. (1988). Diagnosis and treatment of aphasia. *Journal of the American Medical Association, 259*, 1043–1210.

Bardin Ayers, S. K., Potter, R. E., & McDermon, J. R. (1975). Using reinforcement therapy and precision teaching techniques with adult aphasics. *Journal of Behavior Therapy and Experimental Psychiatry, 6*, 301–305.

Barlow, D. H., & Hersen, M. (1984). *Single case experimental designs. Strategies for studying behavior change.* New York: Pergamon Press.

Bellack, A. S., Hersen, M., & Kazdin, A. E. (1993). *International handbook of behavior modification and therapy.* New York: Plenum Press.

Byng, S., & Black, M. (1995). What makes a therapy? Some parameters of therapeutic intervention in aphasia. *European Journal of Disorders of Communication, 30*, 303–316.

Doyle, P. J., Goldstein, H., Bourgeois, M. S., & Nakles, K. O. (1989). Facilitating generalized requesting behavior in Broca's aphasia: An experimental analysis of a generalization training procedure. *Journal of Applied Behavior Analysis, 22*, 157–170.

Fridriksson, J., & Holland, A. (2001). Final thoughts on management of aphasia in the early phases of recovery following stroke. *American Journal of Speech-Language Pathology, 10*, 37–53.

Hillis, A. E. (1989). Efficacy and generalization of treatment for aphasic naming errors. *Archives of Physical Rehabilitation, 70*, 632–636.

Holland, A. L., Fromm, D. S., DeRuyter, F., & Stein, M. (1996). Treatment efficacy: Aphasia. *Journal of Speech and Hearing Research, 39*, S27–S36.

Jacobs, H. E. (2000). Behavioral contributions to brain-injury rehabilitation. In J. Austin & J. E. Carr (Eds.), *Handbook of applied behavior analysis* (pp. 211–230). Reno, NV: Context Press.

Johnston, J. M., & Pennypacker, H. S. (1993). *Strategies and tactics of behavioral research.* Hillsdale, NJ: Lawrence Erlbaum Associates Inc.

Kerr, J. Y. K. (1979). *Photo cue cards.* Austin, TX: ProEd.

Kerr, J. Y. K. (1985). *More photo cue cards.* Austin, TX: ProEd.

Mitchum, C. C. (1994). Traditional and contemporary views of aphasia: Implication for clinical management. *Topics in Stroke Rehabilitation, 1*, 14–36.

Orange, J. B., & Kertesz, A. (1998). Efficacy of language therapy for aphasia. *Physical Medicine and Rehabilitation: State of the Art Reviews, 12*, 501–517.

Poeck, K., Huber, W., & Willmes, K. (1989). Outcome of intensive language treatment in aphasia. *American Speech-Language-Hearing Association, 54*, 471–479.

Purdy, M. H. (2001). Recovery of communication skills following intracerebral hemorrhage: A case study. *Journal of Medical Speech-Language Pathology, 9*, 193–201.

Raymer, A. M. (2001). Acquired language disorders. *Topics in Language Disorders, 21*, 42–59.

Robey, R. R. (1998). A meta-analysis of clinical outcomes in the treatment to aphasia. *Journal of Speech, Language, and Hearing Research, 41*, 172–187.

Sidman, M. (1960). *Tactics of scientific research.* Boston: Authors Cooperative.

Sveinsdóttir, I., & Sigurðardóttir, Z. G. (1999, May). *Modification of conversation behaviors in a patient with communication dysfunction typical of Broca's aphasia.* Poster session presented at the annual conference of Association for Behavior Analysis-International, Chicago, IL.

Thompson, C. K. (1996). Linguistic-specific sentence production treatment for agrammatic aphasia. *Topics in Stroke Rehabilitation, 3*, 60–85.

Thulborn, K. R., Carpenter, P. A., & Just, M. A. (1999). Plasticity of language-related brain function during recovery from stroke. *Stroke, 30*, 749–754.

INTERNATIONAL JOURNAL OF PSYCHOLOGY, 2006, 41 (6), 541–554

Psychology Press
Taylor & Francis Group

The effects of prompting and social reinforcement on establishing social interactions with peers during the inclusion of four children with autism in preschool

Angeliki Gena

National and Kapodistrian University of Athens, Athens, Greece

*I*nclusion in "regular" schools has become a considerable option for children with autism only in recent years, but we are still far from having a global appreciation of the needs that arise upon the inclusion of children with such a severe disability. The main purpose of the present study was to identify empirically supported procedures that may improve the social interactions of children with autism upon their inclusion in the "regular" preschool. The identification of the needs of preschoolers with autism in Greek schools, as well as the specific skills that would be taught, were based on normative data collected and analysed in a series of prior studies. A long-lasting controversy has been going on between professionals who either advocate for "schools for all children," or stress the importance of making individualized decisions based on each child's needs during the inclusion process. The present study demonstrated that social reinforcement in combination with prompting procedures, provided by a shadow teacher, were effective in increasing the social initiations as well as appropriate responding to peers' initiations of four children with autism during interactions with their classmates in preschool. More importantly, the treatment benefits were obtained in a natural setting, and the initiations and replies were not cliché statements but involved generalized language use appropriate to the social context, and generalized to new therapists.

L'insertion dans les écoles régulières est une option considérable pour les enfants autistiques, mais celle-ci est très récente. Néanmoins, nous sommes encore loin d'avoir une appréciation complète des besoins émergeant de l'insertion des enfants ayant de telles incapacités sévères. Le but principal de la présente étude était d'identifier les procédures soutenues empiriquement qui permettent d'améliorer les interactions sociales des enfants autistiques lors de leur insertion dans les écoles régulières. L'identification des besoins des enfants autistiques d'âge préscolaire dans les écoles grecques, ainsi que les habiletés spécifiques à être enseignées, ont été basées sur des données normatives collectées et analysées par une série d'études antérieures. Une controverse existe depuis longtemps entre les professionnels qui préconisent l'accessibilité à l'école pour tous les enfants et ceux qui plaident en faveur de l'importance de prendre des décisions individualisées basées sur les besoins de chaque enfant dans le processus d'insertion. La présente étude a démontré que le renforcement social en combinaison avec des procédures d'incitation, de la part d'un professeur auxiliaire, étaient efficaces pour l'augmentation des initiations sociales tout comme les réponses appropriées aux initiations des pairs de quatre enfants autistiques durant les interactions avec leurs compagnons de classe au préscolaire. Encore plus important, les bénéfices du traitement ont été obtenus dans des milieux naturels; les initiations et les réponses n'étaient pas des clichés artificiels, mais elles impliquaient l'utilisation généralisée d'un langage adapté au contexte social et généralisé aux nouveaux thérapeutes.

*L*a inclusión en escuelas "regulares" sólo en los últimos años se ha convertido en una opción a considerar para el caso de niños con autismo, pero todavía estamos lejos de lograr una apreciación global de las necesidades que surgen de incluir a niños con limitaciones tan severas. El principal propósito del presente estudio fue identificar procedimientos con respaldo empírico que pudieran mejorar las interacciones sociales de niños con autismo al incluirlos en una escuela preescolar "regular". La identificación de las necesidades de los preescolares con autismo en las escuelas griegas, lo mismo que las habilidades específicas que se les iban a enseñar se basaron en datos normativos recolectados y analizados en una serie de estudios. Ha tenido lugar durante largo tiempo una

Correspondence should be addressed to Angeliki Gena, PhD, National and Kapodistrian University of Athens, Athens, Greece (E-mail: agena@ath.forthnet.gr).

© 2006 International Union of Psychological Science

DOI: 10.1080/00207590500492658

controversia entre los profesionales que están de acuerdo con "escuelas para todos los niños" y los que enfatizan la importancia de tomar decisiones individualizadas con base en las necesidades de cada niño durante el proceso de inclusión. El presente trabajo demostró que el reforzamiento social combinado con procedimientos de instigación proporcionados por un maestro auxiliar era efectivo para aumentar la iniciación de interacciones sociales y para responder apropiadamente a las interacciones iniciadas por los compañeritos, en el caso de cuatro niños con autismo estudiados en sus interacciones con compañeros en el preescolar. Aún más importante, vale la pena señalar que los beneficios se obtuvieron en un ambiente natural, las iniciaciones y las respuestas no fueron clichés artificiales, sino que involucraron el uso generalizado de lenguaje apropiado al contexto social y generalizado a nuevos terapeutas.

INTRODUCTION

Since the 1980s, the issue of inclusion of children with disabilities has provoked a long-lasting controversy among professionals who either advocate for "schools for all children" (e.g., Ainscow, 1996; Stainback & Stainback, 1984, 1996; Stainback, Stainback, Courtnage, & Jaben, 1985) or stress the importance of making individualized decisions based on each child's needs during the inclusion process (e.g., Fuchs & Fuchs, 1995; Zigler & Hall, 1995). More recently, however, the types of research questions asked in the area of inclusion attempt "to determine the differential effects of interventions or settings on children having different characteristics" (p. 168, Odom, 2002).

The inclusion of children with autism, specifically, has become prevalent in the past few years, because of the increasing number of children diagnosed with autism in the USA (Autism Society of America, 1999; Chakrabarti & Fombonne, 2001; Yeargin-Allsopp et al., 2003), but also because of the complex clinical picture that children with autism present. They often present severe difficulties, not only in the cognitive, but also in the emotional and social domains (e.g., American Psychiatric Association, 1994). Therefore, the importance of social interactions with peers, which has been identified as a critical aspect for child development in general (e.g., Yang, Wolfberg, Wu, & Hwu, 2003), becomes an even more critical issue for children with autism. A regular school setting is often considered the ideal context for the advancement of children's social skills (Mesibov & Shea, 1996). Inclusive educational practices not only realize the right of children with disabilities for a least restrictive placement, but also that the educational and social benefits of inclusion on children with and without disabilities are great, as a growing research base outlines (e.g., McDonnell, 1998). For children with autism, inclusion in regular schools may present a challenge, but it may also play a significant role in

their overall adjustment. The breadth and severity of the problems that children with autism present make it unlikely that the majority of those children can benefit from the type of education offered to their typical counterparts. When children with autism receive mainstream educational services that do not address their needs, not only may their cognitive and academic skills fail to advance, but their behaviour management skills may even deteriorate (McClannahan, 1996). In addition, as children with intellectual disabilities, they require specialized services in order to succeed in educational inclusion (Hunt & Goetz, 1997; Laushey & Heflin, 2000; Rogers, 2000). Despite the stand one takes regarding the issue of school inclusion, we would all agree that: (1) the conditions under which it is conducted are critical for a successful outcome and (2) providing effective programming for their educational and social advancement is the most sought-after goal for children with disabilities who are mainstreamed in regular education (e.g., McDonnell, 1998; McDonnell et al., 2003; Robertson, Green, Alper, Schloss, & Kohler, 2003). Thus, upon the inclusion of children with autism in "regular" educational settings, we need to address two important questions. First, whether those children would benefit academically and socially in the mainstream and, if not, whether we can provide the proper assistance to the child or make the proper accommodations in the school setting that may contribute to a successful inclusion.

As a large number of studies has demonstrated, the great majority of children with autism lack the skills that would help them benefit from an inclusive educational setting without support (e.g., Evans, Salisbury, Palombaro, Berryman, & Hollowood, 1992; Kamps et al., 2002; Laushey & Heflin, 2000; Ochs, Kremer-Sadlik, Solomon, & Gainer Sirota, 2001). Thus, the research focus in recent years is on identifying intervention procedures that help those children to overcome their social difficulties and begin to interact with peers. Children with autism are challenged in a wide array of academic and social skills, but their most prevalent needs appear to be in the area of social integration and in forming relationships with peers during their inclusion in early childhood education settings (Guralnick, 1999; Odom, 2002). Their limited language and social repertoires contribute to their isolation or minimal social interactions with peers and call for support in the area of social engagement (Odom, 2002).

There are numerous intervention studies attempting to identify strategies that may facilitate the inclusion of children with disabilities in "regular" schools, but the great majority of such studies involve children with mild disabilities. On the contrary, there are very few empirical studies that analyse optimal instructional contexts for students with moderate and severe disabilities in general education classrooms (Logan & Malone, 1998). The literature on children with mild disabilities is not necessarily instructive, nor can it be generalized to children with moderate and severe disabilities. One example in which there were clear differences between the progress of children with mild and severe disabilities during the inclusion process was that of the Waldron and McLeskey study (1998), which demonstrated that children with mild disabilities benefited to a greater extent by inclusion in "regular" rather than special education, whereas children with moderate disabilities benefited equally in both types of settings. Therefore, the findings from research involving children with mild disabilities may not necessarily generalize to children with moderate and severe disabilities. What we certainly know, however, is that for students with severe disabilities such as autism, it is imperative, when we consider inclusion in "regular" educational settings, to adopt the necessary teaching practices that address their diverse educational and social needs. Such teaching practices require either direct input from specialists or their input in training teachers or paraprofessionals to use specific interventions efficiently and effectively (e.g., Lovaas, 1987; Schepis, Reid, Ownbey, & Clary, 2003). Thus, for children with autism, the efforts required for successful inclusion are usually extensive and require well-trained professionals (Lovaas, 1987). We will, therefore, focus our attention on studies that address the inclusion of children with autism or other moderate and severe disabilities.

Harrower and Dunlap (2001) classified the types of procedures used to facilitate the inclusion of children with autism into five broad categories. Three of those categories included procedures that enhanced, specifically, their social skills within "regular" education settings. Those categories were classified as: (1) antecedent procedures, (2) peer-mediated interventions, and (3) multi-component interventions. Peer-mediated procedures appeared to be the most widely used type of intervention and to have the best results.

Peer-mediated interventions, designed to enhance the social skills of children with autism, have been used since the 1980s (e.g., Kamps et al., 1992; Odom, Chandler, Ostrosky, McConnell, & Reaney, 1992; Odom & Strain, 1986), but continue to be used and to be developed to meet the demands of current practices in inclusive education settings (such practices include cooperative learning, peer tutoring, etc.) (e.g., Kamps et al., 2002; Yang et al., 2003; and Hughes, Carter, Hughes, Bradford, & Copeland, 2002). The extensive use of peer-mediated procedures has been attributed to various factors, such as being conducive to the current practices used during inclusion, reducing the financial cost of inclusion as well as the need for continuous one-on-one adult support (Harrower & Dunlap, 2001), at times when the special education support services offered to local national schools are limited (O'Reilly et al., 2002), and promoting maintenance of acquired social skills (e.g., peers may function as mediating stimuli) (Kamps et al., 2002).

Despite the many advantages of peer-mediated procedures, some limitations may also be pointed out with regard to their use toward improving the social skills of children with autism. First, if we take into consideration the importance of early intervention for children with autism (e.g., Fenske, Zalenski, Krantz, & McClannahan, 1985; Lovaas, 1987), the use of peer modelling procedures may not be applicable during the first steps of those children's inclusion in preschools, because for 3- to 4-year-old, typically developing preschoolers, it may be difficult to comprehend and to cooperate in peer tutoring programs, or to use peer-mediating strategies reliably. There is only one study in which such young students were trained as peer tutors, but the tutees were not children with severe disabilities, nor did the peer tutoring goals involve social interactions with verbal exchanges (Robertson et al., 2003). Another issue that needs to be explored with regard to peer-mediated procedures is the quality of interactions that are produced between tutors and tutees as a result of using such procedures. There are a few studies that either examine the relation between teaching procedures and the type of social interactions that they produce (e.g., Cole, Vandercook, & Rynders, 1988) or alert us to the need for qualitative analyses of the types of interactions that develop between children with and without disabilities (e.g., Evans et al., 1992). In that context, Janney and Snell (1996), suggest that peer-mediated practices should be provided in the context of "cooperation" and "mutual assistance" among all classmates, rather than as special procedures offered exclusively to students with disabilities, which may lead to the differentiation and stigmatization of such students. Finally, a very important outcome of the Kamps et al. (2002) study, which had a very large sample of children with autism, was that, despite the great benefits of peer training on the social interactions among students with autism and their classmates, "no changes were noted for language [of verbal students with autism]."

The second type of intervention strategies aiming to enhance the social skills of children with autism in inclusive settings involve the use of antecedent procedures. They are rather scarce, since the majority of behaviour analytic studies incorporate manipulations of both antecedent and consequential stimuli. Such procedures, when used exclusively, often serve a proactive function, as opposed to targeting directly the modification of specific response classes (Harrower & Dunlap, 2001).

The third type of strategies used to facilitate the inclusion of students with autism incorporate multiple treatment components (Harrower & Dunlap, 2001). There are also very few studies of this type that specifically address social skills training (e.g., Hunt, Farron-Davis, Wrenn, Hirose-Hatae, & Goetz, 1997; Yang et al., 2003). It is worth exploring which of those procedures have been found to be effective. First, a promising approach, not yet extensively researched in the area of social skills, is self-management or self-regulation. Self-management procedures have been very effective in improving the performance of children with developmental disabilities in typical classrooms, but mostly on academic tasks (e.g., Koegel, Harrower, & Koegel, 1999; Wehmeyer, Yeager, Bolding, Agran, & Hughes, 2003). Self-management was used for social skills training in one study, but in conjunction with edible reinforcers (Koegel, Koegel, Hurley, & Frea, 1992). Thus, we may not ascertain to what extent each of the procedures—delivery of primary reinforcers or self-management—attributed to the acquisition of the target responses. In addition, acquired responses did not maintain upon the withdrawal of treatment for two of the subjects.

When using systematic treatment procedures during the inclusion of students with moderate or severe disabilities, the presence of a well-trained shadow teacher, who provided direct support to the child during the inclusion process, was one of the critical variables for enhancing both the academic skills of children with moderate disabilities (e.g., McDonnell et al., 2003) as well as the social skills of children with autism (Schepis et al., 2003).

In summary, from a review of the studies that incorporated multicomponent interventions to enhance the social skills of children with autism in "regular" education settings, we may conclude that there is not sufficient empirical evidence to demonstrate the effectiveness of self-management or self-regulation procedures in improving those skills. Yet, direct support from well-trained staff has been clearly identified as a critical variable for such improvement.

Two other points that were stressed in the literature addressing the inclusion of children with autism are, first, the lack of research in promoting social interactions between children with and without special needs in school playgrounds (Nabors, Willoughby, Leff, & McMenamin, 2001), and second, a lack of studies incorporating experimental methodologies (Schwartz, Sandall, Garfinkle, & Bauer, 1998). The majority of published studies on the inclusion of children with autism used nonexperimental methodologies, such as the paradigm of action research, which, though useful for practitioners, do not allow for the identification of causal relations between treatment manipulations and outcome.

The research questions that arise from the literature discussed in the present review, as well as the desire to explore important variables that may be specific to the Greek culture, led to a series of empirical studies conducted in preschools and kindergartens in Greece. The initial studies of this series have attempted to identify the deficits that children with autism presented upon their inclusion in kindergarten, which prevented them from benefiting from the learning and social opportunities offered in the inclusion settings (Gena & Kymissis, 2001; Gena & Logothetis, 2001; Γενά, 2001, 2002). The most important findings of those studies were the following. (1) Preschoolers of typical development interact in very complex ways and their interactions are quite frequent during free play and recess times. More specifically, content analysis of the interactions of typically developing preschoolers, during play activities, revealed that there were about 25 response categories, with several subcategories of interactions (Gena & Kymissis, 2001). (2) Children with autism lag behind their peers on various areas, including on-task behaviour, responding to teachers' requests or questions, etc. Yet, the two areas in which all children invariably demonstrated severe difficulties pertain to the social domain. Making initiations toward classmates, and responding appropriately to their classmates' attempts to interact with them, were the two types of responses that children with autism either did not have at all in their repertoires, or demonstrated minimally. (3) A girl with autism, who was mainstreamed in kindergarten, made excellent progress in all the areas mentioned above and particularly in the social domain. (4) The variables that may have contributed to that progress include intensive behaviour analytic intervention at home and close supervision and guidance in the inclusion setting provided by a shadow teacher with a behaviour analytic orientation (Gena & Logothetis, 2001). The above findings have stimulated the interest to explore the effects of the intervention in an experimental manner. Thus, the purpose of the present study was to assess whether, for children with autism who receive intensive behaviour analytic intervention at home, a multi-component intervention would be effective in helping them to improve the types of social interactions with peers that require generalized language use. Specifically, the purposes of the present study were formulated as follows: (1) to analyse whether the combination of antecedent strategies (i.e., prompting), social reinforcement, and time out from reinforcement contingent on noncompliant behaviour would increase the frequency of social responding that involves generalized language use (i.e., making social initiations and responding to initiations made by peers) in four preschoolers with autism; (2) to provide an experimental analysis of the effectiveness of treatment using a multiple baseline across subjects experimental design; (3) to investigate whether the intervention would be successful with young children, around the age of 4 years; (4) to promote response generalization of the target responses by using diverse and loose training in the sense of not teaching cliché initiation or reply statements, but rather using types of contextually appropriate responses when prompting from the shadow teacher was required; (5) to foster the development of social skills in a natural setting by selecting the preschool playground as the training context, which was considered important since children with autism are often excluded from interactions with peers in settings, such as the playground, where most children their age typically engage in high rates of social exchanges (Nabors et al., 2001); (6) to use a method of direct observation, which may be viewed as a performance-based

assessment, which is considered a more accurate type of assessment to evaluate treatment outcome (Gettinger & Callan Stoiber, 1998); and (7) to assess fluency of appropriate affective responding by comparing the level of social responding of children with autism to that of their typical classmates in the target areas.

METHOD

Participants

The participants of this study were four children with autism. We will also refer to normative data for comparison purposes, without providing a detailed description of the typically developing peers, since it has already been provided in a previous publication (Gena & Kymissis, 2001). There were 12 typically developing preschoolers—3 per child with autism—aged from 3 years and 10 months to 4 years and 7 months. They were matched for gender and age to the children with autism and were selected randomly from the preschools that the children with autism attended.

The target children were two girls and two boys with the diagnosis of autistic disorder. Their diagnosis was based on public hospital evaluations, as well as evaluations of the centre where they received intervention (the Athenian Centre for Child Development and Education), both of which were located in Athens, Greece. Other than having the diagnosis of autism, all four children had been excluded from several private and public preschools because of their behavioural and learning difficulties, according to their parents' reports.

All four participants received behaviour analytic intervention, mostly one-on-one, in dyads or small groups prior to and during their inclusion in "regular" preschool. At the beginning of the study, Lena was 4 years old and had been in therapy for 7 months. Her therapeutic programme included, on the average, 7 hours per week one-on-one, in-home, and intervention by experienced therapists. In addition, her mother received training and was very competent in carrying out Lena's therapeutic goals. Lena's attendance started at a private preschool with 1 hour per day and gradually increased to a full-day attendance (4 hours).

Eva was 4 years and 5 months old at the beginning of the study, and had been in therapy for 3 months receiving one-on-one, in-home intervention for an average of 9 hours weekly. Eva attended a public preschool and her attendance schedule was similar to Lena's.

Andrew was 4 years and 2 months old and had been in therapy for 4 months prior to inclusion. Initially, he attended a day programme for children with autism, where he received behaviour-analytic, mostly one-on-one intervention for 24 hours per week, which progressively decreased to approximately 10–12 hours weekly. His inclusion took place in a private preschool starting with 2 hours per week and increased to 4 hours per day.

At the beginning of the study Cory was 4 years old and had been in therapy for 2 months prior to inclusion. His inclusion took place in a public preschool starting with 4 hours per day with the shadow teacher, whose presence was faded, progressively, to 6 hours per week.

Regarding the participants' overall progress in therapy, it is worth mentioning that all four started out with limited language (mostly one-word utterances), severe delays in communication, inappropriate affective behaviour, and aberrant behaviour. Yet, shortly after intervention, they all showed great improvement in their use of expressive and communicative language, in motivation and in compliance toward parents and therapists. Additionally, behavioural problems, such as temper tantrums and stereotypic behaviour, had decreased dramatically for all the participants prior to their inclusion in preschool. Even though the participants were considered severely disabled and nontestable by standardized assessments before treatment, their intellectual functioning reached age-appropriate levels in the course of treatment, but they continued to demonstrate severe social and emotional difficulties, which led to the need for additional help during their attendance in "regular" preschool. No standardized measures of their intellectual, emotional, or social abilities can be provided, since there are no psychometric tests available for the Greek population of their age group.

Settings and therapists

All data were collected in the inclusion preschool settings, which were located in three middle-class areas of Athens, in Greece. Data were collected during semistructured or free-play activities, because they were considered ideal for social interactions between children, unlike structured activities, which typically require attending and responding mainly to the teacher.

During both baseline and treatment, well-trained shadow teachers were assigned to the participants (one teacher per child). The shadow teachers were experienced therapists who had worked for several years with children with autism, but received additional training for a minimum of 3 months to familiarize themselves with the intervention implemented for the purposes of the present study. Each one of the shadow teachers was familiar with the children she supervised in the inclusion setting. All shadow teachers were college graduates who had majored either in psychology or in education.

Inter-observer agreement data were collected by the shadow teachers, three other therapists of children with autism, who were college students, and the author of the present study. The college students received training on the data collection procedures of the present study.

Definitions of the target responses and collection of normative data

Student initiations toward classmates were defined as statements and gestures that the participants made toward classmates. Those statements and gestures had to be socially appropriate, relevant to the context of the interaction, independent of prompting by the shadow teacher, and made in the absence of inappropriate or stereotypic behaviour.

Student reply statements were defined as verbal and nonverbal responses that followed initiations made by classmates, were relevant to those initiations, were not prompted by the shadow teacher, and were not accompanied by inappropriate or stereotypic behaviour. Initiations and reply statements that were prompted by the preschool teacher or by classmates were scored as independent.

To determine the types of initiation statements that we would teach to children with autism, we used data of typically developing preschoolers. Normative data were collected twice, at the beginning and at the end of the school year, with approximately 8 to 9 months elapsing between the two observation periods. There were a total of 10 half-hour observation periods per child, 5 in the beginning and 5 at the end of the school year. The conditions under which normative data were collected were similar to the conditions under which baseline and treatment data were collected. Namely, independent observers recorded verbatim the initiation statements, as well as the reply statements toward classmates that the 12 typical preschoolers made during free-play or semistructured activities (see Gena & Kymissis, 2001, for further details). Specifically, we analysed the initiation statements of 12 preschoolers matched for gender and age to the target preschoolers.

Independent observers recorded initiations and reply statements addressing classmates during free-play or semistructured activities. The analysis of those data yielded over 20 categories and several subcategories of initiations, but only the 5 most frequently used types of initiations were selected for the purpose of training children with autism. We considered that teaching more than five types could be overwhelming for children who do not initiate interactions at all. The five categories of initiations were as follows: (1) asking questions either to obtain information or to provoke competition, (2) demonstrating affective responses expressed verbally or with gestures, (3) asking a classmate to perform an action or to make a statement, (4) announcing information about their own and others' actions at the present or at a remote time, and (5) inviting classmates to participate in a common activity. Definitions of the response categories selected for the purposes of the present study and examples from each category are presented in Table 1.

Experimental design, data collection, conditions, and procedure

A multiple baseline across subjects single-case experimental design was used to assess the efficacy of the treatment procedure. During baseline, the shadow teachers were present and guided the participants to attend and participate in activities, but neither prompted nor reinforced target social responses.

During treatment, the shadow teachers used prompting and social reinforcement contingent upon target responses, as well as instruction following. Prompting was defined as any kind of verbal prompt or manual guidance provided by

TABLE 1
Response categories of initiations toward peers

Response categories	Definitions and examples
1. Asking questions	Posing questions that pertain to the following areas: (a) seeking information; (b) provoking competition. E.g., "Do you know what we have to do with this worksheet?" or "Can you write 'A' like me?"
2. Displaying affective behaviour	Showing affection toward a peer either verbally or with gestures: (a) with gestures; (b) verbally; (c) offering something with affection (e.g., "Here, you can have my painting"); (d) greeting with affection (e.g., "Hi, I missed you"); (e) asking for one's friendship (e.g., "I want you to be my best friend"); (f) seeking reassurance for one's friendship (e.g., "Am I still your best friend?"); (g) showing enthusiasm (e.g., "I love to sing along with the teacher"); (h) showing sympathy (e.g., "Feel better, Stephania"); (i) showing anger (e.g., "Don't you dare take my marker again!").
3. Giving commands	Making statements that require classmates to perform an action or to make a statement. E.g., "Put this tissue in the garbage" "Tell her what your favorite colour is."
4. Announcing information	Providing information regarding: (a) own actions at present time; (b) own actions at remote time (past or future); (c) others' actions. E.g., "Look, I drew an airplane" or "I am going to go to the playground this afternoon."
5. Inviting classmates	Inviting classmates to participate in activities other than play activities. E.g., "Sit next to me" or "Will you come to my birthday party?"
6. Other	Making any type of initiation that was not included in the five categories on which data were specifically collected. E.g., making welcoming or goodbye statements upon the entrance of a classmate or upon his own entrance or departure from the preschool, or giving a compliment to a classmate.

the shadow teacher for the child with autism to engage in either one of the target responses. For example, to encourage social initiations toward classmates, the shadow teacher might have asked the student to say something like: "Let's play in the backyard," or "Look at my doll, isn't she pretty?"

Social reinforcement was provided contingent upon the participants' spontaneous social initiations, as well as upon their independent responses to peer initiations. Social reinforcement included verbal statements, such as "you are doing a great job!" a pat on the back, and other forms of social approval.

"Instruction following" was used as a behaviour management procedure to reduce the frequency of aberrant behaviour such as noncompliance, inappropriate behaviour toward classmates or the teacher, and having temper tantrums. During "instruction following" the participants were removed from the classroom or the playground and were accompanied to an empty classroom or the preschool kitchen, where they had to follow simple directions, such as to complete a puzzle, to answer social questions given by the shadow teacher, etc. In addition, the shadow teacher reminded the child of their agreement by saying, "When you are ready, we will go back to your friends." The exit criterion from the instruction following procedure was that the child would follow three consecutive instructions without crying or fussing.

Data on initiation statements were collected specifically for each one of the five aforementioned categories. The data collection sheet for initiations included boxes corresponding to each one of the response categories, as well as a separate box for the category of "other." Tally marks under each category were used to indicate the occurrence of initiations per response category. The sum of those tally marks per session was plotted as one data point.

Data on reply statements were collected on a separate data sheet, on which initiation statements of classmates were reported followed by a "+" or "–", indicating the presence or absence, respectively, of an appropriate reply statement provided by the target student. The percentage of appropriate reply statements was calculated by dividing the number of appropriate statements by the total number of appropriate and inappropriate statements and multiplying the quotient by 100. The percentage per session was plotted as one data point.

Generalization data were collected only for two of the participants, because school regulations of the other two preschools did not allow for the absence of the shadow teacher. During generalization sessions, the target child was observed in the absence of his shadow teacher and no type of intervention was provided. The novel therapist was present and collected data discretely, but did not interact with the child.

Baseline, intervention, and generalization data were collected over several months: 9 months for Eva, 13 months for Lena, and 15 months for Andrew and Cory. The intervention was ongoing, but the total observation time for data collection purposes ranged from 12 to 22 hours per child across experimental conditions.

Fidelity of treatment measures were collected on at least 70% of sessions per experimental phase and per child and indicated that research staff implemented experimental procedures 100% as intended across all assessed sessions. The high accuracy of implementing treatment procedures may be attributed to the fact that all the shadow teachers were very experienced in using the experimental procedures, since they had used them, for clinical purposes, for at least 1 year prior to the present research study.

Inter-observer agreement

Inter-observer agreement data were collected on at least 33% of observations for each child and during each experimental condition. The frequency ratio agreement method (Kazdin, 1982) was used to assess agreement between observers for replies and initiations. Specifically, the smaller total number of initiations scored by one observer was divided by the larger number of initiations scored by the second observer and the quotient was multiplied by 100. Respectively, for reply statements, the smaller percentage of appropriate reply statements was divided by the larger percentage of inappropriate reply statements and the quotient was multiplied by 100. Inter-observer agreement across all target responses ranged from 85–100%, with an average of 95% agreement. The same procedure was used to assess the dependent measures and agreement was invariably at 100%.

Social validation

All four participants refused to attend preschool prior to intervention and had severe temper tantrums to avoid going to school. They all preferred to engage in one-on-one, in-home therapeutic sessions, rather than having to go to preschool. Shortly after the intervention, however, attending preschool was

Number of Initiations Toward Classmates

Therapist: _____

Date _____

Student: _____

Time   **Initiation Categories**

Questions	Affective Re.	Commands	Announcements	Invitations	Other

Figure 1. Data sheet for initiations toward classmates.

preferred to one-on-one therapeutic sessions, and going to preschool became highly valued by the participants (e.g., they wanted to go to preschool even when sick). In addition, both parents and preschool teachers reported that the intervention procedure was both highly necessary and critical for the child's social adjustment. Finally, the target responses may be considered socially valid, because their selection was based on normative data.

RESULTS

A detailed description of the normative data pertaining to initiations and reply statements made by preschoolers of typical development has already been published (see Gena & Kymissis, 2001). Therefore, we will only provide a brief account of those data as a means of comparing them to the data collected for the three preschoolers with autism. During the first observation period, the number of social initiations made by classmates of typical development toward peers ranged from 1 to 52 with an average of 22 per half-hour observation, as compared to 14 to 79 with an average of 36 when they were measured 9 months later. The percentage of reply statements during the first observation period ranged from 45–100% with an average of 78%, whereas the corresponding percentages 9 months later ranged from 70–92% with an average of 84% per half-hour observations.

The number of initiations that children with autism made toward their classmates is presented in Figure 2. Lena, during baseline, made 0–4 initiations with an average of 3 initiations per half-hour observation period. During intervention, however, her initiations increased dramatically

with a range of 9–55, showing no overlap with baseline, and an average of 26 per half hour. Eva, Andrew, and Cory did not initiate any interactions with peers during baseline, but during intervention their initiations also showed a dramatic increase. Eva's initiations ranged from 3–31, again with no overlap with baseline points, with an average of 14 initiations during half-hour observation periods. Andrew's initiations ranged from 2–53, with an average of 20 per half-hour session, and Cory's ranged from 4–23 with an average of 14 initiations.

Figure 3 depicts the percentages of replies that children with autism provided to their classmates' initiations. Lena's replies to her classmates' initiations ranged from 0–25% with an average of 15% during baseline, as compared to a range of 42–93% with an average of 72% during treatment. Eva did not reply to any initiations made by her classmates during baseline; neither did Andrew or Cory. Following intervention, however, their replies increased greatly. Eva's replies ranged from 25–71% with an average of 54% during half-hour observation periods, Andrew's from 50–90% with

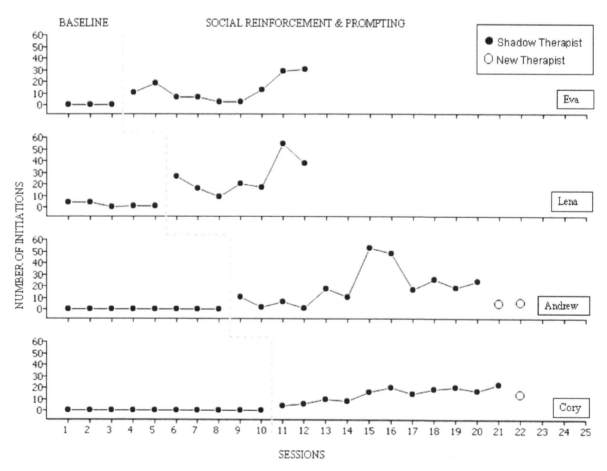

Figure 2. Number of initiations of four children with autism during their inclusion in preschool. The closed circles depict initiations in the presence of a shadow teacher and the open circles depict initiations in the presence of a new therapist.

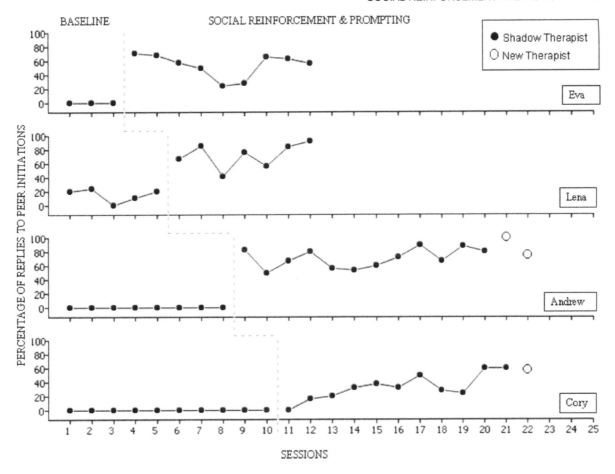

Figure 3. Percentage of reply statements to peer initiations of four children with autism during their inclusion in preschool. The closed circles depict replies in the presence of a shadow teacher and the open circles depict replies in the presence of a new therapist.

an average of 71%, and Cory's from 0–60% with an average of 33%. Overall, it is worth noting that there was no overlap of baseline and treatment points for any of the participants or the categories of target responses.

With regard to generalization across people, Andrew made 5 initiations during the first session and 6 during the second, versus 0 in baseline, but certainly fewer than the initiations he made in the presence of his shadow teacher. Nevertheless, his replies to peer initiations ranged from 75–100%, which are certainly higher than the 0% in baseline, but also as high as the percentage of replies during treatment. Cory's generalization data (14 initiations and 58% replies) are higher than his baseline data (0 initiations and 0% replies) and at approximately the same level as his performance during intervention.

"Instruction following," the behaviour reduction procedure used to reduce temper tantrums and noncompliance, was used as many times as the participants were noncompliant or had temper tantrums. It was implemented, during baseline, 7

times for Lena, 4 for Eva, 2 for Andrew, and 6 times for Cory. There was no need to implement the procedure during treatment.

DISCUSSION

The results of the present study are in agreement with prior research indicating that, during school inclusion, children with autism demonstrate limited communicative or social interactions with their classmates. Specifically, during baseline, three of the participants neither took initiative to interact with their classmates, nor did they respond appropriately when addressed by their classmates. Only one of the participants demonstrated some appropriate interactions, but minimally. Despite their social aloofness, however, they showed dramatic improvement in the target areas. This leads us to conclude that children with autism who receive systematic behaviour analytic intervention from early on and have reached age-appropriate intellectual functioning, like the participants of the present study, may overcome major social difficulties and consequently establish appropriate social interactions with their classmates when provided with systematic treatment by well-trained shadow teachers. Specifically, an intervention including social praise contingent upon the target behaviour and prompting as a correction procedure may be effective in increasing the social initiations toward classmates as well as responding to peer initiations. In addition, compliance to the shadow teacher's instruction and abstaining from inappropriate behaviour, such as temper tantrums, may be critical in obtaining the treatment outcome of the present study. The "instruction following" procedure selected for the purposes of the present study was only used a few times and was sufficient for achieving compliance and for extinguishing temper tantrums.

The increase in appropriate social responding that the participants of the present study noted may not be attributed to maturational factors for several reasons: (1) none of the participants demonstrated improvement in the target responses before intervention was introduced; (2) there was an increase in target responding precisely at the point in time when treatment was introduced for each participant; (3) even though the participants had attended preschool for several months, prior to receiving intervention, they had made no progress in the social domain and had to be excluded from school due to aberrant behaviour; and (4) their typically developing peers did not demonstrate such dramatic progress in the target areas during the school year.

The effectiveness of treatment in the present study may be attributed to several factors. First, the four children with autism who participated in this study, during their inclusion in preschool, were not simply placed in physical proximity to their typically developing counterparts, but were provided with systematic treatment used by competent therapists, well-trained in the use of behaviour analytic procedures. In addition, the intervention in preschool was not the only treatment that the participants received. Before, as well as during, their inclusion, they also received extensive treatment addressing their needs across all areas of development. Furthermore, control of their inappropriate behaviour was attained with minimal intervention, most likely because the shadow teachers were also serving as home therapists for the children and had established a good working relationship with them prior to their inclusion in preschool. Finally, because the participants were trained to use socially validated

initiations, it is very likely that their social responses were also reinforced by natural contingencies (e.g., peer attention and play with peers), rather than by the social reinforcement provided by shadow teacher alone.

The clinical significance of the present study may be high, but there are several limitations and there is certainly a need for further experimental investigation in this area. First, although the internal validity, as well as the reliability, of the results is not in doubt, since a direct measure of the dependent variable was employed (data were collected through direct observations) and the agreement between observers was high, the small sample size and the nonrandom selection of the sample limit the external validity of the findings. Thus, the findings generalize specifically to the sample of children with autism who reach normal intellectual functioning and receive extensive behaviour analytic intervention, rather than the entire population of children with autism. Another limitation of the present study is that stimulus generalization was assessed in only one parameter (across new people) and for only two of the four participants, because of practical considerations. It would be interesting for future research to test for maintenance of the treatment outcome, in the absence of a shadow teacher, at different points in time during intervention, in order to identify a more parsimonious treatment package. For example, it may be sufficient for shadow teachers to limit their presence to progressively fewer hours, rather than to accompany the student to preschool throughout the day for several months. Other types of manipulations could be identified that would lead to a less intrusive intervention or fewer hours of intervention.

Despite the limitations of the present study, we may conclude that the intervention outcome was socially validated by both the parents and the teachers of the participants, who characterized the intervention as both important and necessary for the social adjustment of children with autism in "regular" preschool. In addition, the intervention took place in a natural setting (a "regular" preschool) and the participants interacted with their classmates in a generalized manner and were trained loosely. That is, they did not learn cliché initiations or to respond to specific initiations from their classmates. Rather, they learned to make initiations and to respond to peer initiations in a socially acceptable manner and in various social contexts (e.g., during group games, group activities, while playing with a variety of toys, etc.). It is also important that the preschool teachers were not burdened with making special accommodations for the children with autism, since it was the participants who learned to adjust to preschool routines. For cultures in which the inclusion of children with autism is a relatively new and uncommon practice, making the inclusion process as unobtrusive as possible is important, because it is likely to help teachers and other school personnel to have a more accepting attitude toward inclusion.

The present study is only a small step toward dealing with the complex issues arising from the inclusion of children with disabilities. It sheds some light on the diversity of social skills that children with autism need to acquire in order to be "fluent" in interacting with their classmates. Yet, we are far from identifying the spectrum of criteria that a child and a school have to meet in order for the inclusion of children with autism to be successful and meaningful. The issues of inclusion concern not only children with disabilities, but also the entire school community.

REFERENCES

Ainscow, M. (1996). *Organizing schools for all.* Paper presented at the 2nd National Convention for Special Education in Greece. Athens, February, 1996.

American Psychiatric Association. (1994). *Diagnostic and statistical manual of mental disorders.* (4th ed.). Washington, DC: Author.

Autism Society of America. (1999). Advocate. *The Newsletter of the Autism Society of America, 32,* 3–4.

Chakrabarti, S., & Fombonne, E. (2001). Pervasive developmental disorders in preschool children. *Journal of the American Medical Association, 285,* 3093–3099.

Cole, D. A., Vandercook, T., & Rynders, J. (1988). Comparison of two peer interaction programs: Children with and without severe disabilities. *American Educational Research Journal, 25,* 415–439.

Evans, I. M., Salisbury, C. L., Palombaro, M. M., Berryman, J., & Hollowood, T. M. (1992). Peer interactions and social acceptance of elementary-age children with severe disabilities in an inclusive classroom. *The Journal of the Association for Persons with Severe Handicaps, 17,* 205–212.

Fenske, E. C., Zalenski, S., Krantz, P. J., & McClannahan, L. E. (1985). Age at intervention and treatment outcome for autistic children in a comprehensive intervention program. *Analysis and Intervention in Developmental Disabilities, 5,* 49–58.

Fuchs, D., & Fuchs, L. S. (1995). Inclusive schools movement and the radicalization of special education reform. In J. M. Kauffman & D. P. Hallahan (Eds.), *The illusion of full inclusion.* Austin, TX: ProEd.

Gena, A., & Kymissis, E. (2001). Assessing and setting goals for the attending and communicative behavior of three preschoolers with autism in inclusive kindergarten settings. *Journal of Developmental and Physical Disabilities, 13,* 11–26.

Gena, A., & Logothetis, E. A. (2001, November). Improving the attending and social skills of a girl with autism during inclusion in kindergarten. In A. Gena (Chair), *Improving the social competence of children with autism.* Symposium conducted at the First International Conference of the Association for Behavior Analysis, Venice, Italy.

Gettinger, M., & Callan Stoiber, K. (1998). Critical incident reporting: A procedure for monitoring children's performance and maximizing progress in inclusive settings. *Early Childhood Education, 26,* 39–46.

Guralnick, M. J. (1999). The nature and meaning of social integration for young children with mild developmental delays in inclusive settings. *Journal of Early Intervention, 22,* 70–86.

Harrower, J. K., & Dunlap, G. (2001). Including children with autism in general education classrooms. *Behavior Modification, 25,* 762–784.

Hughes, C., Carter, E. W., Hughes, T., Bradford, E., & Copeland, S. R. (2002). Effects of instructional versus noninstructional roles on the social interactions of high school students. *Education and Training in Mental Retardation and Developmental Disabilities, 37,* 146–162.

Hunt, P., Farron-Davis, F., Wrenn, M., Hirose-Hatae, A., & Goetz, L. (1997). Promoting interactive partnerships in inclusive educational settings. *The Journal of the Association for Persons with Severe Handicaps, 22,* 127–137.

Hunt, P., & Goetz, L. (1997). Research on inclusive educational programs, practices, and outcomes for students with severe disabilities. *The Journal of Special Education, 31,* 3–29.

Janney, R. E., & Snell, M. E. (1996). How teachers use peer interactions to include students with moderate and severe disabilities in elementary general education classes. *The Journal of the Association for Persons with Severe Handicaps, 21,* 72–80.

Kamps, D., Leonard, B. R., Vernon, S., Dugan, E. P., Delquardi, J. C., Gershon, B., Wade, L., & Folk, L. (1992). Teaching social skills to students with autism to increase peer interactions in an integrated first-grade classroom. *Journal of Applied Behavior Analysis, 25,* 281–288.

Kamps, D., Royer, J., Ducan, E., Kravits, T., Gonzalez-Lopez, A., Garcia, J., Carnazzo, K., Morrison, L., & Garrison Kane, L. (2002). Peer training to facilitate social interaction for elementary students with autism and their peers. *Exceptional Children, 68,* 173–87.

Kazdin, A. E. (1982). *Single case experimental design: Methods for clinical and applied settings.* New York: Oxford University Press.

Koegel, L. K., Harrower, J. K., & Koegel, R. L. (1999). Support for children with developmental disabilities in full inclusion classrooms through self-management. *Journal of Positive Behavior Interventions, 1,* 26–34.

Koegel, L. K., Koegel, R. L., Hurley, C., & Frea, W. D. (1992). Improving social skills and disruptive behavior in children with autism through self-management. *Journal of Applied Behavior Analysis, 25,* 341–353.

Laushey, K. M., & Heflin, L. J. (2000). Enhancing social skills of kindergarten children with autism through the training of multiple peers as tutors. *Journal of Autism and Developmental Disorders, 30,* 183–193.

Logan, K. R., & Malone, D. M. (1998). Instructional contexts for students with moderate, severe, and profound intellectual disabilities in general educational elementary classrooms. *Education and Training in Mental Retardation and Developmental Disabilities, 33,* 62–75.

Lovaas, I. (1987). Behavioral treatment and normal educational and intellectual functioning in young autistic children. *Journal of Consulting and Clinical Psychology, 55,* 3–9.

McClannahan, L. (1996). Η υποδομή της συνεκπαί-δευσης παιδιών με αυτισμό [The foundation for the inclusion of children with autism]. In Ε. Τάφα (Ed.), *Συνεκπαίδευση παιδιών με και χωρίς προβλήματα μάθησης και συμπεριφορς [Co-education of children with and without learning and behavior problems]* (pp. 154–167). Αθήνα: Ελληνικά Γράμματα.

McDonnell, J. (1998). Instructions for students with severe disabilities in general education settings. *Education and Training in Mental Retardation and Developmental Disabilities, 33,* 199–215.

McDonnell, J., Johnson, J. W., Polychronis, S., & Risen, T. (2002). Effects of embedded instruction on students with moderate disabilities enrolled in general education classes. *Education and Training in Mental Retardation and Developmental Disabilities, 37,* 363–377.

McDonnell, J., Thorson, N., Disher, S., Mathot-Buckner, C., Mendel, J., & Ray, L. (2003). The achievement of students with developmental disabilities and their peers without disabilities in inclusive settings: An exploratory study. *Education and Treatment of Children, 26,* 224–236.

Mesibov, G. B., & Shea, V. (1996). Full inclusion and students with autism. *Journal of Autism and Developmental Disorders, 26,* 337–346.

Nabors, L., Willoughby, J., Leff, S., & McMenamin, S. (2001). Promoting inclusion for young children with special needs on playgrounds. *Journal of Developmental and Physical Disabilities, 13,* 179–190.

Ochs, E., Kremer-Sadlik, T., Solomon, O., & Gainer Sirota, K. (2001). Inclusion as social practice: Views of children with autism. *Social Development, 10,* 399–419.

Odom, S. L. (2002). Narrowing the question: Social integration and characteristics of children with disabilities in inclusion settings. *Early Childhood Research Quarterly, 17,* 167–170.

Odom, S. L., Chandler, L. K., Ostrosky, M., McConnell, S. R., & Reaney, S. (1992). Fading teacher prompts from peer-initiation interventions for young children with disabilities. *Journal of Applied Behavior Analysis, 25,* 307–317.

Odom, S. L., & Strain, P. S. (1986). A comparison of peer-initiation and teacher-antecedent interventions for promoting reciprocal social interaction of autistic preschoolers. *Journal of Applied Behavior Analysis, 19,* 59–71.

O'Reilly, M., Tiernan, R., Lancioni, G., Lacey, C., Hillery, J., & Gardiner, M. (2002). Use of self-monitoring and delayed feedback to increase on-task behavior in a post-institutionalized child within regular classroom settings. *Education and Treatment of Children, 25,* 91–102.

Robertson, J., Green, K., Alper, S., Schloss, P. J., & Kohler, F. (2003). Using peer-mediated intervention to facilitate children's participation in inclusive childcare activities. *Education and Treatment of Children, 26,* 182–197.

Rogers, S. J. (2000). Interventions that facilitate socialization in children with autism. *Journal of Autism and Developmental Disorders, 30,* 399–409.

Schepis, M. M., Reid, C. H., Ownbey, J., & Clary, J. (2003). Training preschool staff to promote cooperative participation among young children with severe disabilities and their classmates. *Research and Practice for Persons with Severe Disabilities, 28,* 37–42.

Schwartz, I. S., Sandall, S. R., Garfinkle, A. N., & Bauer, J. (1998). Outcomes for children with autism: Three case studies. *Topics in Early Childhood Special Education, 18,* 132–43.

Stainback, W., & Stainback, S. (1984). A rational for the merger of special and regular education. *Exceptional Children, 51,* 102–111.

Stainback, W., & Stainback, S. (1996). *Inclusion: A guide for educators.* Baltimore: Brooks.

Stainback, W., Stainback, S., Courtnage, L., & Jaben, T. (1985). Facilitating mainstreaming by modifying the mainstream. *Exceptional Children, 52,* 144–152.

Waldron, N. L., & McLeskey, J. (1998). The effects of inclusive school program on students with mild and severe disabilities. *Exceptional Children, 64,* 395–405.

Wehmeyer, M. L., Yeager, D., Bolding, N., Agran, M., & Hughes, C. (2003). The effects of self-regulation strategies on goal attainment for students with developmental disabilities in general education classrooms. *Journal of Developmental and Physical Disabilities, 15,* 79–91.

Yang, T. -R., Wolfberg, P. J., Wu, S. -C., & Hwu, P. -Y. (2003). Supporting children on the autism spectrum in peer play at home and school. *Autism, 7,* 437–453.

Yeargin-Allsopp, M., Rice, C., Karapurkar, T., Doernberg, N., Boyle, C., & Murphy, C. (2003). Prevalence of autism in a US metropolitan area. *Journal of the American Medical Association, 289,* 49–55.

Zigler, E., & Hall, N. (1995). Mainstreaming and the philosophy of normalization. In J. M. Kauffman & D. P. Hallahan (Eds.), *The illusion of full inclusion.* Austin, TX: ProEd.

Γενά, Α. (2001). Πρόγραμμα ένταξης παιδιών με αυτισμό στο νηπιαγωγείο και στην πρώτη δημοτι-κού βάσει κανονιστικών δεδομένων [Developing an inclusion plan for kindergarten and first-grade students with autism based on normative data]. *Ψυχολογία, 8,* 221–248.

Γενά, Α. (2002). Ενταξιακό πρόγραμμα φοίτησης ενός κοριτσιού με αυτισμό στο κοινό σχολείο· μεθοδο-λογία και θεραπευτικά αποτελέσματα [An inclusion plan for a girl with autism in a regular education setting: Methodology and therapeutic outcome]. In E. *Κούρτη* (Ed.), *Η έρευνα στην προσχολική εκπαίδευση* [Research in preschool education] (pp. 313–322). Αθήνα: Τυπωθήτω.

INTERNATIONAL JOURNAL OF PSYCHOLOGY, 2006, 41 (6), 555–558

Psychology Press
Taylor & Francis Group

Did Skinner miss the point about teaching?

John Staddon

Duke University, Durham, NC, USA

*T*he Darwinian metaphor, to which Skinner was an early contributor, has been a commonplace for several years. Skinner was sure that much can be learned from experiments with animals, and those strategies that work best for the training of animals can and should be applied to the education of humans. However, his claims about how best to teach people, especially intelligent people who are learning difficult things, have several problems. Operant behaviour is *emitted* (it is spontaneous, at least on first occurrence). Emitted behaviour selected by reinforcement can be compared to the Darwinian idea of selection and variation. Operant learning is seen as interplay between response emission (variation) and reinforcement (selection). In applying his ideas to teaching, Skinner emphasized selection almost exclusively. But the real puzzle posed by non-rote learning, in both animals and humans, is not selection but the sources of variation that cause an action or an idea to appear for the first time. It is in this sense that Skinner's whole discussion of teaching missed the point. The Darwinian framework for behaviour analysis points to the fact that processes of variation exist, even though they have been neglected in favour of an almost exclusive focus on reinforcement and selection.

*L*a métaphore darwinienne, à laquelle Skinner était un premier contributeur, a été un lieu commun pendant plusieurs années. Skinner était certain que nous pouvons apprendre beaucoup des expérimentations animales et que les stratégies qui fonctionnent le mieux dans l'entraînement des animaux peuvent et doivent être appliquées à l'éducation des humains. Cependant, ses prétentions qui portent sur la meilleure façon d'enseigner aux gens, surtout les gens intelligents en train d'apprendre des choses difficiles, présentent plusieurs problèmes. Le comportement opérant est émis (il est spontané au moins à la première occurrence). Le comportement émis sélectionné par renforcement peut être comparé à l'idée darwinienne de la sélection et de la variation. L'apprentissage opérant est vu comme une interaction entre l'émission de la réponse (variation) et le renforcement (sélection). En appliquant ses idées à l'enseignement, Skinner a mis l'emphase presque exclusivement sur la sélection. Cependant, le vrai casse-tête posé par l'apprentissage non mécanique, tant chez les animaux que chez les humains, n'est pas la sélection mais plutôt les sources de variation qui amène une action ou une idée à apparaître pour la première fois. C'est dans ce sens-là que toute la discussion de l'enseignement de Skinner a pu manquer le point. Le cadre darwinien pour l'analyse comportementale souligne le fait que les processus de variation existent, même s'ils ont été négligés aux dépends d'une emphase presque exclusive sur le renforcement et sur la sélection.

*L*a metáfora darwiniana, a la cual Skinner contribuyó desde muy pronto, ha sido un lugar común durante varios años. Skinner estaba seguro de que era posible aprender mucho de experimentos con animales y que las estrategias que funcionaban mejor para entrenar animales podían y debían ser aplicadas a la educación de los seres humanos. Sin embargo sus afirmaciones acerca de cómo enseñar a las personas, especialmente a las personas inteligentes que estaban aprendiendo cosas difíciles, han tenido varios problemas. La conducta operante es emitida (es espontánea al menos cuando ocurre por primera vez). La conducta emitida y seleccionada por el refuerzo puede compararse a la idea darwiniana de selección y variación. El aprendizaje operante se ha visto como un interjuego entre la emisión de respuesta (variación) y el reforzamiento (selección). Al aplicar sus ideas a la enseñanza Skinner enfatizó casi exclusivamente la selección. Pero la verdadera incógnita que surge del aprendizaje no mecánico, tanto en animales como en seres humanos, no es la selección sino la fuente de variación que produce una acción o una idea cuando aparece por primera vez. Es en este sentido que toda la discusión de Skinner en relación con la enseñanza puede haberse equivocado. El marco de referencia darwiniano para el análisis del comportamiento señala el hecho de que en realidad existen los procesos de variación, aunque se hayan descuidado a favor de un énfasis casi exclusivo en el refuerzo y la selección.

Correspondence should be addressed to John Staddon, Duke University, Psychology & Brain Science, Durham, NC 27708, USA (E-mail: staddon@psych.duke.edu).

http://www.psypress.com/ijp

DOI: 10.1080/00207590500492708

ON ANIMALS AND HUMANS

B. F. Skinner was greatly interested in teaching, although he himself was far from charismatic as a lecturer and, in his later years, spent little time with undergraduate students (at least, that was my experience as a teaching assistant in his large Nat. Sci. 114 class at Harvard). Nevertheless, he was quite sure about several points: First and most important, much can be learned from experiments with animals. Strategies that work best for the training of animals can and should be applied to the education of humans. He believed animal experiments to show that positive reinforcement is much better than punishment as a motivator. His errorless-learning experiments with Herb Terrace convinced him that learning without making errors is possible. Since making mistakes is unpleasant, and aversive control is bad, he advocated programmed instruction, which he designed to eliminate errors, as the teaching method of choice.

But do Skinner's claims about how best to teach people, especially intelligent people who are learning difficult things, in fact follow from what we know about behaviour analysis as a science? I don't think so, and as evidence, I offer first a couple of anecdotes. One is about the abilities of an animal, the other about the learning of a schoolboy. They raise obvious questions: Do the most striking examples of animal intelligence in fact show the effect of the kind of training that Skinner advocated? Do the greatest examples of human education exemplify the effects of exclusive positive reinforcement and errorless training?

On February 22, 1818, Blackwood's Magazine published a letter from the "Shepherd Poet" James Hogg, which recounted an extraordinary feat of animal intelligence. Hogg wrote about his dog Sirrah and an experience he had when 700 lambs, newly separated from their dams, escaped at midnight onto the Scottish moor. As Hogg began to search, he could not see his dog in the dark, but spoke and whistled to him nonetheless. He and a companion looked for the lambs until daybreak. Failing to find them, or the dog, they concluded that they must return to their master and tell him that his whole flock of lambs was lost. But then:

> On our way home, however, we discovered a body of lambs at the bottom of a deep ravine ... and the indefatigable Sirrah standing in front of them, looking all around for some relief, but still standing true to his charge ... When we first came in view of them, we concluded that it was one of the divisions of the lambs ... But what was our astonishment, when we discovered that not one lamb of the whole flock was wanting! How had he got all the divisions collected in the dark is beyond my comprehension. The charge was left entirely to himself from midnight until the rising of the sun; and if all the shepherds in the Forest had been there to have assisted him, they could not have effected it with greater propriety.

There are two methods of training a dog. The quickest, least dependent on individual aptitude, and most obviously related to Skinnerian methods, is clicker training. A clicker is sounded every time the dog gets a little "treat." He will associate the clicker with reward and pretty soon the sound of the clicker itself works as a reward—just so long as the clicker–treat pairing is occasionally maintained. If he can't give a treat, the owner can now sound the clicker whenever the animal does whatever is required of him—sit, stay, beg, or whatever. If, as is usually the case, the beast fails to show the correct behaviour full-blown on his own, he can be rewarded for approximations, until the desired behaviour does come about and can be rewarded.

This method of training is called "shaping by successive approximations." It is the method used by circus trainers and the contestants on Animal Stars—we have all noticed the little bit of fish slipped to the dolphin, the treat given to Fifi after each trick. It is effective and reliable, especially if what is to be taught is well-defined and predictable. It is the method of choice for behaviour analysts. It emphasizes reinforcement—selection.

But there is another method of training a dog. It relies much more on the animal's instincts and on his relationship with his owner. Dog trainers often say "the dog wants to please his owner," and there is some truth in this. More important, the dog is social creature. The owner, if he or she behaves properly, will become the "alpha male" (or female: dogs are not sexist). "Positive reinforcement" is still involved, but now the reinforcement is primarily social. Moreover, the dog will behave in a different and more interesting way if he perceives his owner as a fellow creature rather than simply as a source of food. The emphasis now is not on reinforcement, although of course there always is reinforcement, but on variation, on creating an environment where the animal will "show what he can do." This is the approach used by shepherds to train their dogs—animals that already "know" what sheep are and instinctively herd them at first sight. The sheepdog loves to work the sheep and asks only to be shown the sheep and told what to do. Hogg's wonderful dog

Sirrah learned in this way and showed his versatility when circumstances demanded it:

[When I bought him, Sirrah] was scarcely then a year old, and knew so little of herding that *he had never turned a sheep in his life; but as soon as he discovered it was his duty to do so I can never forget with what anxiety and eagerness he learned his different evolutions. He would try everywhere deliberately till he found out what I wanted him to do, and when once I made him understand a direction he never forgot or mistook it again.* Well as I knew him, he often astonished me, for, when hard pressed in accomplishing the task he was put to, he had expedience at the moment that bespoke a great share of reasoning faculty (my emphasis).

Yes, we can learn a lot about teaching from work with animals. But we have attended to only part of the story. Since the early 1950s, it is the first approach—treats, explicit positive reinforcement, and "shaping"—rather than the second, much-harder-to-define method, that has formed the "scientific" basis for education. It is this approach to teaching that was advocated most forcefully, and with the most elegant methods, by B. F. Skinner. It is the origin of "time-outs" as punishment (in lieu of swifter and more vigorous methods), of programmed instruction, and of positive reinforcement as the major engine for behavioural change. It is also the basis for regarding teaching as training in a "skill," like a trick to be taught to an animal. It treats students like dogs, and pretty dim ones at that.

The training of Sirrah is an alternative approach. It means creating an environment in which the animal's natural propensities (which, in an intelligent animal, go far beyond reflex response) can flower to their full extent. Not an easy thing to do, perhaps. Not something that can be reduced to the kind of algorithm represented by the law of effect.

A human illustration is beautifully described by Richard Dawkins in his moving account[1] of "Sanderson of Oundle"—Oundle, a British "public" school famous for its output of talent, and Sanderson, its headmaster early in the 20th century.

Sanderson's hatred of any locked door which might stand between a boy and some worthwhile enthusiasm symbolized his whole attitude to education. A certain boy was so keen on a project he was working on that he used to steal out of the dormitory at 2 am to read in the (unlocked, of

course) library. The Headmaster caught him there, and roared his terrible wrath for this breach of discipline (he had a famous temper and one of his maxims was, "Never punish except in anger")... [The] boy himself tells the story.

"The thunderstorm passed. 'And what are you reading, my boy, at this hour?' I told him of the work that had taken possession of me, work for which the daytime was all too full. Yes, yes, he understood that. He looked over the notes I had been taking and they set his mind going. He sat down beside me to read them. They dealt with the development of metallurgical processes, and he began to talk to me of discovery and the values of discovery, the incessant reaching out of men towards knowledge and power, the significance of this desire to know and make and what we in the school were doing in that process. We talked, he talked for nearly an hour in that still nocturnal room. It was one of the greatest, most formative hours in my life... 'Go back to bed, my boy. We must find some time for you in the day for this'."

Dawkins adds "That story brings me close to tears..."

This story, like the one about Sirrah, shows a kind of creativity in teaching and a kind of spontaneous flowering in learning that seems to lie quite outside the rhetoric of "successive approximations" and the teaching of tricks. Sanderson's pupil was not "shaped" to show an interest in metallurgy. Undoubtedly he had felt Sanderson's ire for past errors, as he felt it now for breaking the school rules. And yet, under Sanderson's tutelage, in the environment Sanderson had created, he developed a passionate interest in learning of the kind we should all love to see in our own students.

WHAT BEHAVIOUR ANALYSIS REALLY IS

But are these examples fair criticism? Behaviour analysts will object that I am merely countering science with anecdote. Isn't this just the anthropomorphism of George Romanes and your grandmother warmed over? I don't think so. To explain why, we need to go back to what the science really is.

Skinner made at least two great discoveries in his analysis of operant behaviour. One was hardly original at all; yet it is the one for which he has gotten the greatest credit—and which he himself thought the most important, namely the principle of reinforcement. But humanity knew about carrots (although they were usually paired with

---

[1] *The Guardian,* Saturday July 6, 2002.

sticks) for countless generations before Skinner came along. And even the scientific version of reward was experimentally demonstrated by Thorndike, some time before *The Behaviour of Organisms* (Skinner, 1938).

So I think that Skinner's second contribution is more important than the reinforcement principle but, because it is still not fully understood, it has received much less attention. It is the idea that operant behaviour is *emitted*; that it is essentially spontaneous, at least on first occurrence. Years ago I compared this dichotomy—emitted behaviour selected by reinforcement—to the Darwinian idea of selection and variation (Staddon & Simmelhag, 1971). Variation was Darwin's term for the then-unknown processes that produced variants (variant phenotypes as we would now call them) from which natural selection would pick the winners. In similar fashion, the processes that govern the emission of operant behaviour produce an initial repertoire from which reinforcement can then select (see Catania & Harnad, 1988, for a selection of articles on the Darwinian theme in operant conditioning).

There are, of course, many differences between Darwinian selection in phylogeny and selection by reinforcement during ontogeny. Behavioural variation (unlike much, but not all, genetic/developmental variation) is far from random. But the most striking difference is that presentation of reinforcement by itself changes the repertoire; not just by selecting from what is available, but also by changing, usually enlarging, the set of behaviours that comprise the repertoire itself. It is as if the operation of selection by itself were to change the range of genotypes. Darwin thought that natural selection worked this way (although he understood nothing of genotypes, of course), when he summarized the sources of variability in the last paragraph of the *Origin*: "Variability from the indirect and direct action of the conditions of life, and from use and disuse…"

We know now that genetic variation is essentially independent of "the conditions of life" and "use and disuse." But the same is not true of behavioural variability: "use and disuse" is just habit, which certainly affects behaviour. And as for the "conditions of life," what are they in the Darwinian metaphor for operant conditioning? Well, I have suggested a few candidates—generalization and Pavlovian conditioning, for example,

in my book *The New Behaviourism* (Staddon, 2001) and earlier articles—but the fact is that we really know very little about the "conditions of life" that produce the kind of behaviour shown by Sanderson's pupil at Oundle—or by the dog Sirrah.

The education establishment, simpleminded as usual, has an obsession with "self-esteem," which is a crude way of addressing the "variation" issue. If a pupil has high self-esteem, we might expect him to be more willing to try out alternatives and to be creative. But, of course, "self-esteem" can just as well lead to smugness and self-satisfaction. It is a poor proxy for the kind of behavioural variation induced by the very best teachers.

All we can be sure of is that the causation involved in generating effective behaviour in challenging situations is complex, involving both nature and nurture in an uncertain mix. But three things seem clear: that there are processes in creative teaching that are understood in an intuitive way by our great teachers, like Sanderson of Oundle and the Shepherd Poet; that the Darwinian framework for behaviour analysis points to the fact that processes of variation exist, even though they have been sorely neglected in favour of an almost exclusive focus on reinforcement and selection; and that behaviour analysts need to take time out from pressing the "reinforcement" lever, and look around for those sources of variation that yield the most exciting kinds of teaching. Such a change of direction would not be an abandonment of behaviour analysis. It would mean only opening a door that has been closed for too long.

REFERENCES

Catania, A. C., & Harnad, S. (Eds.). (1988). *The selection of behaviour: The operant behaviourism of B. F. Skinner*. New York: Cambridge University Press.

Skinner, B. F. (1938). *The behavior of organisms*. New York: Appleton-Century.

Skinner, B. F. (1966). The phylogeny and ontogeny of behavior. *Science, 153*, 1205–1213.

Staddon, J. E. R. (2001). *The new behaviourism. Mind, mechanism, and society*. Philadelphia, PA: Psychology Press.

Staddon, J. E. R., & Simmelhag, V. L. (1971). The "superstition" experiment: A reexamination of its implications for the principles of adaptive behavior. *Psychological Review, 78*, 343.

INTERNATIONAL JOURNAL OF PSYCHOLOGY, 2006, 41 (6), 559–570

Addressing organizational complexity: A behavioural systems analysis application to higher education

Maria E. Malott

*Association for Behavior Analysis,
Kalamazoo, MI, USA*

Wilfredo Salas Martinez

*Universidad Pedagógica de Veracruz,
Xalapa, Mexico*

C ountless demonstrations across a variety of settings have shown how behaviour analysis can alter the behaviour of individuals by manipulating behavioural contingencies. However, changing organizations is more complex than changing specific behaviours. Organizations involve different units of analysis and require distinct interventions. This article describes a higher education change initiative based on a behavioural systems analysis approach. The work was carried out at the National Pedagogical University at Veracruz (México). This large institution presented significant problems, as well as low productivity: enrolment was declining, programs were outdated, and complaints about the administrative processes were frequent. Three types of complexity were analysed: environmental, hierarchical, and component. From the analysis, four improvement strategies were identified and implemented: (1) the incorporation of adult literacy training at the macro system level to attend to the high adult illiteracy and the academic failure of children; (2) the addition of various options to the thesis requirement at the organizational level to increase graduation rate; (3) the development of new programs at the process level to combat the downward enrolment trend; and (4) the re-engineering of the student-centred administrative processes, also at the process level, to tackle the inefficient administration. The designed procedures were partially implemented with great success. This case study points out the application of behaviour analysis to the organizational level.

D 'innombrables démonstrations effectuées à travers une variété de milieux ont montré dans quelle mesure l'analyse du comportement peut modifier le comportement individuel par la manipulation des contingences. Cependant, le changement des organisations est plus complexe que le changement de comportements spécifiques. Les organisations impliquent différentes unités d'analyse et requièrent des interventions distinctes. Cet article décrit une initiative de changement dans l'éducation supérieure basée sur une approche des systèmes d'analyse comportementale. Le travail fut mené à l'Université nationale pédagogique de Veracruz (Mexico). Cette grande institution présentait des problèmes significatifs tels qu'une faible productivité, un déclin des inscriptions, des programmes désuets et des plaintes fréquentes à propos des processus administratifs. Trois types de complexité ont été analysés : environnemental, hiérarchique et de composantes. L'analyse a permis d'identifier quatre stratégies d'amélioration qui ont été implantées : (1) au niveau du macrosystème, l'incorporation d'une formation d'alphabétisation chez les adultes, afin d'assister le haut taux d'analphabétisme chez les adultes et les échecs académiques chez les enfants; (2) au niveau organisationnel, l'ajout d'options diverses d'exigences de thèse afin d'augmenter le taux de graduation; (3) au niveau du processus, le développement de nouveaux programmes afin de contrecarrer la baisse dans les inscriptions et (4) également au niveau du processus, la réorganisation des processus administratifs centrés sur les étudiants afin de s'attaquer à l'inefficacité de l'administration. Les procédures élaborées ont été partiellement implantées avec succès. Cette étude de cas signale l'utilité de l'analyse du comportement au niveau organisationnel.

I nnumerables demostraciones en muchos contextos han señalado que el análisis del comportamiento puede alterar la conducta de los individuos manipulando las contingencias conductuales. Sin embargo cambiar las organizaciones es más complejo que cambiar las conductas específicas. Las organizaciones incluyen diferentes

Correspondence should be addressed to Maria E. Malott, PhD, Association for Behavior Analysis, 6947 Willson Dr, Kalamazoo, MI 49009, USA (E-mail: 71201.1377@compuserve.com).

We thank Carlos Jorge Aguilar Aguilar, Alberto Alarcón Urdapilleta, Ignacio Altamirano, Ricardo Camacho Lozano, Juan Gálvez, Daniel Gómez Fuentes, Tania Muñoz, Marco Antonio Nava Bustos, Ignacio Silva, for their ongoing support and commitment to the change efforts of the Pedagogic University of Veracruz.

DOI: 10.1080/00207590500492773

unidades de análisis y requieren de distintas intervenciones. El presente artículo describe un cambio en la educación superior basado en el enfoque de sistemas de análisis conductual. El trabajo se llevó a cabo en la Universidad Nacional Pedagógica de Veracruz (México). Esta amplia institución presentaba problemas significativos como baja productividad, disminución en el número de matriculados, los programas eran anticuados y abundaban las quejas sobre los procesos administrativos. Se analizaron tres tipos de complejidades: ambiental, jerárquica y de componentes. De este análisis, se identificaron e implementaron parcialmente cuatro estrategias de mejoramiento: (1) la incorporación del entrenamiento de alfabetización de adultos al macrosistema educativo para atender la alta tasa de analfabetismo adulto y los fracasos académicos de los niños, (2) la adición a nivel organizacional de varias opciones a los requisitos de tesis con el fin de aumentar el porcentaje de estudiantes que se graduaban, (3) el desarrollo de nuevos programas a nivel de proceso para combatir la tendencia a la baja en el número de matriculados, y (4) la reingeniería de los procesos administrativos centrados en los estudiantes y también dirigidos a la administración ineficiente. Los procesos diseñados se implementaron parcialmente con gran éxito. Este estudio de caso señala la aplicación del análisis del comportamiento a nivel organizacional.

INTRODUCTION

Behaviour analysis has no geographical boundaries. Countless demonstrations across a variety of settings and subjects around the world have shown how behaviour analysts can alter the behaviour of individuals. Although changing specific target behaviours is essential in many circumstances, changing one behaviour at a time is not sufficient when dealing with relatively more complex entities, such as organizations.

The behaviour of an individual is a different subject matter from the performance of an organization (Brethower, 1999; Glenn & Malott, 2004). A behavioural entity comprises actions of a single individual or group, while an organization, such as a university, involves greater complexity, including: (1) interlocking behavioural contingencies[1] of many individuals (e.g., faculty, students, and administrators) and their interaction with members of external systems (e.g., government officials, representatives of unions and other organizations); (2) insignificant impact of a single behaviour of an individual on the overall output of the organization; (3) aggregate products, such as number of graduates and funding that result from behaviours and products of multiple individuals; and (4) unique dynamic configurations of interlocking behavioural contingencies of multiple individuals that do not reoccur over time.

A behaviour and an organization, therefore, involve different units of analysis. In behaviour analysis, the focus of change is behavioural contingencies. A behavioural contingency describes a functional relation between the behaviour and its consequences that affects the future probability of that behaviour (Baldwin & Baldwin, 1998; Daniels, 1989; R. W. Malott, Malott, & Trojan, 2000; Martin & Paer, 1996). For instance, the relation between returning a recyclable bottle (behaviour) and five cents reimbursement (consequence) will increase the future likelihood of recycling.

In behavioural systems analysis, the focus of change is metacontingencies. A metacontingency consists of a set of interlocking behavioural contingencies that generate an aggregate product that has a demand in its receiving system (Glenn, 1988, 1991, 2004; Malott, 2003). The functional relation between the set of interlocking contingencies and their aggregate product's demand affects their future likelihood. For instance, the multiple interlocking behavioural contingencies of the individuals in a university result in graduates with knowledge and skills. The demand for graduates increases the likelihood that those interlocking contingencies reoccur again, so more graduates are produced. The demand of the organization's product is critical for its survival.

A behavioural contingency is to organizational change like a drop of water is to an ocean. Although behavioural contingencies are the essential components of behavioural systems, focusing on a few behaviours as a way to generate organizational change is too narrow an approach to address a system's complexity. To sustain organizational change, interlocking behavioural contingencies need to be ingrained in the organization's infrastructure—an accomplishment that requires a careful understanding and integration to the organization's complexity (Malott, 2001).

In this article we attempt to illustrate how the study of organizational complexity can guide

---

[1]By interlocking we mean that an element of a behavioural contingency (antecedent, behaviour, or consequence) or its product for one individual also serves as an element of a behavioural contingency for another individual. For instance, turning the light off for individual A serves as an antecedent for leaving the room for individual B—thus, the behavioural contingencies affecting the behaviour of two individuals are interlocked.

change strategies. Based on a behavioural systems analysis approach we engaged in a change initiative for a university in Mexico, the Pedagogic University of Veracruz (UPV) (Malott & Salas Martinez, 2004). The same approach could aid the change process of organizations of all types around the world.

BACKGROUND

During the last quarter of a century, the Mexican government has struggled to raise the educational level of its people by reducing the illiteracy rate and improving the educational level of the country's teachers. Traditionally, to become a teacher in Mexico, a 3-year certificate from a technical educational program was required by federal and state institutions. However, starting in 1979, the federal government demanded that school teachers have at least a BA degree in education. As a result, the National Pedagogic University of Veracruz (UPV) was created to train teachers to the BA level. In 1980, the UPV was founded and its president was appointed by the State Secretary of Education and Culture. The UPV opened with 7000 teachers enrolled in BA and MA degree programs. Today, the UPV continues to offer BA and MA programs to the state's elementary school teachers, located in 15 centres across the State of Veracruz. The central administration is situated in Xalapa, the state's capital. The university employs 360 professors and 160 administrative staff.

By 2000, the university presented significant problems that threatened its long-term survival. Productivity was low, enrolment was declining, programs were outdated, and complaints about the administrative processes were frequent. The UPV needed to undertake a considerable transformation. To help the UPV succeed, the authors and a supporting team engaged in a multiple-year application of the Behavioural Systems Engineering Model, presented in the textbook *Paradox of Organizational Change* (Malott, 2003). The supporting team included individuals reporting direct to the President, who were in charge of the following departments: Legal, Strategic Planning & Evaluation, Organizational Liaison, Academic Programs, Finances, Dissemination, Continuing Education and Information Technology. In addition, a significant number of administrative staff, directors of the university's regional centres, and the directors of five MA programs participated.[2]

Although the project is still in development, this paper focuses on the impact of the analysis of complexity and the results obtained thus far (Malott & Salas Martinez, 2004). Other methodological components, such as strategies for design, implementation, and continuous improvement, have not been included in this article due to space constraints.

COMPLEXITY ANALYSIS

Changing organizations is like engineering (Gilbert, 1996; Malott, 1999; Rummler & Brache, 1995). Building a bridge, for example, requires the unique application of principles from physics, mathematics, and other supporting sciences. Although the underlying principles are the same for multiple applications, no two bridges are alike, as the conditions for each construction are matchless, such as the density of the water, the weather patterns, the natural resources, and available technologies. Likewise, although behavioural systems analysts base their strategies on the scientific principles of behaviour, their applications are also unique, as there are no two organizations exactly the same, even when they generate similar products.

Therefore, the analysis of organizational complexity is essential in planning change, as it helps to identify targets that justify resource utilization, that have an impact on the organization's competitiveness, and that offer opportunities for success. In our efforts to improve the UPV, we found it useful to study the three types of complexity presented by Glenn and Malott (2004)—environmental, hierarchical, and component—to determine the change plan.

Environmental complexity

To contribute to its long-term survival, changes in the university should not be made in isolation without any appreciation of the system in which it operates—its macrosystem (Malott, 2003). Therefore, studying environmental complexity is fundamental. Environmental complexity consists of the variables or conditions existing in the macrosystem that affect the organization's performance. To address environmental complexity, we engaged in a study of the conditions of the State of

---

[2]Various master's theses have been produced addressing components of the change initiative presented in this article (see Aguirre Serena, 1998; Alarcón Urdapilleta, 2001; Alvarado Ruíz, 2000; Nava Bustos, 2001).

Veracruz and identified variables relevant to engineering change. Some of these variables were population characteristics, economic conditions, federal and state regulations, labour unions, and elected governments.

Population characteristics

Out of the approximately 7 million inhabitants of the State of Veracruz, 34% (2,362,869) are 14 years old or younger (*Anuario de Estadística por Entidad Federativa*, 2004). To meet the educational needs of the youngest population, 6500 institutions for pre-schools and primary education exist in the state (*Anuario Estadístico*, 2003). The proliferation of schools increased the demand for capable teachers, which in turn increased the demand for institutions that train educators, such as the UPV. There are 14 public and 8 private institutions that train teachers in the State of Veracruz, which compete with each other for the enrolment of current and potential teachers.

Furthermore, 44% of the state's inhabitants live in rural and indigenous areas, and out of the 580,386 population of indigenous origin, 13% do not speak Spanish (*Anuario de Estadística por Entidad Federativa*, 2004). Higher education institutions are faced with the challenge of adjusting their curricula to meet the different needs of the state's residents.

Economic conditions

There is much poverty in the State of Veracruz. Income per capita is $3600 per year. A significant proportion of the population lacks basic living conditions: 32% lack public water, 32% drainage, and nearly 11% electricity. Such circumstances are worse than the country averages: In Mexico as a whole, 13% of the population does not have public water, 22% drainage, and 5% electricity (*Anuario de Estadística por Entidad Federativa*, 2004). Given such hardship, many parents do not encourage their children to attend school or complete homework, as their children might be more useful helping with essential survival tasks, especially for families working in agricultural fields. Not surprisingly, out of 228,085 children in kindergarten, 5% drop out; and out of 1,064,123 children in primary schools, 8% drop out and 10% fail (*Anuario de Estadística por Entidad Federativa*, 2004).

Federal and state regulations

The Mexican government tends to over-regulate university procedures, creating highly bureaucratic processes. Take, for example, the signatures required to validate a diploma from a higher education institution. Until 2002, the validation of a diploma from the university required the signature of the state's Governor. Today, a diploma must have the signatures of the Secretary of Education and Culture and of the university's President. The diploma's validity must have been previously verified by people in at least four other positions. Such regulations complicate and slow down administrative practices.

Labour unions

The university labour unions in Mexico form a convoluted system. The UPV alone has three labour unions, consolidated in an integrated front of the UPV's union of workers. These unions intermingle with four other higher education unions of the state. One of the most influential unions in the state is the *Sindicato de Trabajadores al Servicio de la Universidad Veracruzana* (FESAPAUV), a union of workers of Veracruz University, the third largest university in the country. The state unions are partly consolidated with the national system of university unions, among them, the *Confederación Nacional de Trabajadores Universitarios* (CONTU) and the *Frente Amplio de Sindicatos Universitarios y de Educación Superior a las Autoridades Federales* (FESUES), which is formed by 72 unions from different universities in the country. The unions have a significant influence in the UPV administration regarding job classifications, employment, compensation, budgets, and student loans. For instance, the state unions demand that blood relations take priority for filling vacancies of teachers who retire, as long as the family member is enrolled in a pedagogic university pursuing a BA degree in education.

Elected governments

The Institutional Revolutionary Party (PRI) dominated Mexican politics at the national, state and local levels as it ruled unchallenged from 1920 to the late 1980s. The other two major political parties—the National Action Party (PAN) and the Party of the Democratic Revolution (PRD)—were formed by dissident leaders of the PRI. In the State of Veracruz, the PRI ruled for 64 years and it has shared state governance in recent years. The state's Governor appoints the Secretary of Education and Culture, who in turn appoints the President of the UPV. The political parties appoint key administrative positions and set direction, thus their role cannot be ignored in change initiatives.

Figure 1 illustrates the concept of environmental complexity. Each variable mutually affects all the others as well as the UPV.

Hierarchical complexity

Hierarchical complexity is determined by the number of part–whole relations of an organization (Glenn & Malott, 2004). A practical way to study hierarchical complexity is by analysing tiers of metacontingencies, from the largest to the smallest—starting with the macrosystem, followed by the organization, and then by the main processes. Figure 2 illustrates the concept of hierarchical complexity.

The macrosystem is the educational system of the State of Veracruz, which contains the UPV. The macrosystem includes the environmental variables discussed above. It also contains the educational system that produces educated citizens (i.e., pre-school, primary, secondary, technical, and higher education) and their dynamic interactions with relevant entities, such as government, industry, and family. The next level is the organization, that is, the UPV, which produces graduates. The UPV includes multiple processes, for instance, the curriculum development process that generates programs and the academic administration process that generates educational records.

Changing the dimensions of aggregate products (e.g., quantity, quality, and timeliness) will affect the configuration of interlocking behavioural contingencies that generate those products. Therefore, we measured critical dimensions of the aggregate products at multiple levels to determine worthy targets for change and the starting points against which the effectiveness of change interventions could be assessed. Table 1 summarizes the analysis of areas of improvement based on measures of aggregate products.

At the macrosystem level, we suspected that the high adult illiteracy rate and the considerable percentage of children who drop out or fail could be related. Parents who cannot read will not be able to help their children with homework and are limited in their support of the academic compliance of their children. Integrating efforts of the university with adult literacy programs could have an impact on the children's academic performance as well as their teachers' success.

At the organizational level, we found that the UPV had low productivity as a significant proportion of the students do not obtain their degrees, even after finishing their course work. Failure to complete the degree is a common problem in higher education in Mexico as well as in countries throughout Latin America (Salas Martínez, Malott, & Gómez Fuentes, 1997).

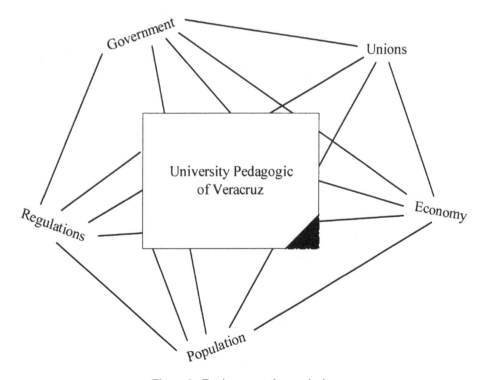

Figure 1. Environmental complexity.

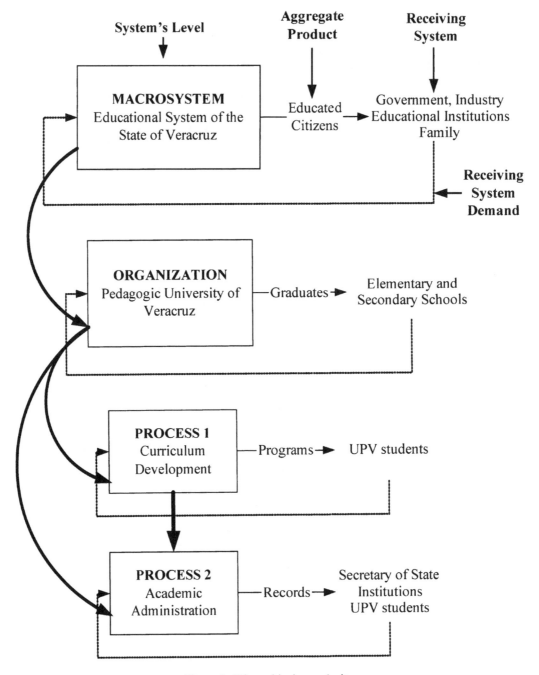

Figure 2. Hierarchical complexity.

That is why most programs in Mexico distinguish those who finish their course work (*egresados*) from those who obtain their degrees (*titulados*). In Mexico, when teachers obtain their degree, their salary is increased in compliance with federal and state regulations. Students contracted by the government to teach in schools will remain employed on renewable contract agreements until they get their degrees. Evidence of the BA or MA degree might result in higher job security, as a graduate would be eligible for regular employment.

At the process level, we found a decreasing trend in the demand for the main programs offered by the UPV. In part, the decline was due to the success of the UPV in training existing school teachers in the BA program—and, therefore, fulfilling the requirements that the federal government established in the 1980s. Enrolment in the BA programmes of the UPV was 7000 in 1980, 5000 in 2000, and 2324 in 2004.

However, the UPV could still maintain high level of enrolment as new vacancies result from the creation of new schools, expansion of existing

TABLE 1
Analysis of areas of improvement (1997–2000)

Levels	Interlocking behavioural contingencies	Aggregate product	Measures of aggregate product	Areas of improvement
Macrosystem: State's educational system	Pre-school, primary, high school, technical, higher education and their interaction with other entities, such as government, industry, and family.	Educated population	- Illiteracy: 13% of population 15 years or older can't read. –Out of 7 million inhabitants in the State, 80% had primary education, 10% high school, 7% technical, 6% higher education. –5% children in kindergarten drop out. –10% of children in primary education fail, 8% drop out.	–High adult illiteracy –Significant academic failure of children
Organization: Pedagogic University of Veracruz	Processes and interactions among UPV employees and students.	Graduates	–77% of students finish course work. –14.6% of the students graduate in the BA programs; and 1.2% in the MA programs.	Low graduation rate
Process 1: Curriculum development	All interactions that generate new BA, MA, or special academic programmes.	Programmes	Declining enrolment trend: –Two BA programs in education (67% decline). -BA in physical education (25% decline). Stable enrolment trend –MA in education (90% enrolment per year).	Downward enrolment trend
Process 2: Academic administration	All interactions that generate student records: grades, student identification cards, certificate of courses and social service completion, titles, certificates of professional texts, transcripts, and grades.	Academic records	–The UPV produces 7000 document a year, 10% of them with errors. –70% of UPV students evaluated the university administrative services as ineffective and inefficient. (20% of the 1400 students surveyed responded).	Inefficient administration

ones, and turnover of the current teacher population (approximately 1000 teachers alone retire from the school system in Veracruz every year). New vacancies require at least a BA degree from updated programmes that could provide adequate knowledge and skills to satisfy the needs of children across the state.

At the process level, we found that UPV students often complain about the student-centred services the university provides, especially those processes that generate student records. The process infrastructure is convoluted and inefficient, and administrators have lost sight of the fact that the students are the university's major clients. Other institutions with better services could compete effectively for the student market.

Component complexity

The number of elements that constitute an organization determines component complexity.

The more parts a system has, the more complex it is (Glenn & Malott, 2004). Analysing component complexity is essential to developing effective interventions that can survive in the dynamic environment of organizations. Relationship maps are useful tools in the analysis of component complexity, as they show functional relations between components of a system (e.g., departments or tasks) by outlining their output–input stream of aggregate products.

Figure 3 illustrates a functional analysis of the UPV internal organization that produces teachers with degrees. Each department represented in Figure 3 generates an overall aggregate product received by other departments. As at the macrosystem and the organizational levels, the demand of each department's aggregate product maintains the set of interlocking behavioural contingencies that generate that product.

We can distinguish between three types of departments: core, supporting, and integrating.

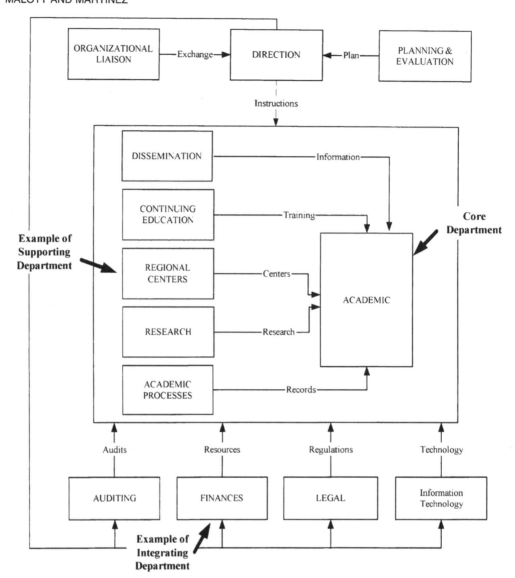

Figure 3. Component complexity.

The core department's function is essential for the university's existence as it generates the graduates—the product for which the university was created. The supporting departments provide aggregate products that serve as critical inputs to selected departments: For instance, the academic process department generates academic records, such as grades, and the regional centres provide practicum sites. Both academic records and practicum sites are critical for the academic department to function properly. Integrating departments generate products that all the departments of the organization need to function properly: For instance, the finance department generates financial records and transactions that affect the functioning of all the UPV departments.

The landscape of functional relations can be analysed at various levels of hierarchical complexity. Figure 3 is like a view of the organization from 20,000 feet above. It can guide us to grasp the big picture of major troubled functional relations and prioritize areas of improvement. To study the component complexity of all processes in an organization would be too time-consuming and unnecessary. But to re-engineer a process, we would need a more detailed view of the interactions so we can identify what each individual does and produces in the process. This analysis can be accomplished with very detailed process maps.

The study of complexity helps to identify levels of analysis and variables critical in the design of effective interventions. The analysis of

TABLE 2
Summary findings in the analysis of complexity

Types of complexity	Findings
Environmental	–High proportion of young and rural/Indian population. –High level of poverty. –Government excessive regulation over administrative processes. –Considerable influence of unions on policy and administration. – Political parties' role in leadership and direction.
Hierarchical	Macrosystem: –High illiteracy rate. –High drop-out and failure rate of kindergarten and primary school children. Organization: –Low productivity. Process: –Decreasing demand for specific programmes. –High number of complaints about administrative processes.
Component	Inefficient and ineffective administrative processes.

environmental complexity facilitates the identification of trends that might affect the organization's long-term survival; hierarchical complexity helps to appreciate whole–part relations; and component complexity aids the understanding of the parts of a process in enough detail to engineer change. Table 2 summarizes the major findings of the analysis of the three types of complexity.

CHANGE INTERVENTIONS

Based on our analysis of complexity, we identified four change initiatives: (1) the incorporation of adult literacy training at the macrosystem level to attend to the high adult illiteracy rate and the academic failure of children; (2) the addition of various options to the thesis requirement at the organizational level to increase the graduation rate; (3) the development of new programmes at the process level to combat the downward enrolment trend; and (4) the re-engineering of the student-centred administrative processes, also at the process level, to tackle the inefficient administration.

Macrosystem: Literacy training

We implemented an adult literacy training programme to address the high proportion of adult illiteracy and the related high drop-out and failure rate of kindergarten and primary school children found at the macrosystem level. By teaching parents to read, we hoped that they would be able to support their children's academic performance. In addition, literacy training could contribute to raising the state's education level of its people—a priority set forth by the Governor of the State of Veracruz and aligned with the direction from the Mexico's President. The training is carried out by the students enrolled in the BA program in Education as part of their practicum. Each student is required to teach 15 adults how to read and their practicum is assessed by testing the reading ability of the participant's adults. As a result of this effort, thus far 6809 adults have learned to read. At this point we have not assessed the adults' support of their children's training.

Organization: Terminal requirements

To graduate, students had to complete a thesis. Because the thesis requirement often involves little or no structure in comparison to academic courses (e.g., regular classes, ongoing evaluation of faculty), students tend to complete their course work but fail to finish their theses and therefore do not obtain their degree. This is known in Latin America as the "all but thesis" syndrome, similar to the well-known "all but dissertation" phenomenon typically observed in doctoral programs (Valarino, 1994, 1997). The problem was evidenced by the low productivity found at the organizational level in the study of hierarchical complexity. In an attempt to improve the number of graduates, we added five additional and more structured options for the terminal requirement of the BA program in Education: qualitative research, passing a national accreditation test, equivalence of advanced studies, bibliographic research, and practicum report. As a result, in a period of 4 years, 55% (1876) of the students in the BA programmes graduated—an increase of 35%. Encouraged by these results, similar alternatives are being incorporated into the MA programs.

Process: New programs and streamlined processes

Several new programs were designed in response to the downward enrolment trend. The new programs were tailored to meet the needs of the high proportion of the state's population living in rural and Indian areas and in poverty conditions—as we found in our analysis of environmental complexity. The new programs also incorporated the most recent educational technologies. In 2000, a BA in Indian and Rural Education program was launched. In 2003, certificate programs in Primary Education, Kindergarten, and Administration of Educational Systems, and MA programs in Teaching Development of Higher Education and Pre-School Education were initiated. In 2004, a certificate program in Special Education and BA programs in Administration of Educational Systems and Liberal Arts were introduced; and MA programs in Physical Education and Teaching in Higher Education are scheduled to start in 2005. In 1993, enrolment in the newly created programs was over 1700 and in 2004 it reached 2324.

Another initiative at the process level, still in early stages, was started: A redesign of student-centred administrative processes to increase process efficiency and reduce complaints. The scope of the analysis extended from admissions until follow-up after graduation. So far we have completed a detailed process map so we can appreciate the current process. The map includes over 400 tasks and the following subprocesses: pre-registration, student selection, admissions, program assignment, course enrolment, training

(courses, seminars, and workshops), social services, certification of studies, professional exam, generation of diplomas and student identification cards, employment, job performance, and continuing education. Special emphasis is being given to the subprocesses that generate student records. We are in the early stages of process redesign and plan to take into account constraints imposed by political parties, unions, and government identified in the analysis of environmental complexity. Table 3 summarizes the results of our change efforts thus far based on the analysis of complexity.

DISCUSSION

The change efforts of the UPV constitute a case study of how analysing complex systems can guide interventions aligned to external and internal environments. Our analysis guided the main strategies of the university's strategic plan, which is still in operation. Considerable accomplishments have been achieved thus far, including a significant number of adults who learned to read, an increased proportion of graduates, creation of new programs, and comprehensive appreciation of student-centred administrative processes.

TABLE 3
Interventions and results of change effort

Level	Interventions	Results
Macrosystem	Adult literacy program	–Developed program. –Incorporated literacy package to the BA programme in Education. –6809 adults have learned to read.
Organization	Terminal degree requirement	–Developed and implemented the following terminal requirement options in addition to a thesis in the BA program of Education: qualitative research, passing a national accreditation test, equivalence of advanced studies, bibliographic research, and practicum report. –55% (1876) of the students in the BA programs graduated—an increase from 35% in 4 years.
Process	Diversification of programs	New programs: –BA in Indian and Rural Education program (2000). –Certificate programs in Primary Education, Kindergarten, Administration of Educational Systems (2003). - MA programs in Teaching Development of Higher Education and Pre-School Education (2003). –Certificate program in Special Education; BA programs in Administration of Educational Systems and Liberal Art (2004). –MA programs in Physical Education and Teaching in Higher Education (scheduled for 2005). Enrolment: –In 1993, enrolment in the newly created programs was over 1700 and in 2004 reached 2324.
	Academic process redesign	–Detailed process map of all student-centred processes developed.

Our hope was to focus on the analysis of complexity and its impact on setting direction for improvement, while showing the value of the analysis. The analysis tools included in this article have been used with a variety of businesses and settings (Malott, 1992, 2003). We believe that this analysis can aid organizations in different cultures and in unique circumstances.

In this article we have not addressed behavioural systems analysis strategies for intervention design and implementation. Each of these topics in itself deserves a separate article. Indeed, we have been engaged in the UPV's change efforts for many years. So we hope that our emphasis does not portray a simplistic view of organizational change. Designing and implementing change interventions involves much more than simply identifying strategies, although identifying the right target of change is important and also requires much effort. Designing implies engineering metacontingencies, including planning the dynamics of what people do and produce, specifying job responsibilities, revising the organizational structure, re-engineering the information technology infrastructure, upgrading quality of products and services, and much more. Consider, for instance, the adult literacy program. Its design alone required significant endeavours such as analysing the current training system, developing effective instructional materials, figuring out how to include the training in the curriculum, and planning logistics.

Furthermore, there is a big gap between design and implementation. Without successful implementation there is no real change, as change means that the people in the organization engage in different tasks and generate different products from what they were doing before. Implementation requires that supporting contingencies and metacontingencies be ingrained in the organization infrastructure. For instance, to implement the literacy program, a set of supporting contingencies were put in place for the students to apply the program, for the adults to attend the courses, and for the administrators to manage the system.

Because organizations are dynamic and constantly changing, the analysis of complexity presented here represents an X-ray of the organization at a given time. The changes generated by our strategies will cause other systems alterations, and more changes will be generated by the interactive evolution of external and internal systems. Therefore, managing complexity requires ongoing evaluation and assessment and continuous analysis, design, and implementation.

REFERENCES

Aguirre Serena, M. E. (1998). *Aplicación del sistema de supervisión de tesis en la línea de investigación curricular en la Facultad de Psicología y Educación de la Universidad Veracruzana de la Región de Veracruz*. Unpublished master's thesis, Universidad Veracruzana, Veracruz, Mexico.

Alarcón Urdapilleta, A. F. (2001). *Un modelo organizacional aplicado a la normatividad de la Universidad Pedagógica de la Universidad Veracruzana*. Unpublished master's thesis, Universidad Veracruzana, Veracruz, Mexico.

Alvarado Ruíz, S. E. (2000). *Propuesta de un sistema de supervisión para incrementar la titulación de alumnos de psicología*. Unpublished master's thesis, Universidad Veracruzana, Veracruz, Mexico.

Anuario de Estadística por Entidad Federativa. (2004) México, DF: INEGI.

Anuario Estadístico (2003) Xalapa, Mexico: Departamento de Estadística y Evaluación, SEC, Veracruz.

Baldwin, J. D., & Baldwin, J. I. (1998). *Behavior principles in every day life* (3rd ed.). Upper Saddle River, NJ: Prentice-Hall.

Brethower, D. M. (1999). Specifying a human performance technology database. In P. J. Dean (Ed.), *Performance engineering at work* (pp. 17–142). Washington, DC: International Society for Performance and Instruction.

Daniels, A. C. (1989). *Performance management* (3rd ed.). Tucker, GA: Performance Management Publications.

Gilbert, T. F. (1996). *Human competence: Engineering worthy performance*. Amherst, MA: HRD Press (Original work published 1978).

Glenn, S. S. (1988). Contingencies and metacontingencies: Toward a synthesis of behavior analysis and cultural materialism. *The Behavior Analyst, 11,* 161–179.

Glenn, S. S. (1991). Contingencies and metacontingencies: Relations among behavioral, cultural and biological evolution. In P. A. Lamal (Ed.), *Behavioral analysis of societies and cultural practices* (pp. 39–73). New York: Hemisphere.

Glenn, S. S. (2004). Individual behavior, culture, and social change. *The Behavior Analyst, 27,* 133–151.

Glenn, S. S., & Malott, M. E. (2004). Complexity and selection: Implications for organizational change. *Behavior and Social Issues, 13,* 112–115.

Malott, M. E. (1992). Planning the well-being of a culture: An analysis of the Cuban experiment. *Behavior and Social Issues, 2,* 99–118.

Malott, M. E. (1999). Creating lasting organizational changes. *Performance Improvement, 38,* 33–36.

Malott, M. E. (2001). Putting the horse before the cart. In L. Hayes, R. Fleming, J. Austin, & R. Houmanfar (Eds.), *Organizational change* (pp. 297–320). Reno, NV: Context Press.

Malott, M. E. (2003). *Paradox of organizational change*. Reno, NV: Context Press. [Spanish edition: Malott, M. E. (2001). *Paradoja de Cambio organizacional*. Mexico: Trillas.]

Malott, M. E., & Salas Martinez, M. W. (2004). Strategic organizational change in higher education. *OBM Newsletter, 18,* 9–11.

Malott, R. W., Malott, M. E., & Trojan, E. A. (2000). *Elementary principles of behavior* (4th ed.). Upper Saddle River, NJ: Prentice-Hall.

Martin, G., & Paer, J. (1996). *Behavior modification: What it is and how to do it* (5th ed.). Upper Saddle River, NJ: Prentice-Hall.

Nava Bustos, M. A. (2001). *Un modelo para evaluar la licenciatura en educación física de la Universidad Pedagógica Veracruzana.* Unpublished master's thesis, Universidad Veracruzana, Veracruz, Mexico.

Rummler, G. A., & Brache, A. P. (1995). *Improving performance: How to manage the white space on the organizational chart.* San Francisco, CA: Jossey-Bass.

Salas Martínez M., W., Malott, M. E., & Gómez Fuentes, A. D. (1997, Julio-Diciembre). La evaluación de un sistema de supervisión de tesis en alumnos universitarios. *Revista del Consejo Nacional para la Enseñanza e Investigación en Psicología, 2,* 45–56.

Valarino, E. (1994). *Todo menos investigación.* Caracas, Venezuela: Equinoccio.

Valarino, E. (1997). *Tesis a tiempo.* Caracas, Venezuela: Equinoccio.

INTERNATIONAL JOURNAL OF PSYCHOLOGY, 2006, 41 (6), 571–579

Psychology Press
Taylor & Francis Group

INTERNATIONAL PLATFORM FOR PSYCHOLOGISTS

Annual Report of the International Union of Psychological Science (IUPsyS) to the International Council for Science (ICSU)

Pierre L.-J. Ritchie

Secretary-General

This report covers the period January to December 2005.

INTRODUCTION

The International Union of Psychological Science is an organization composed of National Member organizations (national societies/associations/committees of scientific psychology, national academies of science, or similar organizations), comprising not more than one National Member per country. Eleven charter Members founded IUPsyS in 1951. At December 31, 2005 the number of National Members was 70. As a Union, IUPsyS holds membership both in the International Council for Science (ICSU) and in the International Social Science Council (ISSC), Special Consultative status with the United Nations Economic and Social Council (ECOSOC) and Consultative status with the United Nations Department of Public Information (DPI) as well as Official Relations with the World Health Organization.

MEMBERSHIP

Countries with National Membership in IUPsyS in 2005 were: Albania; Argentina; Australia; Austria; Bangladesh; Belgium; Bulgaria; Canada; Chile; China; Colombia; Croatia; Cuba; Czech Republic; Denmark; Dominican Republic; Egypt; Estonia; Finland; France; Georgia; Germany; Greece; Hong Kong; Hungary; India; Indonesia; Iran; Ireland; Israel; Italy; Japan; Jordan; Korea; Lithuania; Malta; Mexico; Mongolia; Morocco; Netherlands; New Zealand; Nicaragua; Nigeria; Norway; Pakistan; Panama; Peru; Philippines; Poland; Portugal; Romania; Russia; Singapore; Slovakia; Slovenia; South Africa; Spain; Sudan; Sweden; Switzerland; Turkey; Uganda; Ukraine; United Kingdom; United States of America; Uruguay; Venezuela; Vietnam; Yemen; and Zimbabwe. At the end of the year, several potential applications were at varying stages of preparation.

Thirteen organizations are now affiliated with IUPsyS. The complete list of Affiliates is: Association de Psychologie Scientifique de Langue Française (APSLF); European Association of Experimental Social Psychologists (EAESP); European Association of Personality Assessment (EAPA;) European Association of Personality Psychology (EAPP); European Association of Work and Organizational Psychology (EAWOP); European Society for Cognitive Psychology (ESCP), Interamerican Society of Psychology/Sociedad Interamericana de Psicologia (SIP); International Association of Applied Psychology (IAAP); International Association for Cross-Cultural Psychology (IACCP); International Council of Psychologists (ICP); International Neuropsychological Society (INS); International Society for the Study of Behavioural Development (ISSBD); International Society of Comparative Psychology (ISCP). In

http://www.psypress.com/ijp

DOI: 10.1080/00207590601020713

addition, special liaison relationships have been established with the European Federation of Professional Psychologists Associations (EFPPA) and the International Test Commission (ITC).

VITAL STATISTICS

Number of National Members: 70
Number of Affiliated Organizations: 13
Number of Publications: 2

- *International Journal of Psychology*
- *Psychology: IUPsyS Global Resource*

Number of Scientific Meetings:

- 1 quadrennial International Congress
- 1 biennial Regional Conference

ORGANIZATIONAL MATTERS

This section summarizes some items of business not otherwise presented elsewhere in the Annual Report. Highlights of 2005 included the transition to a new Editor of the *International Journal of Psychology* and continued success of the journal, research activities and special projects reported below, in particular the large grant awarded from ICSU, as well as the Union's response to the Tsunami disaster in Asia, further enhancements of the *Psychology Resource File*, and continued work on revision of the Statutes as well as on the administration, management and structure of the Union. Special emphasis was given to implementation of the strategic planning framework adopted by the Assembly in 2004.

Assembly and Executive Committee Meetings

The Assembly of the Union last met in Beijing, China in August, 2004. The details were summarized in the 2004 Annual Report. The Assembly will next meet in Athens, Greece in July, 2006 in conjunction with the International Congress of Applied Psychology.

The Executive Committee met in July, 2005 in Berlin, Germany. Excellent arrangements for this meeting were coordinated by EC member Professor Rainer Silbereisen and the Union's Liaison to the Berlin Congress, Professor Michel Denis, with the assistance of colleagues Union's German National Member.

The 2004 Assembly adopted a Policy Directive that the Union will function on the basis of a Strategic Plan and the process of strategic planning will be a fundamental principle for the Union's governance and management. It also adopted a Procedural Directive that at each Assembly, the EC will submit a progress report on the Strategic Plan as well as any proposed revisions. In 2005, the EC was guided by the initial strategic priorities adopted by the 2004 Assembly:

1. Implement the policy and procedures for strategic planning (including development of a strategic vision).
2. Pursue permanent sources of new funding and augmenting short-term project funding.
3. Evaluate the Union's requirements for human resources.
4. Identify and maintain current core functions and ongoing short-term special projects.

A progress report will be presented to the 2006 Assembly.

For the short-term, the EC and Officers have concentrated on priorities 1, 2 and 3. Until the prospects for additional permanent funding or of substantial increases in project-based funding have been further determined, it was decided not to focus priority 3, notwithstanding sustained pressures and new demands on the Union's limited human resources. In the course of its work on priority 1, the EC held broad discussions on how the mission and goals of the Union were reflected in present, planned and possible activities. The intent is to better articulate a vision of the Union's role, aims and function. The next step was to examine the Union's structure to determine what structural changes are needed to match the vision, thereby enhancing its ability to carry out strategically-based activities.

The vision, reflected in the Union's mission, is to be the voice of psychological science and its application in the international arena, and to serve as a conduit for interfacing with other sciences to advance human welfare. In its deliberations, the EC considered how the vision can best be accomplished. The EC determined that the Union is best serve as: (i) a conduit (for information, exchange); (ii) a catalyst (in the development of international activities, national organized psychology, standards and training activities); and (iii) a convenor (as a sponsor of international and regional meetings).

Regarding Priority 2, "pursue permanent sources of new funding and augmenting short-term project funding", a significant achievement in 2005 was the creation of the International Psychology Development Fund (IPDF). This initiative was originally proposed by Union President Overmier who has also made a substantial donation to spearhead fund-raising. To meet certain legal requirements, the Fund has been administratively lodged with the American Psychological Foundation. Many members of the EC have made pledges; active fund raising will begin in 2006.

Under the leadership of EC member Professor Rainer Silbereisen, the Union is working on an agreement with the Dogan Foundation to establish a quadrennial award to be granted at each International Congress of Psychology. It is hoped that the agreement will be signed in 2006 and that the first award can be made at the Berlin Congress in 2008.

As part of its work on Priority 4, "identify and maintain current core functions and ongoing short-term special projects", the EC and Officers worked on a proposal for re-structuring the ongoing work of the Union to enable a more strategic focus. The essence of the proposal is to organize work around one continuing Standing Committee (Communications and Publications) and two new ones (Capacity Building, Strategic Planning). The work of the new Standing Committees would largely be carried out by focal Work Groups. The President also allocated to each EC member liaison responsibility for designated National Members.

As part of the work on strategic planning, the EC concluded that the Statutes needed relatively minor revision to be congruent with the vision and to make certain structural changes. The 2006 Assembly will be asked to consider proposed amendments to the Statutes and Rules of Procedure.

Among other matters, the EC received a progress report from Assembly delegate, Professor J. Gauthier, on a joint IUPsyS–IAAP initiative on the development a universal declaration of ethical principles for psychologists. The International Association for Cross-Cultural Psychology has also joined this project as a collaborating body. It is expected that the 2006 Assembly will receive a further progress report. The EC also continued to carefully monitor the current UNESCO Framework Agreement. As noted in recent annual reports, the Union remains very concerned about the implications for research and special project of possible changes in funding received from UNESCO via ICSU and ISSC.

The priority accorded to capacity-building and to regional development is concretized in several activities, including the 2005 Regional Conference

(see below), and planning for the 2006 Advanced Research Training Seminars. An unanticipated tragedy gave rise to a raid response capacity-building activity in the aftermath of the tsunami that struck parts of Asia in late 2004. As chair of the National Capacity Building Work Group, EC member Dr. Elizabeth Nair initiated immediate discussion within the EC about an initiative to facilitate the establishment of collaborative and consultative networks among key psychologists in the countries most severely affected by the tsunami. The objective was to develop and facilitate training programs for evidence-based psychosocial intervention, paying heed to maintaining high standards in ethical practices, applying a "best practices" approach in service delivery, utilizing program evaluation and feedback, and incorporating local cultural perspectives and approaches. The EC agreed to support development of a workshop for participants from the tsunami affected countries and other interested psychologists. Funds for this endeavor were provided by a major grant from the American Psychological Association (APA), with additional funding from the ISSBD, the Chinese Academy of Science and Technology and the Australian Psychological Society. The IAAP provided funding for follow-up activities held in Bangkok in November 2005 in conjunction with the Asian Regional Psychology Congress.

The main workshop, *Building Psychosocial Interventions in the Tsunami Aftermath* was held in Singapore, 15–18 May 2005. Instrumental in the planning and implementation of the workshop were Dr. Nair (Workshop Chair), the President of the Union Professor Overmier, and Deputy Secretary-General Dr. Bullock (also APA tsunami relief activities coordinator), and Dr. G. Jacobs (Director, Disaster Mental Health Institute, University of North Dakota). Workshop leaders were Dr. Jacobs and Dr Nair as well as Dr. A. Oyungerel (Mongolian Red Cross) and Professor M. Wessells (Randolph Macon University). The workshop was highly rated by the participants who came from Australia, China, India, Indonesia, Sri Lanka, and Thailand. A follow-up activity, sponsored by the International Association of Applied Psychology (IAAP) was planned in conjunction with the November 2005 Asian Applied Psychology Conference held in Bangkok, Thailand. This activity focused on participants from India, Indonesia, Sri Lanka, and Thailand. Follow-up activities at the national level have also occurred in these countries. A symposium on the overall project is planned for the International Congress of Psychology to held in Athens and the First Asian Regional Union of Psychological Science Congress to be held in Jakarta, both in 2006. The EC is continuing to review implications for future capacity-building activities.

The Executive Committee reviewed activities of the Union's several international research networks and projects. Activities of the past year are reported below in the highlights of specific projects. As already noted, the emphasis in 2005 was on the tsunami project as well as on the water project (see below). Activities for 2006–2007 are under active consideration. Longer-term planning of special projects is now contingent on the directions and priorities to be set in the course of strategic planning.

The Executive Committee for the current quadrennium (2004–2008) is: President, Prof. Bruce Overmier (USA); Secretary-General, Prof. Pierre Ritchie (Canada); Past-President, Prof. Michel Denis (France); Treasurer, Prof. Michel Sabourin (Canada); Vice-Presidents, Profs. Saths Cooper (South Africa) and Ingrid Lunt (United Kingdom); Deputy Secretary-General, Dr. Merry Bullock (USA); Members: Profs. Helio Carpintero (Spain); James Georgas (Greece); Hassan Kassim Khan (Yemen); Sonoko Kuwano (Japan); Patrick Lemaire (France); Elizabeth Nair (Singapore); Juan José Sánchez Sosa (Mexico); Rainer Silbereisen (Germany); Barbara Tversky (USA); and Kan Zhang (China).

The Officers are the President, Secretary-General, Treasurer, Vice-Presidents, Past-President, and Deputy Secretary-General.

Finances

Detailed financial statements, independently audited, have been submitted to the ICSU and ISSC Secretariats.

The Treasurer, Professor Michel Sabourin, presented a comprehensive report to the Executive Committee. While the financial base of the Union remains sound, in recent years, the Treasurer reported increasing concern about the prospect of deficits in future years, an experience that already occurred in the past quadrennium. Current operational finances remain very tight and provide little margin for new initiatives. As noted previously, the budgets of some National Members continues to affect their capacity to render timely dues payments; this is typically due to economic and currency problems in their respective countries. The 2004 Assembly approved

a dues increase, being implemented in two steps, US$20 in 2005 and a further US$10 in 2006, except that National Members in Category A are exempted from the increase. It is recognized that this is modest step toward stabilizing the Union's finances. As noted above, a strategic priority is to increase the Union non-dues based revenues. The establishment of the International Psychology Development Fund to build an endowment is an important first step in this direction. For the short-term, the Treasurer confirmed that fiscal prudence in the management of the Union's affairs has allowed it to maintain financial viability. He again noted that financial reporting requirements continue to increase, adding to the administrative load of the Union.

Secretariat

Progress on electronic communication to facilitate internal communications has been sustained, especially within the Executive Committee and externally with the more established international organizations as well as increasingly with the Assembly, National Members and broader communities. Nonetheless, this mode of communication remains difficult to access for a number of National Members.

As noted in recent Annual Reports and in the Secretary-General's report to the 2004 Assembly, the administrative burden of the Union continues to be greater than available resources. The result is a noteworthy overload, typically prompting a short-term priority-setting orientation. The volume of communications as well as the expectation of rapid responses is an ever increasing challenge relative to available administrative resources. This attenuates the general advantages afforded by electronic communications. It is also compounded by the unlikely prospect of additional resources being allocated to the secretariat in the immediate future. The Secretary-General recommended that internal resources be an important consideration in strategic planning.

No new work on the Archives was initiated in the past year. However, the Secretary-General plans to begin work on an electronic archive in 2006.

The work of the Secretary-General has been ably complemented by the assistance of the Deputy-Secretary-General, Professor Merry Bullock who also continues to provide valuable service as web master of the Union's web site (www.iupsys.org).

ACTIVITIES UNDERTAKEN DURING 2005

Scientific meetings

XXVIII International Congress of Psychology
The Final Report of the XXVIII International Congress of Psychology, held in August, 2004 in Beijing, China was received by the Executive Committee. It was organized under the leadership of Congress President, Professor Q. Jing, then Union Vice-President, Professor H. Zhang and Congress Secretary-General, Professor K. Zhang (now a member of the Union's EC), with former Past-President, Professor G. d'Ydewalle as the Union Liaison. As reported in 2004, the Congress was a complete scientific success. The final report also confirmed that the Congress succeeded financially, achieving a small surplus that will be shared with the Union according to the provisions of the contract between the Chinese National Member and the Union.

XXIX International Congress of Psychology
The XXIX International Congress of Psychology will be held in Berlin, July 20–25, 2008. The organizational structure of the Congress is now in place. The new Congress President, Professor Peter Frensch and key colleagues made a progress report and held extensive discussions with the Officers and the EC in conjunction with the Executive Committee meetings held in Berlin. The EC also conducted a site visit of the Congress venue. Union Past-President M. Denis, is the Union Liaison to the Berlin Congress.

XXX International Congress of Psychology
The 2004 Assembly voted to hold the XXX International Congress of Psychology in Cape Town, South Africa in 2012. The incoming Executive Committee appointed Secretary-General P. Ritchie as the Union's Liaison to the Capetown Congress. An initial liaison visit and meetings with Congress organizers is planned for 2006.

2005 Regional Conferences
Regional Conferences are held during every two years in collaboration with IAAP. The 2005 Asia Regional Conference was held in Bangkok, Thailand in November, 2005 under the primary auspices of the IAAP, with support from IUPsyS and IACCP. In addition to the contribution of the scientific programme, it is anticipated that Thailand will become a member of the Union. In addition, this Conference enabled preparations for the anticipated First Asian Regional Union of Psychological Science Congress to be held in Jakarta in August, 2006. More than 400 participants from 25 countries attended, predominantly from Asia but including delegates from North Africa and the Middle East as well as Sub-Saharan Africa, the Americas and Europe as well.

It is expected that a decision on the 2007 Regional Conference will be made in the coming year.

ICSU General Assembly
The Union was represented at the 2005 ICSU General Assembly meeting in Shanghai and Suzhou, China by Union President, Professor B. Overmier, Secretary-General, Professor Pierre Ritchie, Past-President Michel Denis, and EC member, Professor K. Zhang. The main work of the GA was deliberation on and adoption of ICSU's first ever Strategic Plan. During the Scientific Forum preceding the GA, Secretary-General Ritchie made an invited presentation on the Contributions of Psychological Science to Health and Well-being. At the GA, Professor Denis was re-elected to the ICSU Executive Board. Later in 2005, Professor Ritchie was re-appointed to the ICSU Committee on Scientific Planning and Research that had been charged with development of the Strategic Plan and that will now play coordinate its implementation.

Publications

The IUPsyS publications program is guided by the **Standing Committee on Communications and Publications** chaired by current Past-President M. Denis.

The past year was one of transition for the *International Journal of Psychology*, from outgoing editor, Professor Laura Hernandez to incoming editor, Professor Claudia Dalbert. The *IJP* remains the major regular scientific publication channel of IUPsyS. The International Platform Section of the Journal (Editors: Professors P. Ritchie and M. Bullock) continued to serve as a quick-access information forum on major national and regional developments in scientific psychology. A continuously updated calendar of international congresses and conferences in psychology was again part of that section as well as posted to the web-site. Special issues were again an important feature of the Journal. In 2005, these were 'Environmental Perception and Cognitive Maps' edited by Professors Mira and Deus, and 'Social Psychology Around the World', edited by Professor John Adair.

The sixth edition of the *Psychology Resource Files* (Co-Editors: M. Stevens and D. Wedding) was published in 2005, the first one published by the new editorial team. This initiative, the Union's first venture in publishing in CD-Rom format, continued to be well received. The sixth edition, as with the immediate prior edition, now takes advantage of the likelihood that users of the CD-Rom will have concurrently available access to the internet. However, such access is not required for the use of the databases. Among the resource tools, users will find a historical time-line for psychology, with integrated links to the internet, an organized list of useful internet websites that are primarily meta-sites offering access to further sites, review of the origins and developments of scientific psychology in various regions of the world, as well as updates of materials which were included in preceding editions.

The IUPsyS Website (www.iupsys.org), under the direction of the Deputy Secretary-General, M. Bullock, continues to be enhanced. It is a rich source of current information on the Union and activities of international significance.

The Union's newsletter *Keeping You Posted* under the direction of Deputy Secretary-General, M. Bullock facilitates communication with National Members.

It is expected that a comprehensive, internationally oriented conceptual history of psychology, *Psychological Concepts: An International Historical Perspective* (Editors: K. Pawlik and G. d'Ydewalle), will be published in 2006.

The **Standing Committee on Research and Special Projects**, chaired by Professor B. Overmier, continues to assist the Assembly and Executive Committee in providing general oversight and a policy framework. Alternatives to current procedures for development, monitoring and reporting of projects by the committee remain under consideration. As noted previously, the need for often rapid response to externally controlled factors, has led the committee's historic functioning to become increasingly marginal to effective decision-making. During the EC deliberations on strategic planning (see above), it was concluded that the work of this Standing Committee can be better carried out through different structures. This recommendation is part of the general recommendations and progress report on strategic planning being submitted to the Assembly in 2006.

The **Standing Committee on the Development of Psychology as a Science and a Profession** chaired by former Vice-President J.J. Sanchez Sosa worked primarily through the **Work Group on National Capacity-building**. During the EC deliberations on strategic planning (see above), it was concluded that the work of this Standing

Committee can be better carried out through a Standing Committee on Capacity-building. This recommendation is part of the general recommendations and progress report on strategic planning being submitted to the Assembly in 2006.

The **Task Group on Women's Issues** met during the Beijing Congress. Several projects are under consideration. A list serve has been established.

The Union's **Standing Committee on the Psychological Study of Peace**, previously chaired by Professor D. Bretherton (University of Melbourne) is now chaired by Prof D. Christie (Ohio State University). The committee is actively developing a new work plan that will be reviewed by the Executive Committee in 2006.

Special Projects

The **Advanced Research Training Seminars** (ARTS) continues to be a centre-piece of the Union's capacity-building program. ARTS are held every even-numbered year, in conjunction with the major international congresses of the Union and of IAAP. For the 2006 ARTS, the Co-Coordinators were Professors I. Lunt and Heidi Keller. A strong ARTS programme is again expected for 2006, with three offerings: (i) Design and Methods in Cross-cultural Psychology (Professor Fons van de Vijver, Convener); (ii) Stress, Health and Well-being in the Face of Major Trauma (Professor Stevan E. Hobfoll, Convener); (iii) Universal and ethnocyncratic couple patterns: From evolution to culture and from theory to research (Rolando, Diaz-Loving, Convener).

In the previous quadrennium, the creation of the Union's **Work Group on Capacity-Building for National Psychology** chaired by EC member Dr. Elisabeth Nair in this quadrennium, resulted from the Executive Committee authorization to develop additional capacity-building activities to address the national and regional development of psychology as a science and as a profession. The short-term priority was accorded to the countries of Asia and of the Middle East. The contributions of this Work Group to the Tsunami Project and to the 2005 Regional Conference were described above.

The **International Network on Psychological Dimensions of Global Change** built on the foundations of the previous project **Perception and Assessment of Global Environmental Change** (PAGEC), chaired by former Union President K. Pawlik (University of Hamburg). In the previous quadrennium, it established a new initiative focused on **Psychological Aspects of Global Change** that resulted in a scientific conference held in Istanbul, Turkey focused on evaluation of PAGEC and on research planning for psychological aspects of global change.

As an outcome of the very successful Istanbul meeting, priority was accorded to the development of a large-scale project on sustainable water use. The project coordinators for this new endeavor are Professors M. Bonnes (University of Rome) and G. Moser (University of Paris V). Under their leadership, in 2004 a new activity, **Human Dimensions of Global Change: Human Perceptions and Behavior in Sustainable Water Use**, was launched that continued into 2005. This two-year research project received financial assistance from UNESCO and the USA State Department via ICSU. This innovative project includes a team of scientists from France, India, Italy, Germany, Spain, and Turkey. The International Geographic Union is the principle external partner for this endeavor. In 2004, pilot work was completed in four communities in France, India, Italy, and Mexico. The main outcomes and achievements of the research activities conducted to date are the implementation and timely completion of the four pilot studies composing the first phase of the project. The data gathered through these four pilot studies allow a very informative (although necessarily partial and preliminary) picture of possible cultural, social psychological and geographical variations existing in the human use and perception of fresh water resources, according to the different national contexts considered in the present research project. The second stage of the project is now being implemented. Final results and analysis are expected by early 2006.

The Research Network Project **Psychology in a Multi disciplinary Environment** is an extension of the former project, **Psychology and Cognitive Science**. It was launched to provide a framework for engaging contacts with international bodies representing other disciplines related to psychology. The objective is to explore the possibilities for IUPsyS and other organizations whose objectives partly overlap to join their efforts in launching activities and stimulate collaborations that promote an interdisciplinary view of science. The project remains based with the Human Cognition Group under the direction of IUPsyS Past-President, Professor M. Denis (LIMSI-CNRS, France). It also continues to be a broad-based international endeavor drawing on the strong 31 country network already identified in Stage I of the project. Particular attention is being accorded to the capacity building value of this project in countries where psychology can contribute to new

technologies which may promote sustainable research and attendant economic benefits. Prior activities and support from UNESCO, the US National Academy of Sciences and ICSU were described in detail in previous Annual Reports.

The objective remains the pursuit of common scientific issues through joint initiatives which are currently being considered. IUPsyS continues to evaluate this project as an important success of recent years. The capacity-building dimension has been particularly well achieved by the work to date. Future multi-disciplinary endeavors will build and expand on the scholarly and training activities undertaken by this project since its inception.

The **International Network of Psychology and the Developing World** (INPDW), is coordinated by EC Member, Dr. S. Cooper. Activities continued to centre on facilitating communication between individual psychologists who work in the developing world, helping to make IUPsyS more visible in the developing world, supporting psychological research in different areas of the planet, and enhancing participation in the International Congresses of Psychology and in the Regional Congresses held in developing countries or countries in transition. The Advanced Research Training Seminars (ARTS) are regarded as very important in helping to facilitate research and international networks. Recent efforts have focused on expanding the network in sub-Saharan Africa and in South Asia. The INPDW has also contributed to the National Capacity-building activities.

The IUPsyS **HealthNet**, co-ordinated by Professor J.J. Sánchez Sosa (National University of Mexico), continued its renewal and expansion in this quadrennium. It has grown steadily with participants in more than 30 countries. It is a network of psychologists working as clinicians and scientists on a wide range of health problems. They develop and implement illness prevention and health promotion programs as well as specific clinical interventions. HealthNet was instrumental in creating the Latin American Network of University Health Research Programs as well as the Latin American Association of Schools and Institutes of Psychology. Currently, HealthNet plays an instrumental role in both organizations. This Network also provides collaboration and assistance to Union and to the World Health Organization (WHO) in implementing the IUPsyS–WHO Work Plan. The HealthNet web site is fully operational with assistance from the General Directorate for Academic Computing of UNAM. The Health Net web page may be found at: http://www.unam.mx/healthnet. The hard copy

Health Net Newsletter is also published periodically and disseminated world-wide.

Official Relations between the Union and the **World Health Organization** (WHO) were established in the current quadrennium (2002). Secretary-General, Professor Pierre Ritchie, serves as the Union's Main Representative to WHO. The (2002–2005) **WHO–IUPsyS Work Plan** (2002–2005) had several foci. Consistent with the generic WHO goal of "Achieving Health for All" and to reducing the burden of disease and illness as well as current WHO priorities, the Work Plan supports and enhances:

(1) Capacity Building;
(2) Evidence Based Change;
(3) Transferability of Knowledge.

Specific activities included collaboration on Adherence and Compliance to Therapeutic Regimes, contributing to policy development and projects in the Non-Communicable Diseases and Mental Health and Substance Abuse cluster (with emphasis on behavioral and psychological risk factors for health) as well as to the Organization of Health Services Delivery in the Evidence and Information for Policy cluster (with emphasis on reducing the burden of diseases of poverty as well as the role and functions of Psychology in national health systems, including Primary Care). In 2005, the Union continued to support the development of the next edition of the International Classification of Diseases (ICD), with particular focus on the Mental health section. This activity is under the auspices of the Evidence and Information for Policy cluster of WHO. The Union has appointed Dr. Geoff Reed (USA) as its member of the Core Group coordinating this activity in WHO. The Union's strong contributions to the ICD project are made possible by an allocation of financial and human resources from the American Psychological Association.

In the latter part of 2005, WHO and the review were reviewing previous Work Plan and considering the renewal of Official Relations. This decision is expected in early 2006.

BRIEF REPORT ON USE OF 2005 ICSU GRANTS, UNESCO AND US STATE DEPARTMENT SUBVENTIONS AND FUNDING FROM OTHER SOURCES

A description of activities supported by UNESCO and the US State Department through the 2004–2005 ICSU grant as well as those also receiving support from other sources was provided in the report of special projects and in separate, elaborated reports to the granting bodies. This included the project on **Human Dimensions of Global Change: Human Perceptions and Behavior in Sustainable Water Use**.

A separate detailed report and financial statements for the project as well as audited financial statements for 2005 will be submitted to the ICSU and ISSC secretariats.

CONCLUSION AND FUTURE PLANS

In the 2004 Annual Report, a broad perspective was offered in the context of the Union celebrating its first half-century. For this report, the Union's strategically oriented planning and concomitant changes to the way it conducts its business. Capacity-building has emerged as a central priority, not only for this quadrennium, but as part of the core vision of the Union. Historically, through its International Congress and in the past decade through regional conferences of psychology, the Union has demonstrated the importance it accords to capacity building. Nonetheless, through the national capacity-building initiative and other projects, the Union has reaffirmed its commitment to this area. Furthermore, the choice of Cape Town, South Africa well illustrates the Union's intent to devote resources to supporting the development of psychology in Africa.

As in the 2000–2004 quadrennium, the Union is making a sustained contribution to international development through strong relations with ICSU, ISSC, the UN secretariat, and WHO. It will be evaluating opportunities to further enhanced interdisciplinary collaboration in the advancement of science and its application for human well-being.

As reported above, the 2004 Assembly mandated that the Union function on the basis of a Strategic Plan. Henceforth, the process of strategic planning will be a fundamental principle for the Union's governance and management. The Executive Committee and Officers have embraced this process in the first year of the new quadrennium. Initial progress will be reviewed at the 2006 Assembly in Athens, Greece. The Union requires a well crafted approach to strategic planning. A major challenge of the new quadrennium will be to make noteworthy strides toward realizing this objective.

Annual reports in recent years have noted the heavy demands placed on the Union to mobilize the capacity to make possible the achievements reported here. With the sustained growth in activity and the continued dramatic increase in external as well as internal communications, the Union's small part-time secretariat receives demands beyond the limits of its resources. Although the detailed review of the Union's human resource needs was deferred to a later point in the strategic planning process, this dimension will ultimately have to be a fundamental consideration in the review of the Union's functions and structure. Without practical solutions to managing the Union's overall workload, it is unlikely that strategic priorities can be achieved.

The International Union of Psychological Science through the actions of the Assembly, together with the leadership of the Executive Committee and Officers, in concert with National Members, Affiliates and Liaisons is now implementing the orderly renewal begun in the previous quadrennium. Determining the policy framework and strategic vision along with securing the financial means and human resources needed to realize the full potential of the Union's priorities remain the challenges faced by those charged by the 2004 Assembly to provide leadership in the new quadrennium. Notwithstanding the reservations about internal capacity, the results of the first year of the new quadrennium confirm that the prospects for the Union remain positive.

INTERNATIONAL JOURNAL OF PSYCHOLOGY, 2006, 41 (6), 580–581

Psychology Press
Taylor & Francis Group

Congresses and scientific meetings

February 7 - 10, 2007
International Neuropsychological Society (INS) Annual
Conference
Portland, Oregon, USA
URL: www.the-ins.org/meetings

March 5 - 6, 2007
9th International Helping Families Change Conference
Charleston, South Carolina, USA
URL: www.hfcc07.net

March 15 - 18, 2007
First Symposium of Pedagogy and Psychology PhD
Students
Wroclaw, POLAND
URL: http://www.conference.dawid.uni.wroc.pl

March 24 - 31, 2007
3rd European Spring Conference on Social Psychology
St. Moritz, SWITZERLAND
URL: http://132.187.160.5/download/StMoritz07.pdf

March 29 - April 1, 2007
Society for Research in Child Development Biennial
Meeting
Boston, Massachusetts, USA
URL: www.srcd.org/biennial.html

April 17 - 21, 2007
2nd International Congress or the World Federation of
Societies of Biological Psychiatry
Santiago, CHILE
URL: www.wfsbp.org

April 18 - 21, 2007
Society for Behavioral Medicine Annual Meeting
Miami Beach, Florida, USA
ULR: www.sbm.org

April 29 - May 1, 2007
Second Middle East and North Africa Regional Conference
of Psychology (MENA RCP);
Preconference workshops April 27-28
Amman, JORDAN
URL and call for papers forthcoming as of 9.1.2006

May 9 - 13, 2007
5th Biennial Conference of the International Academy for
Intercultural Research
URL: http://www.interculturalacademy.org

May 9 - 12, 2007
European Congress of Work and Organizational Psychology
Stockholm, SWEDEN
URL: www.eawop2007.org

May 31 - June 2, 2007
Jean Piaget Society Meetings
Amsterdam, NETHERLANDS
URL: www.piaget.org

June 21 - 22, 2007
Small group meeting on social stigma and social
disadvantage
Oud-Poelgeest Castle, THE NETHERLANDS
Contact: barreto@fsw.leidenuniv.nl
Deadlines: Abstracts due November 15

Summer, 2007
International Association for Research in Economic
Psychology (IAREP) Annual Conference
Ljubljana, SLOVENIA
URL: http://www.iarep.org/conferences.htm

July 1 - 5, 2007
31st Interamerican Congress of Psychology: Integrating
the Americas
Mexico City, MEXICO
URL: www.sipmexico2007.org.mx

July 3 - 6, 2007
Xth European Congress of Psychology
Prague, CZECH REPUBLIC
URL: www.ecp2007.com/intro.htm

July 3 - 8, 2007
3rd International Congress of Psychology and Law
Adelaide, South Australia, AUSTRALIA
URL: http://www.sapmea.asn.au

July 9 - 13, 2007
Eighth Annual Conference, International Stress
Management Association
Montreal, CANADA
URL: www.isma-usa.org

August 16 - 19, 2007
International Council of Psychologists (ICP)
Location: San Diego, California, USA
URL: http://icpsych.tripod.com

August 17 - 20, 2007
112th Annual Convention of the American Psychological
Association (APA)
Location: San Francisco, California, USA
URL: www.apa.org/convention

August 21 - 25, 2007
13th European Conference on Developmental Psychology
(ECDP)
Jena, GERMANY
URL: www.esdp2007.de

---

* Please send details of forthcoming events as far in advance as is possible to Dr Merry Bullock, Deputy
Secretary-General, International Union of Psychological Science and Associate Editor of the *International
Journal of Psychology*, Science Directorate, APA, 750 First Street NE, Washington DC 20002, USA;
E-mail: mbullock@apa.org; URL: http://www.iupsys.org

August 23 - 26, 2007
2007 World Conference of Stress
Budapest, HUNGARY
URL: www.stress07.com

October 17 - 21, 2007
Society for Physiology Research, 47th Annual Meeting
Savannah, Georgia, USA
URL: http://www.sprweb.org

November 15 - 18, 2007
48th Psychonomic Society Annual Meeting
Long Beach, California, USA
URL: http://www.psychonomic.org/meet.htm
2008 AND BEYOND

February 6 - 9, 2008
International Neuropsychological Society (INS) Annual
Conference
Waikoloa, Hawaii, USA
URL: http://www.the-ins.org/meetings

June, 2008
Second Annual Convention, Asian Psychological
Association (APsyA)
Kuala Lumpur, MALAYSIA
URL: www.apsya.org

Summer, 2008
International Council of Psychologists (ICP)
St. Petersburg, RUSSIA
URL: http://icpsych.tripod.com

July, 14 - 16, 2008
6th International Conference, International Test
Commission: The Public Face of Testing
Liverpool, UK
URL: www.intestcom.org

July 20 - 25, 2008
XXIX International Congress of Psychology
Berlin, GERMANY
URL: http://www.icp2008.de

July 27 - 31, 2008
4th Latin American Regional Congress of Cross-Cultural
Psychology
Mexico City, MEXICO
Contact: loving@servidor.unam.mx

August 14 - 17, 2008
116th Annual Convention of the American Psychological
Association
Boston, Massachusetts, USA
URL: www.apa.org/convention

November 20 - 24, 2008
49th Psychonomic Society Annual Meeting
Chicago, Illinois, USA
URL: http://www.psychonomic.org/meet.htm

February 11 - 14, 2009
International Neuropsychological Society (INS) Annual
Conference
Atlanta, Georgia, USA
URL: http://www.the-ins.org/meetings

April 1 - 5, 2009
Society for Research in Child Development Biennial
Meeting
Denver, Colorado, USA
URL: http://www.srcd.org/biennial.html

July 7 - 10, 2009
11th European Congress of Psychology
Oslo, NORWAY
URL: www.ecp2009.no

August 6 - 9, 2009
117th Annual Convention of the American Psychological
Association
Toronto, Ontario, CANADA
URL: www.apa.org/convention

July 11 - 16, 2010
International Congress of Applied Psychology
Melbourne, AUSTRALIA
URL: www.icap2010.com

August 12 - 15, 2010
118th Annual Convention of the American Psychological
Association
San Diego, California, USA
URL: www.apa.org/convention

August 4 - 7, 2011
119th Annual Convention of the American Psychological
Association
Washington, DC, USA
URL: www.apa.org/convention

Summer, 2012
International Congress of Psychology
Cape Town, SOUTH AFRICA

August 2 - 5, 2012
120th Annual Convention of the American Psychological
Association
Chicago, Illinois, USA
URL: www.apa.org/convention

July 31 - August 4, 2013
121st Annual Convention of the American Psychological
Association
Honolulu, Hawaii, USA
URL: www.apa.org/convention

August 7 - 10, 2014
122nd Annual Convention of the American Psychological
Association
Washington DC, USA
URL: www.apa.org/convention

International Journal of Psychology
Volume 41, 2006, Contents

Issue 6
Special issue on *Behaviour analysis around the world*
(Guest editor: Rubén Ardila)

International Journal of Psychology
Volume 41, 2006, Author index

International Journal of Psychology
Volume 41, 2006, Guest reviewers

The Editor and Associate Editors of the *International Journal of Psychology* would like to thank the following experts for their participation as invited reviewers for 2005–2006.

Hisham Motkal Abu-Rayya
Jüri Allik
Mikayo Ando
Judit V. Arends-Toth
Yasmin Asvat
Winton W. T. Au
Kaisa Aunola
Adriana Baban
Karen Barrett
Daphne Bavelier
Martin Beaupré
Eni Becker
Terry Beehr
Corina Benjet
Yossef S. Ben-Porath
Steven Berman
Danny Bernstein
John Widdup Berry
Robert Biswas
Klaus Boehnke
Marc Bornstein
Pablo Brinol
Jim Brockmole
Freek Bucx
Steven D. Caldwell
John Caldwell
Dora Capozza
Gian Vittorio Caprara
Alan Dan Castel
Margarida Silva Cesar
Raymond M. C. Chan
Kamal Abou Chedid
Cecilia Cheng
Terry Childers
Yang-Seok Cho
Xenia Chryssochoou
Timothy Church
Laurence Claes
Adam B. Cohen
Lucian Gideon Conway III
Marie Coppola
Isabel Correia
Kai Schnabel Cortina
Mark Coulson
Sarah Coyne
David Crystal
Vera Cubela Adoric
Teresa Daza Gonzalez
Maria Vidal de Haymes
Anton de Man
Boele de Raad
Serdar M. Degirmencioglu
Martijn DeGoede
Paul Delfabbro

Jan Delhey
Jean Descoteaux
Lisa Di Blas
Mark R. Dixon
José Miguel Fernández Dols
Robert Eisenberger
Hillary Anger Elfenbein
Andrew Elliot
Mehmet Eskin
Dorothy Espelage
Alexander von Eye
Jörg Felfe
Kristin Finn
Ronald Fischer
Gerard Fogarty
Luis J. Fuentes
Eamon Fulcher
Tomas Furmark
Carl Gabbard
David Gallo
Masha Gartstein
Jeremy Genovese
Carol Gohm
Rapson Gomez
Mohammad Ali Goodarzi
Robert Gordon
Mikel Gorriti
Patrick Gosselin
Luc Gossens
Louis Gottschalk
John Grable
Elena Grigorenko
Melissa J. Guynn
Chad Gwaltney
Simon Handley
Martin Hänze
Lesley Hart
Toshikazu Hasegawa
Brad Hastings
Henriëtte Hendriks
Matthew Hickmann
Helmut Hildebrandt
Robert Ho
Gabriel Horenczyk
Nuran Hortaçsu
Anke Huckauf
Alycia M. Hund
Eric Raymond Igou
Derek Isaacowitz
Heidi Ittner
Lynne Jackson
Steve Jex
Gary Jones
Paul E. Jose

Patricia Kahlbaugh
Michael P. Kaschak
David Kember
Elizabeth Kensinger
Gerben van Kleef
Sara Knight
Guenther Knoblich
Kalevi Korpela
Justin Kruger
Anton Kuehberger
Asiye Kumru
Ute Kunzmann
Sonoko Kuwano
Marco Lauriola
Stefan Lautenbacher
Mark Le Fevre
Kibeom Lee
Luigi Leone
Irwin Levin
Lynn S. Liben
Karmela Liebkind
Elizabeth F. Loftus
Ederaldo Lopes
Fabio Lorenzi-Cioldi
Richard Lucas
Heather MacDonald
James N. MacGregor
Gina Magyar-Russel
Vanessa Malcarne
Richard L. Marsh
Chad Marsolek
David Matsumoto
Ellen Matthies
Eugene Matusov
Robert R. McCrae
Sam McFarland
Dennis McInerney
Sanjay Menon
Elizabeth Midlarsky
Padraic Monaghan
Gary Morgan
Elias Mpofu
Tatjana Nazir
Drew Nesdale
Craig Neumann
Franz Neyer
Gabriele Oettingen
Shigehiro Oishi
Thomas Ollendick
Kathleen Otto
Frank Pajares
Mark Pancer
Joel Paris
Nansook Park

Crystal Park
James Parker
Manuel Perea
Lars-Eric Petersen
Urmila Pillay
Ursula Piontkowski
Katarzyna Popiolek
David Popivanov
Stephanie Sandra Pourcel
Raija-Leena Punamäki
Joël Pynte
Kopano Ratele
Sonia Roccas
Jérôme Rossier
Peter Rossmann
Jean-François Rouet
Steven Rouse
Pagona Roussi
Floyd Rudmin
Martha Rueter
Marcos Ruiz
Clara Sabbagh
Lilach Sagiv
Carlos Santamaría
Gabriel Schui
Seth Schwartz
Simone Seemann
Juan Segui
Miri Shacham
Alex Yeung See Shing
Michelle Shiota
Winston Sieck

Sandra Sigmon
Dean Keith Simonton
Saulo Sirigatti
Oi-ling Siu
Einar M. Skaalvik
Peter Bevington Smith
Mark Smith
Laura Snodgras
Robert Sorkin
Elmar Souvignier
Jörn Sparfeldt
Stephen Sprinkle
Rajalakshmi Sriram
John Staddon
Mark Stemmler
Joachim Stoeber
Sven Strömqvist
Eunkook Suh
Vesa Hannu Suutari
Laurence Taconnat
Vicky C. W. Tam
Li Hai Tan
Junko Tanaka-Matsumi
Thomas Li-Ping Tang
Eugene Tartakovsky
Femke ten Velden
Colin Tredoux
Edison J. Trickett
Ewa Trzebinska
Brunna Tuschen-Caffier
Haci-Halil Uslucan
Fons J. R. van de Vijver

J. P. L. M. van Oudenhoven
Karen Ivette van Oudenhoven-van
    der Zee
Fritz van Wel
Ekant Veer
Chiara Volpato
Daniel Voyer
Ulrich Wagner
David A. Waller
X. T. Wang
Oi Wang
Philip Watkins
Paul Joseph Watson
Sheila Webber
Duane Wegener
Hildegard Weiss
John Welte
Michael Wenzel
Michèle Wessa
Grażyna Wieczorkowska
Ross Wilkinson
Uwe Wolfradt
Daniel B. Wright
Zohreh Yaghoub Zadeh
Chin Lung Yang
Yamazaki Yoshitaka
Rene Zeelenberg
Melanie Zeintl
Rene Ziegler

T - #0197 - 270225 - C0 - 271/201/9 - PB - 9781841698205 - Gloss Lamination